EVIL AND CHRISTIAN ETHICS

Genocide in Rwanda, multiple murder at Denver or Dunblane, the gruesome activities of serial killers – what makes these great evils, and why do they occur? In addressing such questions this book, unusually, interconnects contemporary moral philosophy with recent work in New Testament scholarship. The conclusions to emerge are surprising. Gordon Graham argues that the inability of modernist thought to account satisfactorily for evil and its occurrence should not lead us to embrace an eclectic postmodernism, but to take seriously some unfashionable pre-modern conceptions – Satan, demonic possession, spiritual powers, cosmic battles. Precisely because it strives to observe the high standards of clarity and rigour that are the hallmarks of philosophy in the analytical tradition, the book makes a powerful case for the rejection of humanism and naturalism, and for explaining the moral obligation to struggle against evil by reference to the New Testament's cosmic narrative.

GORDON GRAHAM is Regius Professor of Moral Philosophy at the University of Aberdeen. His books include *Historical Explanation Reconsidered* (1984), *Politics and its Place: a Study of Six Ideologies* (1986), *Contemporary Social Philosophy* (1987), *The Idea of Christian Charity* (1989), *Living the Good Life: an Introduction to Moral Philosophy* (1990), *Ethics and International Relations* (1997), *The Shape of the Past: a Philosophical Approach to History* (1997), *Philosophy of the Arts* (1997) and *The Internet: a Philosophical Enquiry* (1999). He has also published numerous journal and newspaper articles.

D1630910

NEW STUDIES IN CHRISTIAN ETHICS

General editor
Robin Gill

Editorial board
Stephen R. L. Clark, Stanley Hauerwas, Robin W. Lovin

Christian ethics has increasingly assumed a central place within academic theology. At the same time the growing power and ambiguity of modern science and the rising dissatisfaction within the social sciences about claims to value-neutrality have prompted renewed interest in ethics within the secular academic world. There is, therefore, a need for studies in Christian ethics which, as well as being concerned with the relevance of Christian ethics to the present-day secular debate, are well informed about parallel discussions in recent philosophy, science or social science. New Studies in Christian Ethics aims to provide books that do this at the highest intellectual level and demonstrate that Christian ethics can make a distinctive contribution to this debate – either in moral substance or in terms of underlying moral justifications.

EVIL AND CHRISTIAN ETHICS

GORDON GRAHAM

University of Aberdeen

CAMBRIDGE UNIVERSITY PRESS

PUBLISHED BY THE PRESS SYNDICATE OF THE UNIVERSITY OF CAMBRIDGE
The Pitt Building, Trumpington Street, Cambridge, United Kingdom

CAMBRIDGE UNIVERSITY PRESS
The Edinburgh Building, Cambridge CB2 2RU, UK   www.cup.cam.ac.uk
40 West 20th Street, New York, NY 10011–4211, USA   www.cup.org
10 Stamford Road, Oakleigh, Melbourne 3166, Australia
Ruiz de Alarcón 13, 28014 Madrid, Spain

© Gordon Graham 2001

First published 2001

Printed in the United Kingdom at the University Press, Cambridge

Typeface Baskerville 11/12.5 pt   *System* 3b2   [CE]

A catalogue record for this book is available from the British Library

ISBN 0 521 77109 9 hardback
ISBN 0 521 79745 4 paperback

For the
Bishop,
Clergy and People
of the
Diocese of Aberdeen and Orkney

We pieced our thoughts into philosophy,
And planned to bring the world under a rule,
Who are but weasels fighting in a hole.

W. B. Yeats
from *Nineteen Hundred and Nineteen*

Contents

General editor's preface

This book is the twentieth in the series New Studies in Christian Ethics. It is very good to have another professional philosopher writing for the series and this is indeed a very unusual and challenging book. Several of the books in the series have combined philosophical and theological skills as this book does: notably, Kieran Cronin's *Rights and Christian Ethics*, Jean Porter's *Moral Action and Christian Ethics*, Garth Hallett's *Priorities and Christian Ethics* and Stephen R. L. Clark's *Biology and Christian Ethics*. All of these books closely reflect the two key aims of the series – namely to promote monographs in Christian ethics which engage centrally with the present secular moral debate at the highest possible intellectual level and, secondly, to encourage contributors to demonstrate that Christian ethics can make a distinctive contribution to this debate.

Gordon Graham's concern here is that evil should be taken seriously. He argues at length that secular accounts of evil are inadequate, either because they seek to explain away evil as some disorder or malfunction, or because they maintain that there is no such thing as absolute evil, or because they offer no hope beyond evil. In contrast, he presents a powerful case for thinking that a Christian narrative can provide a more adequate basis for understanding and overcoming evil and that to believe coherently in the existence of absolute evil requires us to believe in a providential God. Now, of course, such claims will immediately be greeted with much scepticism since it is widely assumed that the problem of evil presents theists with a unique and insurmountable problem. Gordon Graham is well aware of this and offers an extended account of this 'problem', arguing in the process that secularists actually have a greater problem of evil and that theologians do not lack rational and cogent responses to secularists at this point. After a fascinating account of gross moral evil in the form of multiple murderers, he concludes that 'humanism cannot explain (so to speak) the evil of evil, and naturalistic science, even of a well-informed psychological kind, cannot explain its occurrence'.

One way to understand this beautifully written and challenging book is to compare it with Jonathan Glover's recent book *Humanity*. A number of reviewers have noted that Glover gives a very full account of human evil in the twentieth century but a very inadequate (secular consequential) response to it. His well-researched empirical accounts of the evils perpetuated in Hitler's Germany and Stalin's Soviet Union, as well as those more recently in Rwanda, are not matched by the philosophical explanations that he offers. Parts of Gordon Graham's book also give meticulous, and sometimes harrowing, accounts of evil, but his theological explanations finally dominate. Not every theologian will agree with the latter – I remain more sceptical than he is about the ontological status and explanatory power of Satan – but they will need to be considered very seriously.

In short, this is an interdisciplinary book on an important theme which should make readers think. It is a very welcome addition to New Studies in Christian Ethics.

ROBIN GILL

Preface

Weary of the historicism, psychologism and relativism of
the scientific study of religion, people long for revelation
and demand a scientific approach to the Bible which does
justice to its claim to be revelation.

Otto Eissfeldt (Quoted in Watson 1997: 19)

In his book *Facing Evil*, a book that addresses many of the
themes with which I am concerned here, John Kekes remarks
that 'Christianity is another way of succumbing to false hope'.
This book, though not a point by point response to Kekes (to
whom I shall refer only occasionally), aims to refute that
contention – not just to deny it, or to represent another point of
view, but to *refute* it, and to do so in a way that makes my
reasoning as transparently open to criticism as I can make it.
There is no better task that philosophy can perform, in my view,
than to construct clear and rigorous arguments about peren-
nially important topics.

'Refute' overstates the case perhaps. To be realistic, my aim
is the slightly more modest one of providing compelling (admit-
tedly not conclusive) reasons for thinking Kekes's view to be
false. The way in which I propose to do so, however, cannot
claim any fundamental originality. With considerable adapt-
ation and extension, the elements of the line of thought I shall
pursue are to be found in Kant's second Critique, the *Critique of
Practical Reason*. My argument is essentially a version of his so-
called 'moral argument for the existence of God'. Kant was one
of the towering geniuses of Western thought. I am not. How
then could I expect to improve on what he has to say?

I should say at the outset that this is not a work of Kantian exposition or interpretation. I have neither the requisite ability nor expertise. The reader who wants to know a lot about Kant will not find much illumination here. Rather, I aim to *deploy* some of Kant's conceptions and ideas. What marks out my treatment of the relevant subjects from Kant's, and will I hope commend it, is first, my attempt to provide the detail which his argument requires but which he does not himself supply, and second, my presentation of this amplified version in a new cultural context.

This context is new in at least two respects. Since Kant wrote, Christian theology has faced almost unprecedented challenges from the application of historical criticism to the New Testament, and from the sweeping success of evolutionary biology. The result is that compared with the period in which Kant formulated his philosophy, the present time is one in which theological conceptions cut little real intellectual ice. This condition is compounded, in my view, by the fact that, beginning with Schleiermacher's *Speeches to the Cultured Despisers of Religion*, the general tendency of those aiming to revitalise Christian theology and give it 'relevance' to 'the modern mind' has been anti-metaphysical and anti-orthodox. That is to say, a very great deal of contemporary Christian writing and reflection holds out little hope that the ideas and conceptions which have characterised Christian theology through most of its history can be made to apply directly to the intellectual and moral concerns of the contemporary world. Their aspiration is, rather, a 'new' theology, better adapted to post-Enlightenment, post-Darwinian times.

By contrast, my aim is to swim against both these currents. Lest I be accused of ante-deluvianism, however, I hasten to point out that my purpose is neither to defend biblical literalism nor play up the merits of Creationism. Nor is this new. Long ago Augustine also wrote for cultured despisers, and sought to undermine their *jejeune* interpretation of the Scriptures, an interpretation which Christians no less than pagans were inclined to project. In a similar vein, despite lacking the brilliant and illuminating intelligence of St Augustine, I aim to identify certain signal failures in contemporary secular thought, scientific as well as philosophical, and to show that it is only by re-invoking much older, broadly theological, conceptions that these deficiencies can be remedied. In other words, I want to focus on the explanatory tasks that modern thought has set itself, in the shared and firm conviction that the questions it addresses are crucially important – the nature of evil, the value of human life and the meaningfulness of morality – and to demonstrate as best I can that the naturalistic and humanistic presuppositions of modernity are inadequate to its own purposes. On the other hand, I have none of the inclination some Christian thinkers have shown to join the ranks of the postmodernists. Postmodernism, in so far as it is one thing, seems to me a new flight to unreason. I might better describe my intention as that of revitalising the pre-modern.

The odds are stacked against such an endeavour, as it seems to me, and I do not suppose that I have the ability to turn a powerful tide, though there are some signs, I think, that the tide is indeed turning. Still, however cogent, all such arguments will inevitably be thought to fly fruitlessly in the face of 'the march of modern history' (Marx). My inclination, I should admit, an inclination common to philosophers in all generations, is to uncover radical alternatives to contemporary truisms and to make them plausible, to put to the test what Alasdair MacIntyre has called the *Self-images of the Age*. Since I accept the Hegelian dictum that philosophy cannot 'leap over Rhodes', inevitably these alternatives are derived from conceptions with an ancient history. They have thus the advantage of being radically critical of modern ideas while at the same time calling upon the venerability of the accumulated wisdom of the ages, another reason for denying them any very great originality.

I do not expect to find many converts to my point of view. To most readers, I imagine, even if my arguments appear cogent enough, the conclusions I arrive at will seem absurd, to the postmodern no less than to the modern mind. I shall be satisfied, therefore, if both Christians and non-Christians who read this book come to the more modest view that some strands of philosophical theology they have hitherto dismissed, may not be as otiose as they have been inclined to suppose.

I am by training, occupation and intellectual disposition a moral philosopher in the Anglo-American tradition. By conviction I am a Christian. Inevitably, in the contemporary world, these are in tension. Still, I hope the present work will show that this tension can be creative.

Acknowledgements

In the course of preparing the material in this book I have had to engage in a number of areas of inquiry in which I am less than expert. Chief among these is New Testament scholarship. Let me here record my very great debt to the writings of N. T. Wright. The historical Jesus is a subject in which I have been interested for many years and some of the views I expound here I came to partly because of my chancing across a book to which I have found little reference elsewhere – E. F. Scott's *The Validity of the Gospel Record.* But reading Wright's impressive volumes (and those of other scholars to which they pointed me) led me to the opinion that between the 'cutting edge' of biblical scholarship and the concerns of contemporary philosophy there is a largely unremarked consonance and, accordingly, the possibility of fruitful exchange. This opinion was strengthened by the presence of Professor David Fergusson (now at the University of Edinburgh) and Professor Francis Watson among my academic colleagues at Aberdeen. Both the books they have written, and their comments on draft chapters of this one, have produced a marked improvement in what I have to say. Whether the prospects of collaboration between biblical theology and moral philosophy are as bright as I think, I leave the reader to judge.

I am also grateful to the incisive comments of my colleague in philosophy, Dr Jonathan Friday, and, as on many previous occasions, to my daughter Lindsay Graham for invaluable editorial assistance.

I must also acknowledge my debt to members of the Philosophy Department at Calvin College, in Michigan, especially Dr Kelly Clarke. They accorded me the very great distinction of election to the Jellema Lectureship in Philosophy and Religion for 1998. The lectures, under the title 'Ethics and the Real Jesus', gave me the occasion to put my thoughts on these matters into order for the first time, and conversations at Calvin with Professor John E. Hare, author of *The Moral Gap*, greatly enriched them. The subsequent suggestion from the editors of *New Studies in Christian Ethics* that I write a book in this series presented me with the opportunity to try and spell them out in a reasonably extended and rigorous form. The comments of both an anonymous reader and of Professor Robin Gill, the General Editor, have still further improved the final result.

An earlier version of chapter six was read to a conference on 'The Biblical Theology of Hope', and subsequently appeared in *The Evangelical Quarterly*. I am grateful to the Editor, Professor Howard Marshall, for permission to reproduce some of it here.

King's College
Aberdeen

CHAPTER I

Christian ethics or moral theology?

The intellectual position of Christianity in the modern world, by which I mean Western Christendom at the turn of the twenty-first century, is largely one of retreat. As it seems to me, theologians, and believers more generally, have lost confidence in the relevance of Christian theology to the explanatory endeavours of intellectual inquiry. This is evidenced by the fact that in physics, biology, history, law, social theory and psychology, less and less (almost nothing indeed) is heard of the role of theological conceptions, conceptions which at one time dominated all these disciplines to the point where theology could be described as 'the queen of the sciences'. So far have we moved away from that condition, that hardly anyone confidently deploys theology in the discussion of intellectual problems in cosmology, evolutionary biology, historiography, jurisprudence or metaphysics. It is true that there are exceptions, but for the most part it is so. Even human health, both physical and mental, is held to be the province of physiology, microbiology, neurology and psychiatry, and social well being is the subject of political and economic science. The generalised behaviour of people is investigated by sociology and anthropology, that of individuals by psychology. In short, furthering our understanding of the world in which we find ourselves is thought to lie with something called 'science', both natural and social, while theology is widely regarded as 'unscientific'. Indeed, 'theological' is used by the media (in political commentary for example) as a label for the doctrinaire and the irrelevant, or worse obscurantist. Consequently, anyone who, in almost any context, appeals to divine activity or religious experience is dismissed by the experts and, in so far as they receive public attention, are regarded with embarrassment by many, perhaps most, of their co-religionists.

This is not to say that natural theology – theology based on scientific and historical knowledge rather than on revelation – has itself been in retreat. On the contrary, natural theology has undergone a remarkable revival in recent years, notably at the hands of Richard Swinburne, and, in a different way, Alvin Plantinga. As a result, especially of Plantinga's robust deployment of what has come to be known as 'reformed epistemology', there are considerable numbers of philosophers, especially in the United States, who manage to combine their philosophical expertise and their Christianity in a way that has won for their religious beliefs a significant measure of contemporary intellectual relevance. The membership of the Society of Christian Philosophers has grown to thousands.

But this is atypical. Although a glance at publishers' catalogues will reveal that systematic theology, biblical scholarship and popular religious reflection continue to appear in quantities probably larger than ever before, such work is written very largely in intellectual isolation from the currents of thought characteristic of the academy. The important point to stress, moreover, is that this academic isolation is one way. Modern theology and biblical scholarship generally think themselves under an obligation to attend and respond to the methods of science and history, to take account of and adapt themselves to the latest innovations in cosmology, biology, anthropology, philosophy, literary theory, or whatever. By contrast, neither contemporary science, whether natural and social, nor modern historiography feels in anyway constrained by the investigations of natural or systematic theology. Still less do they await their 'results'. Secular historians, for example, do not scruple to write about the history of religion, believing, more likely, that their indifference to religious and theological questions works to their advantage.

In short, Laplace's view that God is an hypothesis of which the scientist has no need is endorsed by nearly everyone. This includes most Christian theologians. For many theologians, in fact, the study of theology has become primarily the study of its history, albeit its very recent history. Those who wish to engage in something more contemporary and creative generally pin their hopes on replacing metaphysical theology with an apologetic which turns to literary study of the 'metaphorical' or 'figurative' function of religious language, and thus converts it into an interpretative 'slant' on the world that is not, in the end, in conflict with, but accommodated to, modern secularised ways of thinking. Or else (sometimes, as well) they focus upon 'the Christian ethic', and thereby construe Christianity not as an explanatory understanding at all, but a code by which to live, with, perhaps, 'radical' implications for social criticism as well as for the behaviour of individuals. Such is the self-conception, and distinguishing mark, of what is called 'liberation theology'.

I shall have more to say about the 'figurative', but for the moment it is this second response to modern secularism with which I am concerned. It is a response to be found at work well beyond the confines of academic theology. In accordance with it, preachers are regularly heard to assert that Christianity is not a 'theory', but a way of life, and in so saying they unconsciously reflect an important feature of Western Christianity's history in the course of the twentieth century, its move away from 'dogmatics' to 'ethics', a change tellingly recorded by Phillip Gosse in *Father and Son*. In short, most latter-day Christian exponents believe that, whatever historical interest there may be in traditional theological debates, if Christianity is to speak to the contemporary world it is in its ethic that a meaningful message is to be found, and not in any theological-cum-metaphysical explanation of existence and experience that Christian theology has hitherto been thought uniquely to supply.

I

This focus on 'Christian ethics' is often motivated by an apologetic retreat to the 'relevant'. But it is a retreat that receives confirmation from a supposition about the modern world widely endorsed by both secularists and the religious, namely the belief in its moral pluralism. It is a commonplace, held on nearly every side, that Western societies of today are marked by extensive moral variety in belief and lifestyle. Contemporary societies, so this common supposition holds, are to be contrasted with the much more monoglot societies of the past. While once upon a time (not so very long ago perhaps) there was general consensus about the values which make for a good human life, now there is competition between a host of alternatives. This is true, it is held, regardless of whether by 'good' we mean objectively worthwhile or subjectively satisfying.

It is upon the assumption of pluralism that the dominant political philosophy of the twentieth century – Rawlsian liberalism – has been built. This is a political philosophy that gives priority to 'the right' over 'the good', separates law and morality, strives to provide a rational foundation for a shared political neutrality, and aims to formulate social principles which are not intended to adjudicate between competing 'conceptions of the good' but whose purpose is to find an 'overlapping consensus' between them. In particular, it expressly leaves metaphysical and theological commitments behind.

Rawlsian liberalism is not without its critics. The alternative position generally goes by the name of communitarianism. But 'communitarianism' is not in fact a single view, except negatively. Indeed it can only be characterised in terms of the rejection of liberal individualism; the grounds of this rejection are many and varied – feminism, environmentalism, MacIntyrean traditionalism and so on. If there is more common ground than this it lies in alternative communitarian attacks on the political neutralism that underlies the modern liberal conception, rather than the value pluralism it seeks to address.

Now there are issues in the liberalism/communitarianism debate with which Christian writers concerned with ethics may engage directly. This is evidenced, in fact, by at least two of the volumes that appeared earlier in this series, Ian S. Markham's *Plurality and Christian Ethics* and David Fergusson's *Community, Liberalism and Christian Ethics*. The point to be emphasised for present purposes, however, is not so much that there is a connection between the liberal/communitarian debate and specific issues in Christian ethics – there undoubtedly is – but that the general picture of moral pluralism as 'the way we live now' is a background assumption of most of those engaged in this debate, Christian or non-Christian. The *general* impact this has had on Christian thinking is a retreat from the metaphysical to the ethical. Its principal effect is to provide a cultural and intellectual context which allows Christians to claim an identity that is precisely independent of their theology, and for that very reason one that can claim the same status as every other participant to the pluralist debate. If to be 'a Christian' is a matter of endorsing a particular 'way of life', one which stands alongside, but also out from, many others, this can readily come to be seen as having a certain integrity and validity regardless of any suspect theological trappings it may have inherited.

The thesis of moral pluralism does not logically imply moral relativism, though it is frequently thought to do so, and the two are often to be found in each other's company, so to speak. By moral relativism I mean the idea that there is no ultimate moral 'truth', no demonstrably 'right' way of living, no provable set of ethical principles, no 'absolute' values. Moral relativism (surprisingly to me), has its Christian sympathisers. This is largely, I think, because it fits in well with the modern existentialist idea that human existence is characterised by the need to make fundamental choices, choices with respect to which the individual chooser is radically free. Though the atheist Sartre is the name most immediately associated with existentialism, it is a philosophy with Protestant roots. These are to be found in the writings of the modernistically fashionable Christian thinker, Søren Kierkegaard, whose most famous slogan unambiguously declares that 'Subjectivity is truth' and the title of whose best known book is *Either/Or*. My concern here is not with moral relativism, however. I believe it to be false, but this is not such a novel view since relativism is commonly, if not widely, still regarded as philosophically controversial. More interesting as a target, then, is the fashionable belief in moral pluralism, a far less controversial view, but one which I also think, and hope to show, to be false.

It is worth emphasising that the pluralistic thesis, which underlies so much contemporary thinking, both Christian and non-Christian, is essentially an empirical one. It holds that, as a matter of fact, the state of contemporary culture is this way rather than that. Yet there is good reason easily arrived at to question the truth of this familiar assumption. We should begin, though, by citing some of the evidence which seems to support it. It is true that there are a variety of 'lifestyles' evident in the modern Western world; in contrast to most other times and places, the natural family is no longer the standard household. It is also true that some of these lifestyles may be said to express (somewhat) different 'value systems' – gay alternatives, for instance. There are also different religions, as there always have been, but these are now to be found side by side in a way that they were not in previous centuries. In part this is a result of post-colonialism, but it is also true that the United States has, over a century or more, developed into a multicultural society which in turn has become a pattern for other parts of the world.

These are the chief observable differences that sustain the belief in pluralism, yet their significance can be, and is, exaggerated. For one thing, those who point to value pluralism will just as often point to the phenomenon of 'globalisation'. In particular, if the US has set a pattern for elsewhere, it is a surprisingly homogeneous one. The rapid spread of American consumerism – the way in which we shop, travel, eat and entertain ourselves – is if anything even more obviously standardising values than varying them, right across the world, and the emergence of the Internet shows every sign of intensifying this. Even the multiplicity of religions may not be what it seems. Possibly because religion as such, and not just Christianity, is somewhat threatened by materialism, there is increasing emphasis on 'inter-faith dialogue'. This, certainly, is something for which modern pluralists generally show enthusiasm, but it is far from clear that they can do so consistently. Inter-faith dialogue in the face of a common secular enemy makes most sense if it is based on the idea that the evident differences between religious traditions are largely a matter of surface appearance, an appearance that disguises the underlying unity of different paths to the same spiritual goal. I do not myself say that this is correct. In fact, I am inclined to believe that it is not, or at least that the underlying unity is exaggerated. But my point here is only that it is a belief which, if true, throws doubt on the significance of perceptible religious differences in multicultural societies.

However, interesting though they are, these are not matters I propose to investigate further. My target is not the hypothesis of value pluralism writ large, but the rather narrower, if scarcely less important claim, that modern Western societies are *morally* pluralistic. Now when this claim is pressed, it turns out that the points of difference that are supposed to illustrate this moral pluralism are rather few in number. Of course, there is a question about what is to count as a *moral* difference, in contradistinction to differences of some other sort. This is an issue to which I will return at length in a later chapter, but for the moment, we can rest content with trading on intuition – moral differences are differences about such issues as abortion, euthanasia, capital punishment, suicide, homosexuality, the treatment of animals, respect for the environment, and so on.

The commonest example which the proponents of moral pluralism cite is abortion, a topic around which, they allege, there are deep and irreconcilable differences. Now it is sufficient for my purposes simply to register a doubt about this, though a doubt of a reasonably sophisticated sort. Arguments about abortion turn almost exclusively, in my experience, on the relative importance of the right to life on the one hand and the right to moral freedom of choice on the other (Pro-life *versus* Pro-choice), and on how these two, when they come into competition, are to be prioritised. What is *not* (or rarely) in dispute, is that *both* rights have a proper claim to our attention, that they both have moral weight. No one denies that the life of the potential child is of *some* importance; no one (or hardly anyone) thinks that abortion is on the same level as removing a tooth or an appendix. And no one asserts that the mother's desire in the matter is *wholly* irrelevant; her connection with the pregnancy clearly gives her a special interest, and her choice to persist to term, everyone acknowledges, should be respected.

But precisely because this is so, it is plausible to claim that the dispute between the pro-life and pro-choice positions is not really about fundamental values at all, but about their application. Individual freedom of choice and the preservation of life *both* matter; differences only arise when they come into conflict. In short, it is not the case that the values of one party are held to be of no account by the other, but that they are ordered differently. In the midst of disagreement, in fact, we have, at a minimum, mutual understanding.

It is likely that this last claim will be disputed, for the pictures of pro- and anti-abortionists at campaigning rallies strongly indicate to the contrary. I might observe that the fiercest moral and political disputes tend to take place between those who are close rather than those who are distant, but fortunately I neither need nor intend to explore this particular example further, nor defend my interpretation of it, because less contentious evidence against the pluralist's assumption is just as readily available. While there are normative issues over which people in the modern world divide no doubt (though in which world did they not?), there are predominantly many more about which there is virtually no dispute at all – opposition to racism, condemnation of torture, theft, fraud, child abuse, murder, rape. Social opprobrium attaches almost everywhere to lying, cheating (especially in sport), bribery, blackmail and the abuse of public office. This is not to say, of course, that such things do not go on. They do. But their common occurrence is compatible with their being *judged* bad by everyone's moral code. The evidence for this is that cheats and child abusers cannot ordinarily withstand public exposure. Where torturers (say) prevail, despite exposure, this is almost always a result of political oppression, and not a result of differing standards of moral acceptability. It is striking, and of the greatest relevance to the point at issue, that even the most despotic and violent regimes regularly deny (and perhaps more significantly feel constrained to deny) that they are despotic and violent, claiming, usually, democratic credentials and/or urgent political necessity for their actions. Real moral pluralism would lie in this, I think, not that such acts were performed by some and not by others (which has always been the case) but that they were *condemned* by some and not by others, and this simply is not how it is. No one openly owns up to torture, racism, fraud, abuse and terror, still less do they do this with pride. On the contrary, everyone, truly or not, denies such accusations. There are countries, unfortunately, in which slavery is a reality, but no countries in which this fact will be openly admitted.

If this is true, if the extent and depth of moral difference is not as it is popularly imagined, what explains the widespread belief in moral pluralism? Can such a widespread belief be so evidently mistaken, so easily shown to be erroneous? This is an important question. The belief in moral pluralism is indeed widespread, yet if I am right, moral pluralism, which is to say wholesale competition between competing or conflicting moral values is not in fact a mark of contemporary life. The belief in moral pluralism, more closely considered, does not expressly deny this; it *assumes* it. Why so? The answer I think is twofold. First, the history of North America and Western Europe in the second half of the twentieth century was marked by a striking change in *sexual* morality. Up to 1960, say, it was widely thought that sex outside marriage was 'improper' in some sense or other. Cohabitation, fornication, and adultery, though they were known to occur widely, were frowned upon to the extent that they could rarely be admitted openly without significant personal and social cost. Similarly, while the existence of homosexuality was acknowledged, it, too, was rarely admitted to, and coming out, as a matter of 'gay pride', would have been unthinkable in the first half of the twentieth century. Subsequently all this changed. The very concept of 'fornication' has fallen into almost total obsolescence (and correspondingly the concept of chastity), and what is now called 'sexual orientation' has come to be regarded as a matter of individual choice (or genetic destiny) entitled to equal freedom and respect. Laws relating to both these issues, in part reflecting and in part contributing to the change, have been passed in almost all Western countries. Opinion on moral issues that are related to sexuality – such as abortion and contraception – has also undergone significant change, with corresponding amendments in the law.

Now part of my point about moral pluralism is that such change does not necessarily imply, and is not in fact to be interpreted as, evidence of moral plurality. Indeed, the most plausible interpretation of these important changes, it seems to me, is that people quite widely have come to believe that the censure which formerly attached to fornication and homosexuality is without foundation, that there is nothing actually wrong with these practices. In other words, the change is not indicative of moral difference at all, but of a new moral consensus, a common agreement that Victorian attitudes to sexuality were indefensibly confining, and caused in large part by the fear of unwanted pregnancies which effective birth control has eliminated to a great extent.[1]

It is not to the purpose here to ask whether this change in sexual *mores* is correct or incorrect, a product of moral enlightenment or of moral degeneration. The point rather is that it signals a widespread alteration in beliefs about moral right and wrong; it does not signal a fragmentation of moral opinion. Of course, there are some who still take a view opposed to what is now the common consensus, who still think badly of sexual promiscuity and will not acknowledge the validity of homosexual relations. But even the continuing existence of such people does not serve to undermine the point I am making. This is for two reasons. First, anything properly called 'a common consensus' will never amount to universal agreement; there will always be some differences of opinion. Second, such differences as do remain on these issues must be set within a much wider framework of moral agreement. This is the framework I earlier described in fact – the common condemnation of torture, theft, fraud, child abuse, murder, rape, lying, cheating in sport, and so on. Those in the moral minority with respect to sexual liberty, are nevertheless at one with their opponents in the condemnation of this much longer list of other things.

---

[1] There are intriguing and perplexing historical questions here. 'Effective birth control' cannot mean 'the pill'. What demographers know as 'the demographic transition' – a substantial drop in the number of children per family – began in Western Europe well before the pill was invented. For a recent discussion in one particular context see Devine (1999), ch. 22.

The general demise of sexual ethics, it can be argued, arose not so much from a positive view that greater sexual freedom was good (though this was a view expressed by some) as from a sense that the old restrictions had proved groundless, that they rested on nothing better than a shared but merely conventional *feeling* of disapproval. (A similar point might be made about racial or gender discrimination.) Inspected by the cold light of reason, it was not that traditional arguments were opposed by alternative sets of values, but that there appeared to be no justifying arguments at all. (This is the strategy adopted by John Stuart Mill in his pioneering attack on *The Subjection of Women*, for instance.) In short, the change in beliefs about sexual morality brought with it a sense of the *groundlessness* of the moral censure hitherto applied.

This growing sense about the morality of sex, as it seems to me, both re-awakened and made credible a very ancient view, one to be found in the Sophists with whom Plato argued, and to be found at issue between David Hume and his critics in the eighteenth century, that quite generally 'morality is more felt than reasoned of' (Hume 1967: 416), and that accordingly moral beliefs are matters of personal 'opinion'. The belief in moral pluralism, if all that I have been saying is correct, does not rest upon the empirical observation of widespread moral disagreement. It could not do so, since there is in fact no such disagreement. The reality, more closely considered, is that in fact there is relatively little disagreement, and such disagreement as does exist does not run either very wide or very deep. The truth, rather, is that moral pluralism is an *inference*, an inference drawn from the contingently related belief that there is no firm foundation for moral values and principles; that they are not rooted in anything more secure than personal choice and subjective opinion. Hume, of course, who also believed this, did not draw the same inference. He did not subscribe to the idea of widespread moral pluralism because he thought that, as a matter of fact, most people's moral feelings tend to coincide, and that this coincidence is part of that human nature which his *Treatise* set out to describe. Thus while ' 'tis not contrary to reason for me to prefer my total ruin, to prevent the

least uneasiness of an *Indian* or person wholly unknown to me'
(Hume 1967: 416), no normal person would actually have such a
preference. Or so Hume thought. Modern Humeans, by contrast, though they do not explicitly contend that moral feelings
differ widely, are inclined to hold that there is nothing stopping
them doing so; they do not have the same conception of a
'fixed' human nature that Hume had. As a result, they generally
expect that the differences we see in sexual *mores*, where things
that shock some people fail to shock others, will spread ever
wider into other areas of human conduct. But, if we view the
matter without the neo-Humeans' philosophical prejudice, we
have no good reason to share their expectation. What we
actually find in the modern world is an increasingly liberal
attitude to sex combined with near uniform attitudes (of condemnation) to rape, racism and so on. Only this explains the
possibility, and the prevalence, of the moral conformity known
as political correctness.

II

The modern world, then, is marked both by a fairly widespread
moral consensus, and at the same time an accompanying belief
in moral pluralism. The second of these is not, and obviously
cannot be, grounded on the first. If there are in fact few deep
moral disagreements, there can be no good empirical reason to
hold that morality is fragmented. The belief in pluralism arises,
rather, from a certain widespread assumption about the nature
of morality, an implication of philosophical theory not a result
of empirical social study. This is an observation of considerable
interest in its own right with several important consequences for
the understanding of contemporary culture. But my principal
purpose in drawing attention to it, and thus to a peculiarity of
modern society, is not to refute the ill-founded assumption of
moral pluralism which has coloured and shaped contemporary
thinking on so many levels (however much this may be worth
doing), but to focus on one product of it – the identification of
Christianity as just one among a number of 'ways of life', an
identification that is usually taken to imply a distinctive *moral*

component. It is against the background I have been describing (while rejecting) that it becomes plausible to think of and to represent Christianity as primarily one moral code among many, a moral code which both conflicts with and competes alongside several other 'secular' moralities in a highly pluralistic context. And, importantly, it is this component that is held to be the subject of what is called 'Christian ethics'.

As a conceptual model of the relation between moral principles and being a Christian – to be a Christian is to subscribe to certain dos and don'ts – the simplicity of this way of thinking is attractive, but at the same time deceptive. To promote Christian belief as chiefly a matter of adherence to a distinctive ethical code, rather than subscription to a set of theological doctrines, relies in large part upon the belief in moral pluralism which, I have argued, is an erroneous description of the modern condition. But odd though it may sound, an even greater challenge to this evangelising strategy lies in the fact that it presupposes that there is indeed such a thing as Christian ethics.

The assumption, often (as I have suggested) one welcomed by Christians, that the heart of Christianity lies not in its metaphysics but in its ethics, is common but not universal. Some very recent writers on these topics have denied that this separation is possible. Chilton and McDonald, for example, begin their study of *Jesus and the Ethics of the Kingdom* with the claim that 'Jesus of Nazareth is probably most famous, among believers and non-believers, as a teacher of morality.' Although they concede that this is a 'fully justifiable reputation' they also think that 'caution must be exercised in order to avoid drawing an overly generalized portrait of Jesus as teacher of human love' (Chilton and McDonald 1987: 1). In defence of that caution they go on to draw attention, correctly in my view, to the fact that what the Gospels record Jesus as having said has far more to do with eschatology than with ethics, and they infer from this that 'a consideration of Jesus' sayings in the Synoptic Gospels therefore raises the issue of how his ethical teaching is to be reconciled with his preaching of the Kingdom' (5).

Now I too shall be concerned with eschatological themes of

the New Testament and with their relation to morality, but I want to start from a more radical position than that of Chilton and McDonald. The most interesting task we can engage upon in this area is not that of relating two elements of Jesus' teaching – his eschatology and his ethics – but rather that of placing moral endeavour in general within the explanatory context of Christian eschatological theology. I describe this as a more radical position because, as I shall argue, there is in the first place good reason to think that Jesus was not primarily a teacher at all – about ethics, eschatology or anything else – and in the second, that there is no such thing as Christian ethics. I propose, however, to defend these claims in reverse order. The remainder of this chapter will be concerned with the existence/ non-existence of Christian ethics, and the next with what we should think about Jesus.

My contention about Christian ethics will strike many as absurd because so common and so widespread are references to 'Christian ethics' that only a monumental effort could displace the idea. Yet, somewhat surprisingly perhaps, this is not so; no major effort is required. Even if my previous doubts about pluralism in general were to be discounted, it would remain relatively easy to cast doubt on the idea of a Christian ethic. Consider this simple question. If there is such a thing as a distinctively Christian 'code of conduct', what is it? According to Chilton and McDonald it lies in the pre-eminence Jesus gave to the commandment 'You shall love your neighbour as your-self.' But what exactly makes this *Christian*? This is a question to be considered at greater length in the next chapter. For the moment, we need to ask what exactly such a command implies. There needs to be a translation of this general rubric into specifics before we can speak of an ethic or a code – Christian dos and don'ts, we might say. What are they?

One point with which to begin is this: the moral world has not stood still in the last two thousand years. In the ancient world, when Christianity first made its appearance, there were differences between Christians and pagans about what ought and ought not to be done, that were probably quite striking; the Christians' austerity with respect to marriage and sexual morality, for instance, was then unusual and in marked contrast to the more relaxed attitudes of the world around them. Early Christians also tended to be pacifists. It is not quite clear why this was so,[2] but at any rate it was an attitude that the ancient world would have found very strange. They also had an aversion to oaths of loyalty to the emperor; they made a song and dance about state religion and civic requirements which pagan people regarded as an insignificant part of the ordinary run of things. It was these features, among others, that allowed St Paul to call new Christians 'out' from the world and the same features that made 'the Christian way' peculiarly different. And precisely for this reason, there is evidence to think, it was regarded by many as troublesomely perverse. There were many causes of Christian persecution no doubt, but one of them was certainly the fact that the Christian code of conduct was anti-social, that is to say, incompatible with ordinary ways of life and conduct in the world of the first two centuries AD. In short, the early Christians made awkward and untrustworthy citizens.

But in the contemporary world, two thousand years on, the position is quite different. It is an ascertainable fact of almost everyone's experience that on most ethical issues Christians can be found on opposing sides. This needs no special sociological research; it is confirmed daily in the newspapers. Moreover, the views they espouse or denounce are shared and rejected by significant numbers of non-Christians. To return for a moment to the much quoted example of abortion: Christians can be found to be ranged on both sides in almost equal numbers. It is true even of Roman Catholics, despite the pronouncements of Rome, that there is no single view common to all. In the United States there is even an organisation entitled 'Nuns for Abortion'. The same point can be made about birth control, sex outside marriage, homosexuality, euthanasia, suicide and capital punishment. Who could plausibly claim that there is 'a' Christian view on these issues, if by that we mean a view that all thinking Christians conscientiously hold? The fact is that con-

---

[2] On this see Bainton (1964), ch. 5 entitled 'The Pacifism of the Early Church'.

temporary Christians disagree with each other over these issues just as much as they disagree with the secularists around them.

Like it or not, this is how it is in the modern world, but even looking back to the past will not make much difference. The indiscernability of an exclusively 'Christian' ethic is confirmed, not eroded, as we extend the picture across time. The extent to which present and past Christians disagree with each other and agree with non-Christians in almost equal proportions on ethical issues is, if anything, even more striking than the degree to which modern Christians disagree. For instance, contemporary Christians believe that slavery is utterly wrong. This is a belief contemporary secularists share no less firmly; there is nothing distinctively Christian (in the modern world) about anti-slavery. But just as importantly, on this point both they and the secularists disagree fundamentally with Christians of most earlier periods (up to the nineteenth century) for whom slavery was not an obvious evil (a view Christians shared with non-Christians of course). The same is true of attitudes to war. Early Christians may have been largely pacifist, but subsequently there have been Christian militarists and Christian theorists of the just war. There have also been non-Christian militants, pacifists and just war theorists, however, and today, I speculate, while there are hardly any Christian militarists, there are also hardly any secular militarists either.

Consider another example. The Roman Catholic catechism (at one time) declared the four sins that 'cry out to heaven for vengeance' to be wilful murder, sodomy, failing to help the poor, and depriving the worker of a just wage. The first of these identifies an act *every* human ethical and legal system has condemned, the second (homosexuality) an act that many contemporary Christians (including Roman Catholics) no longer believe to be wrong, and the third and fourth identify actions which are in conflict with the values of large numbers of non-Christians just as much as they may be with Catholicism. Where then is the distinctively *Christian* 'way of life' to be found?

There are answers to this question which need to be explored before it can be said confidently that the idea of a Christian ethic has been undermined. One such answer invokes the conception of Christian *character* rather than Christian *principles*. Such a view focuses not on the classes of action which Christianity uniquely forbids or enjoins, but on the virtues of character which Christianity commends. That there are such virtues seems incontestable. What is more contestable is that they are distinctively Christian. Let us agree that charitableness and generosity are among the Christian virtues. But can it seriously be suggested that they are exclusively Christian, not in the sense that only Christians possess them, but in the sense that only Christians believe in them?

Perhaps these are not the principle contenders. What then are? There is no fiercer critic of Christian morality than Nietzsche, and he provides a good focus on this point, precisely because he wants to contrast (to its detriment) Christian 'morality' with the 'aristocratic' virtues that preceded it. A good deal of his wrath is centred on Christian humility which lies at the heart of what he most hates – 'the morality of the herd'. Now humility, it seems to me, is the strongest case for a distinctively Christian virtue, and certainly one that is absent from the list of Aristotelian virtues by which, apparently, Nietzsche is impressed. Yet it is not one that all Christians have espoused, for, despite Christ's fairly explicit remarks about meekness and turning the other cheek, there is a decidedly 'muscular' Christianity to be found at regular periods in the Church's history; a belief in humility and loving one's enemies hardly marks the aspiration (or conduct) of the Crusades, for example. Even if we were to grant that this exception is an aberration, and may reasonably be discounted in any plausible description of 'the Christian way', it has to be remarked that the single virtue of humility cannot provide a sufficiently broad basis on which to construct an entire, and distinctive, Christian 'ethic'. Humility has no very obvious connection, for instance, with the elements that are most frequently cited as parts of that idea – charitable works, integrity, chastity, truthfulness and faithfulness. It does not require humility to engage in charitable works, and integrity, chastity and faithfulness are all compatible with a strong sense of self-esteem. They could all be readily endorsed, indeed,

by the ancient alternative to Christian humility – the Aristotelian '*megalopsychos*' or 'great-souled man'.

In short, whatever may have been true of Christians at the
foundation of the Church, what is true *now* is that they agree
and disagree in pretty much equal measure with non-Christians
on which actions are morally permissible and which are not.
And in the light of the last few paragraphs, we may add to this
that their estimation of what counts as a morally praiseworthy
character, even where it reveals a greater degree of consensus, is
too thin to constitute a distinctively different ideal.

III

Enough has been said, I hope, to cast doubt *both* on the idea
that Christianity can plausibly be identified as one 'ethic'
competing amongst others in a pluralistic moral sea, *and* that it
has its own peculiar and distinguishing features. There are
points about these claims that will be returned to, but the more
important question for the purpose of this book is this. Suppose
it is true that there is not in fact any distinctive Christian ethic.
Do Christians have any reason to worry about this? The answer
is 'yes' for Christians who have retreated from the role of
theological theorists to ethicists. Having confined themselves to
advancing the cause of Christianity in terms of its ethic, it
cannot but be a blow to this enterprise if there is no special
'ethic' to advance. Somewhat ironically, given their aspiration,
they have put themselves in the position of having nothing to
say relevant to morality in the modern world. But the answer is
'yes' more generally, *only* if it is the case that the Christian
approach to morality must lie in a distinctive account of its
content. That is to say, the interest and relevance of Christianity
to morality is threatened only if we suppose (as 'ethical' Christianity has generally done) that interest and relevance reside in
the identification of actions and attitudes that Christians, in
contradistinction to non-Christians, commend and condemn.
What remains unscathed by the contention that there is no such
thing as a Christian ethic, is another, quite different interpretation of the way in which Christianity provides a distinctive

approach to morality. This interpretation points to the explanation Christianity gives, not of the *content* but the *meaning* of morality.

To offer an alternative explanation of the meaning of morality, however, is to depart from contemporary trends because it means reintroducing and taking seriously several of those very theological conceptions from which a focus on Christian 'conduct' has generally sought to retreat. In other words (to draw a somewhat factitious distinction) the emptiness of Christian *ethics* does not imply the otioseness of Christian *moral theology*, and to hold that there is no such thing as a Christian ethic (as I have been arguing) is quite consistent with holding that the best explanation of the meaning of morality is to be found in Christian theology.

This distinction – between Christian ethics and moral theology – is factitious because it does not accord with everyone's usage, or even with a common one. For instance, in the second chapter of a book already referred to, *Liberalism, Community and Christian Ethics*, David Fergusson expounds Karl Barth's account of 'Christian Ethical Distinctiveness'. But on examination, it turns out that what he means by ethical distinctiveness does not have to do primarily with the content of morality but with its meaning. 'The fundamental setting determines the moral universe of the Christian. As Webster remarks [in *Barth's Ethics of Reconciliation*] "For Christian ethics, the world is a different place, and part of the Christian theory of morality, is a careful delineation of that difference"' (Fergusson 1998: 27). To speak in this way is to use the terms 'Christian ethics' and 'the Christian theory of morality' interchangeably. Since there is no philosophical objection to anyone's doing so, it follows that the value of the contrast I have drawn between Christian ethics and Christian moral theology rests entirely on the cogency of the argument of subsequent chapters. I am not recommending any stipulations in this respect. It is for the sake of the present analysis that I shall mark an important conceptual difference by drawing a contrasting terminological distinction between 'Christian ethics' and 'Christian moral theology'.

To appreciate the importance of the conceptual difference

this distinction is meant to reflect, it is helpful to return to my
earlier contentions about moral pluralism. Can it really be that
this very widespread belief is to be undermined, refuted even, in
a few brief paragraphs? It is natural to wonder whether such a
firmly entrenched opinion can be so easily overthrown. Yet I
stand by my contention that the moral variety in the modern
world is hugely exaggerated, and repeat the point that even a
fairly casual inspection of contemporary evidence, if it is not
deflected by philosophical preconceptions, will confirm this.
Moreover, as I suggested, in such vexed issues as abortion, we
can readily observe far more agreement than disagreement, not
at the level of prescription perhaps, but at the level on which
such prescriptions are based. Modern morality consists in a set
of values and principles that, despite the allegations of the
pluralists, are broadly endorsed by almost all humankind,
Christian and non-Christian. That is to say, every modern
culture deplores child sacrifice and female circumcision, decries
dishonesty and disloyalty, outlaws slavery, forbids murder and
theft, deplores racial discrimination, condemns corruption,
praises generosity and human kindness, appeals to rights,
accepts the prevention of harm to others as proper grounds for
legal proscription, seeks to promote health, happiness, freedom
and democracy, and hopes to extend the benefits of education.
Say, if you like, that these are the outworking of the Christian
'law of love', but if they are, no one seriously doubts that law
any more, and consequently, no one can claim it as their
peculiar 'teaching'. It may well be true that many of these
values have Christian origins, but once they have been appro-
priated by the world at large, this is of historical interest only.

Of course, there are a few marked differences in codes of
acceptable conduct even yet, particularly between (some)
Muslims and most non-Muslims. Western attitudes to animals,
for instance, are simply not shared in many parts of the world,
and the horror with which Europeans and Americans regard
punishment by mutilation just is not felt in those countries
(mostly Islamic) where it is practised. Nevertheless, such differences of opinion and practice, however striking, are greatly
outnumbered by points of commonality.

If this is so, realistically speaking there is not much to discover or to dispute about the *content* of morality. What feeds the belief in radical pluralism, I have argued, is a deep uncertainty about moral foundations. On what, if not in personal choice and subjective opinion, *could* morality rest? This is the characteristic doubt of the present age, and it has been elevated to the status of an explanatory philosophy by the range of theories that have gathered strength under the general label of 'postmodernism'. Contemporary Anglo-Saxon moral philosophy (in contrast to that of a 'continental' sort) is not short of answers to this question, and thus has its stock of replies to postmodernism. Indeed, there are several rival theories actively canvassed whose aim precisely is to explain satisfactorily the foundations of morality. These theories tend to proceed at somewhat different levels, a difference that can be described as one between the ethical and meta-ethical. The dispute between utilitarianism and rights-based moralities, between the successors of John Stuart Mill and the successors of Immanuel Kant, for instance, may be described as a dispute between theories of *ethics*, whereas the disputes between realism, anti-realism and quasi-realism (where Kant makes a further appearance of course) are disputes about *meta-ethics*. The ethical (in this sense) concerns fundamental moral principles by which conduct is to be guided; the meta-ethical concerns morality's metaphysical-cum-epistemological basis and status.

Some writers have attempted to introduce, or perhaps re-introduce, Christian theology into both these debates. Fergusson is one. Generally speaking, however, this attempt has not been effective, whatever its intellectual merits. One has only to make a cursory examination of the literature to see that few professional philosophers concerned with these issues can be found to make direct appeal to Christian doctrine. The explanation is not far to seek. To do so at the ethical level sooner or later requires an appeal to revealed theology – the Ten Commandments or the Sermon on the Mount, for instance – and thus to take as foundational the authority of the Bible, and as I alleged at the start at the start of this chapter, in this respect Christianity has for some time been in retreat. There are of course plenty of people who claim to look to the Bible as a source of moral guidance, but they are not those engaged in the philosophical debate between utilitarianism and deontology and the like. To appeal to theology at the meta-ethical level, i.e. in the debate between realism and anti-realism, on the other hand, though it has had more of a hearing perhaps, is widely thought sooner or later (usually sooner) to fall foul of the *Euthyphro* dilemma. This is the dilemma posed by Plato in the dialogue of that name, which shows, or at least is widely regarded as having shown, that the divine cannot underwrite the moral since, to put the matter very briefly, it either pre-supposes the goodness of the good (God declares things to be good *because* they are good), or makes the good rest upon the arbitrary fiat of a heavenly dictator (the good is *whatever* God declares it to be, including, should He choose to, acts that ordinary moral consciousness abhors).

These remarks are brief, peremptory and (to a degree) contentious. However, for all that I do not propose to elaborate upon them further or offer any defence (though the *Euthyphro* dilemma is one to which I shall return). This is because I think the most plausible and interesting context in which to attempt a re-introduction of Christian theology is at neither the ethical nor the meta-ethical level, but at what I shall refer to as the level of moral motivation.

Consider these distinctions. We can ask: 'Which things are moral, which immoral, and why?' These I take to be ethical questions. We can ask: 'What is the status of moral propositions, and can the moral be *known*, or only believed?' These I take to be meta-ethical questions. But there is this further issue: Even if we are all agreed about what is moral and immoral, and even if this can be shown to be something we can know, there remains this question: why should I *be* moral? Or, as I shall put it: what is the importance, the meaning, of morality?

There are a good many answers to this question, but two seem recurrent in the history of moral philosophy and specially prominent at the present time: (i) morality is the necessary foundation of social co-operation and hence of law, a view I shall refer to as the 'social contract' account; (ii) morality is the outcome of natural impulses in personal endeavour, a matter of how human beings most 'naturally' live, a view that in its modern version can be described as that of 'evolutionary' or 'socio-biological' ethics. If we take the first of these interpretations, the 'social contract' view (by which I mean to include 'Kantian reconstructionism'), morality is most importantly linked to interpersonal behaviour, and the range of concepts it involves (and is to be expressed in) is some combination of terms such as action, principle, consequence, harm, duties, happiness and rights. If we take the second, the 'evolutionary' approach, morality is linked to biological inheritance. We may thus raise this question: In trying to understand the significance of morality, which is to say moral endeavour, moral fault and moral accomplishment, should we think in terms of the requirements of social order, or should we think in terms of the natural workings of human kind?

Now it is in this third context, the context of moral motivation rather than that of the ethical or the meta-ethical, that there is scope for a return to Christian moral theology, and moreover a moral theology biblically based. This, I shall argue, is because both contract theory and socio-biological naturalism aim to address a fundamentally important question about human experience and existence, and fail to do so adequately. This fundamentally important question is the nature and existence of evil. It is in their explanations of evil that they founder, and as a result of that failure, and despite the presuppositions of modernism, we have good reason to re-think some elements of traditional and (largely) orthodox Christian moral theology. In short, while there may be no such thing as Christian ethics, Christian theology might nevertheless be the best explanation of the meaning of morality that we have.

IV

At any rate, this is what I hope to show, and it will be obvious that describing the task ahead in this way returns us to the opening theme of this chapter, the role of the theological in the intellectual explanation of existence and experience. The issue to be addressed in the course of this book can be summarised as the meaning of morality in the light of experience. My purpose is to make a convincing case for thinking that substantial theological conceptions are our only recourse if we are to make sense of morality. In short, without God, and theologically interpreted conceptions of good and evil (some of them premodern), what we call moral endeavour is fruitless, and all references to moral *obligation* are, consequently, without adequate foundation. Another way of putting this point is to say that only a theological (which is to say supernatural) account of experience can explain and justify the requirement to take morality *seriously*. This claim and the issues it gives rise to are quite independent of the *content* of morality. They do not change our ideas about what is good and what is evil, what is right and what is wrong. This is why it is the philosophical source of the modern belief in moral pluralism that is the principal subject of the inquiry, and not the fact (were it one) that there is a plurality of moral values in the contemporary world. *Whatever* we include in our moral code, or in our conception of the morally good person, and whatever we think the epistemological status of such things, we still have to determine what morality amounts to in the context of explaining and evaluating human experience. And indeed, bearing in mind the possibility of a certain sort of nihilism, we must even ask whether it amounts to anything. Or again, more modestly but more interestingly in my view, we can wonder whether it amounts to what it is customarily thought to. Adapting a question that the Italian philosopher Benedetto Croce raised with respect to art and the aesthetic, we can ask 'what function belongs properly to morality in the life of the spirit?' And we can even ask: does it have *any* function?

More explanation is needed on this point before the argument can proceed. I have used the expression 'taking morality seriously'. What does this mean? Consider a contrast between morals and manners (or ethics and etiquette). Politeness is important, and rudeness unpleasant. These are matters of good manners, but there seems to be a yawning gap between them and those concerns properly described as 'moral'. Being rude to people is indeed objectionable, but it is (or so we commonly believe) in a quite different league to torturing them. Intuitively we sense an important difference here, but what is it exactly? Take another example. It is certainly bad to bore your guests. This is something the good host has a duty to avoid, and prevent. Even so, failure to do so falls far short of subjecting them to humiliation by exploiting their personal vulnerability in the company of others. This seems to involve us in bad behaviour of a different order.

So most of us hold at any rate. We hold, in other words, that while manners have *some* claim upon us, but they do not have anything like the same claim as morality does. One way of trying to capture the difference is to think of two spectra on which human conduct can be judged – good *versus* bad, and good *versus* evil. Ordinary ways of speaking bear out this distinction; we *reserve* the term evil for deeds of a certain sort. Yet, if we are really to sustain this distinction, not just intuitively but reflectively, we have to give a convincing account of the difference. What *is* the difference between the merely bad and the truly evil? If we *can* explain it, then we have indeed explained why morality should be taken seriously, and why morality is significant in a way that manners are not. If, however, we *cannot* offer any convincing explanation of this difference, we will be forced to conclude that however deep our intuitive conviction to the contrary, morality does not actually amount to what we thought, that, even if we know and agree what it is, there is no more compelling reason to be moral than there is to be well mannered.

The full force of this issue may still not be evident. Surely, many will be inclined to think, even if we cannot explain the difference between manners and morality, and even if as a result we cannot really be said to know what it is, it is not a live option to cast doubt on the meaningfulness of morality. Torture, child molestation and rape are horrible things; loyalty, generosity and self-sacrifice are good things. Beside them, the rules of etiquette are of little consequence. Philosophical argument cannot bring us to doubt these matters *seriously.*

The trouble with this line of argument, if such it can be

called, is that it is not philosophy which calls these 'indubitable' contentions into doubt but the unquestionable existence of alternative ways of thinking in the record of intellectual history. The right-thinking but relatively unreflective person may suppose that the meaningfulness of morality is not a matter open to real discussion. But as a matter of fact there are several alternative opinions readily to hand – egoism, amoralism, aestheticism and the pursuit of glory, are just some – and all of them have commanded the adherence of serious thinkers. We can find almost innumerable examples in history and in literature which illustrate the real and not merely logical possibility of rejecting the claims of morality in preference to something else. Faust's pact with Satan is illustrative of a knowing preference for personal power; Machiavelli is amongst the most widely reputed instance (if not in point of fact the clearest) of the position which puts moral integrity in second place to political expediency, thereby, given the normal conception of morality as pre-eminent or over-riding, effectively according it no place at all; Oscar Wilde in some of his writings (*The Portrait of Dorian Gray* may plausibly be thought to advance a contrary view) shows a marked preference for the aesthetic over the ethical and seems to hold that the beautiful is more important than the good, a view other 'aesthetes' (Edmund Burke to a degree) have held; the attractions of a military prowess which favours the glory of conquest over even the most basic moral scruples appears to have had regular exemplification, not only in Genghis Khan, but also (coming nearer to home) in those who sang, in adoring praise, 'Saul has slain his thousands, but David has slain his tens of thousands' (1 Samuel 18:7). In our own time close study of some of the century's most notorious serial killers (about which I shall have more to say at a later stage) reveals an indifference to morality which is not easily dismissed as madness or psychological deformity.

These are just some of many possible examples. It is in my view naive to think that egoism, amoralism, aestheticism and militarism are merely logical possibilities in the philosopher's lexicon, to be invoked only to any purpose in the relatively idle business of exploring the foundations of morality. They are, rather, realities in both history and contemporary experience, demanding responses from what, borrowing a phrase of Onora O'Neill's, we might call 'the friends of virtue'. So it is a real, and a pressing question: on what is that response to be based?

What exactly is it that the friends of virtue have to show? They have to demonstrate that what has been called the over-ridingness of morality is grounded in something that can properly command the motivational reason of anyone who is not deranged. This way of putting it, together with my reference a few lines above to serial killers, alerts us to the interconnectedness of a number of issues. Amoralism, whether it takes the form of aestheticism, egoism or militarism needs to be explained. Might it not, though, be explained *away*? This question raises the possibility that some form of science – psychology, sociology or anthropology, perhaps – might take care of the aberrant cases, and leave us free to return to the assertion that the seriousness of morality cannot be in doubt for normal human beings, a view close to that of David Hume's alluded to earlier. What this suggestion signals, in effect, is that the rationality of morality is not challenged by evil because, once we understand it aright, evil properly so called simply does not exist. All that exists are aberrant, or defective people, human beings who are not evil so much as malfunctioning. This is, in my view, a very important, if largely unacknowledged, implication of the naturalistic humanism to which the modern mind subscribes, and both disclosing and questioning this implication is a major part of the purpose of this book. There is further the challenge with which Nietzsche presents us, in several places, that we *ought* to go *Beyond Good and Evil*, the title of one of his best known books, a topic with which I shall also, briefly, be concerned.

To state the matter in this way is to make use of the shortest of summaries. What it signals is a set of highly important issues which will be addressed in far greater detail at later stages. The questions 'Why should we take morality seriously?' and 'Is there such a thing as evil?' require us to consider the alternatives to doing so from both a normative and an explanatory point of view. As a result we must engage with several interconnected issues – the motivating basis of morality, the reality of evil, and the viability of naturalistic explanation. All of these will be of major concern in subsequent chapters. So, too, will the interpretation of the New Testament.

Why so? The answer will not be clear until much more has been said, but to start the process of clarification it is necessary to turn away from the question of morality. This does not mean that we are turning away from the question of Christian ethics, however. In fact, the relation of Christian ethics to the New Testament is the subject of the next chapter.

CHAPTER 2

The real Jesus

The previous chapter introduced the principal claim of this book, a somewhat ambitious one, that only a theological context can adequately account for the seriousness of morality and the reality of evil. But, to take only the first claim, if theology does explain the seriousness of morality, how does it do so, and in particular, how does *Christian* theology do this?

I

The model of Christian ethics as one distinctive code amongst the many competing and conflicting 'moral systems' within a pluralist world (a model about which substantial doubts were raised in the first chapter) has an appropriately straightforward answer to this question. Christian ethics is the code of conduct that approves the actions and attitudes Christ commended, and rejects those which He condemned. There is a parallel here with Mohammed and the Koran, but if we combine with this the Doctrine of the Incarnation the implication is that the words of *Jesus* are the words of *God*, from which we can conclude that the basis of Christian ethics is divine commandment, the law of God. One major objection to this way of thinking, the objection canvassed in the previous chapter, is that there simply is no list of moral principles or injunctions which can accurately be described as distinctively and exclusively Christian. If this is true, then we are lacking at least one crucial element in the model – a determinate content to 'Christian ethics'. But radical though this objection may be, it is not the only difficulty the commonplace model of Christian ethics encounters. Nor, arguably, is it even the most important from a Christian point of view. An even more devastating objection lies in the suggestion that we do not actually know much, or possibly anything, about what the historical Jesus commended and condemned. If so, Christian ethics not only lacks distinctive content; it lacks any biblical foundation.

The first point to be made in support of this more damaging contention is a relatively minor one. Anyone who examines the Gospels with a reasonable degree of care will find that the list of actions *expressly* commended or condemned by Jesus is very short. Any possible list, moreover, is completely silent on most of the issues that concern the modern world – racism, the environment, contraception, homosexuality, abortion, euthanasia, capital punishment, genetic engineering – all of which can be given a Christian 'spin' only by implication, often of a rather strained kind, though there are not lacking Christians anxious to demonstrate the contemporary 'relevance' of the Gospel by straining for just such implications. Secondly, in the issues on which the Gospels record Jesus as pronouncing directly, his *dicta* largely incorporate and endorse actions and attitudes which traditional Judaism *also* commended and condemned. Furthermore, the authority of the Jewish law in this regard seems not only to have been accepted, but to have been invoked by Jesus. Where there is some variation, it is said (by him) not to be an abolition but a 'fulfilment' of the Judaic Law. A third point is this. Alongside the particular pronouncements (about divorce for instance) which can be found in the Gospels, there are two explicit general principles, the two great commandments, to love God and love your neighbour, the second of which has generally been given a strongly ethical interpretation. (There is, of course, in St John's Gospel, a third 'great commandment' – to love one another – but I am not directly concerned with it at this point.)

Now neither of these first two commandments is unique to Jesus, nor (even more significantly) held by him to be such; he is quoting from the Jewish scriptures and must have known that he was doing so. In fact, if not exactly commonplaces in first century Palestine, the requirement to love God and neighbour would have been thoroughly familiar to most of his audiences. And several times, these and other injunctions are expressly acknowledged to be so by Jesus himself – 'You have heard it said . . .' In his response to the rich young ruler, for instance, Jesus simply reminds him of that which he has always known. In short, despite the claims of many, on a fairly plain reading of the Gospels, Jesus was neither an innovative moral teacher nor a moral reformer in any very obvious sense. Even the injunction to love one's enemies, often cited as a specially novel addition, is not wholly without precedent in older Jewish thinking.

The absence of a substantial core of novel moral doctrine is something we can deduce just by taking the Gospels at, relatively speaking, face value. If Jesus' main claim to fame is that of being a moral teacher (as Chilton and McDonald assert), we seem forced to conclude that it is somewhat flimsy. But there is a still greater obstacle yet in the way of thinking that Christian ethics is to be identified as a distinctive moral code embodying 'the ethics Jesus taught'. It is here that the profound challenge of modern historical inquiry alluded to at the start of chapter one comes prominently into view. The story of New Testament scholarship in the last hundred and fifty years or so is one in which a growing consensus has held the 'historical' Jesus to be an ever more elusive figure about whose actual doings (and hence about whose teaching) we can only be very uncertain, if indeed we can know anything at all. Though it is a story that will probably be familiar to many of those reading this book, its importance to my argument is such that it requires to be set out once more. To keep it within manageable bounds however (for it is a very large subject), I shall focus on the work of the five most famous contributors to this history – Strauss, Renan, Wrede, Schweitzer and Bultmann.

II

The most powerful influence on modern New Testament scholarship is to be found in a work by the nineteenth century German scholar/theologian David Friedrich Strauss (1808–74). It is not an exaggeration to say that Strauss's book *Leben Jesu*, though much less well known, is as important a work in cultural history as Darwin's *Origin of Species*. First published in 1835–6, it occasioned much opposition, an English translation (by the novelist George Eliot), *The Life of Jesus Critically Examined*, appearing in 1846. Like Darwin's, Strauss's book did not spring unprecedented from an intellectual vacuum. Importantly, Strauss was a student of Friedrich Schleiermacher (1768–1834), to whom brief reference was made in the Preface. It was Schleiermacher who began the theological effort at *rapprochement* with the 'scientific' trends of the Enlightenment, an effort which has characterised a great deal of 'liberal' theology ever since. Strauss both learned from and rejected the outlook of Schleiermacher. However, Strauss rejected not only orthodox interpretations of the Bible, but the 'liberal' theology of his time as well. His book drew together a number of strands of thought that had been fermenting for some years, and for this reason, despite the furore it provoked, was less a wholly radical departure than the culmination of a process of intellectual revision which had begun quite some time before, most notably in the work of Hermann Reimarus (1694–1768) to whom Strauss makes explicit reference. Indeed it can be argued that Schleiermacher was no less radical than Strauss. 'The consistency with which Schleiermacher is willing to sacrifice the particularities of the Gospel texts to his single christological idea is in its own way just as ruthless as the *Kaltblütigkeit* of which D. F. Strauss boasted in the first volume of his *Life of Jesus*' (Watson 1997: 133). Nevertheless, in the case of both Strauss and Darwin (though for the moment it is Strauss with whom I am more concerned) the new work seemed to encapsulate and endorse all the dramatic implications of ways of thinking that had, so to speak, only been in the air hitherto. The original shift 'occurred in the world of the German universities during the second half of the eighteenth century: the resources of learning were increasingly deployed in the service of non-orthodox positions, which thereby attracted to themselves not only the inevitable controversy, but also the prestige of *Wissenschaft*' (130). By its remarkable propagation of this trend *Leben Jesu* constituted one of those historical *fulcra* on which great changes turn. And so, indeed, it was perceived at the time of its publication, with the result that from the conservative side it attracted a powerful religious opprobrium, an opprobrium which up to this point had not yet been able to focus itself upon a single object. On the liberal side it provoked something of a crisis, because it made explicit implications of liberal theological thought that many liberals were unwilling openly to acknowledge. This explains, in large part, Strauss's contemporary infamy and his subsequent fame.

What is specially interesting, and remarkable, about Strauss's work is that we can find in it, set out for the first time possibly, very many of the categories by which study of the New Testament has been structured for a long time since. Strauss approached the Gospel stories with a resolve to sift the historically and scientifically respectable elements from the 'supernatural' elements, to separate the 'history' from the 'myth', the real from the fantastical, accepting the first as 'fact' and understanding the second as 'mythological' interpretation. This was an application of the Hegelian philosophy in which he was educated and to which he subscribed. According to Hegel, traditional Christianity incorporated in symbolic form truths which his (Hegel's) philosophy revealed in their rational form. Accordingly, Strauss set out to rescue the believable from the incredible. He was not, initially, a religious sceptic. Rather, he held that popular Christianity embodied the truth, but in symbolic form, symbol which orthodox religion mistakenly interpreted literally. Furthermore, he attributed the 'mythological' elements in the Gospel to additions which the early church made to the basic, underlying story, and in the title of a subsequent book (*Der Christus des Glaubens und der Jesu der Geschichte*) Strauss expressly draws the distinction which has so dominated later thought, the distinction between the Christ of faith and the Jesus of history.

It would be wrong to suggest that this new line of thought swept all before it. There continued to be serious, respected and highly influential Biblical scholars who were not part of the same movement, Adolf Schlatter (1852–1938) being a specially notable case. Yet Strauss is of enormous importance for intellectual history, and cultural history more broadly, because, if the *Origins of Species* threw doubt on a major element in natural theology – the design argument, that the order we see in nature implies an orderer – *Leben Jesu* constituted (or at any rate seemed to constitute) a direct attack on the authority of the Bible and the inerrancy of Scripture. This was an attack felt much more closely by the faithful and the religious establishment than the subsequent Darwinian assault (conducted not by Darwin but by his admirer Huxley), because the cogency of natural theology, being by and large less important in the pew and the pulpit, could be held to be a more 'academic', and thus more remote, concern. *Leben Jesu*, by contrast, seemed to attack the Christian religion at its most widely believed, and hallowed, foundation – the person and authority of Jesus himself.

Strauss was condemned for his work and dismissed from his post at Tübingen. Later he was nominated for a chair of theology at Zurich, only for the nomination to be withdrawn because of adverse public opinion. His personal intellectual history presages that of so many subsequently – from pastor, to scholar, to sceptic, to scientific materialist. The message most Christians drew was clear, and in many quarters incontrovertible: turn the critical light of scientific history on the Bible itself and what emerges from the process is a destructive separation of core history – history proper – from accumulated (and probably invented) myth. Better then to resist the advances of modern scholarship altogether, an attitude which still motivates some branches of conservative Christianity, especially in North America. There thus began with Strauss, more so than with Darwin in my view, the 'conflict' between 'science' and religion, one in which 'science' includes empirical history.

This same tension, and anxiety, was exhibited in another (celebrated) instance much later in the century when William Robertson Smith, Professor of Hebrew and Old Testament at the Free Church of Scotland College in Aberdeen was arraigned before the General Assembly of the Church for heresy, on account of his interpretation of the Old Testament. Robertson threw doubt on both the historical primacy and the Mosaic authorship of the first five books of the Bible. Today, his explorations seem nothing more adventurous than the sort of careful examination of real evidence that any decent historical scholarship requires. But at the time, to many minds they represented a threatening scepticism, and an exercise in rationalism which would inevitably lead to the undermining of the faith.

In the modern world, this conservative reaction, to Strauss, Robertson Smith and several others, can only appear anti-intellectual and irrational, a preference for dogma over untrammelled inquiry. These descriptions are broadly correct, in my view. However deep one's attachments to the Christian religion, no one who is intellectually serious can adopt such a conservatism. Honest intellectual investigation, 'science' if you like, advances (at least in part) by the free exercise of critical reason, which must therefore be unconstrained by dogmatic requirements. If Christian doctrine is to be relevant to the wider human endeavour of understanding experience it must hold its own, and make some sort of contribution, to the intellectual excursions of the human mind in a broader framework. It cannot be artificially confined within the prejudices of the comfortable and the familiar. Even more importantly, from a religious point of view, there is good theological reason not to accept intellectual isolation, however much it might offer credal security. There is an old perception, but an accurate one (unfashionable at present certainly), that while error may take many forms, truth is essentially unitary. The accurate and adequate explanation of one aspect of experience cannot conflict, but must cohere, with every other. It follows that if God is indeed a reality and if Jesus really is His unique revelation – the Eternal come into being in Time (to quote Kierkegaard) – the honest pursuit of truth in science or history cannot in the end controvert this. Curiously, it is only a deep uncertainty about the truth of Christianity that could make us think otherwise, and it is this uncertainty which has generated a retreat to the theological ghetto, a retreat evidenced in the 'liberal' embrace of pluralism and 'symbolic interpretation' no less than in a 'conservative' refusal to entertain the investigations of science and history.

At the same time, there is a danger that in the spirit of liberal, undogmatic inquiry, the views that conservative opinion sought to protect come to be regarded, just for that reason, as intellectually indefensible. Don Cupitt (one of the most prominent radically 'liberal' theologians) approvingly quotes a passage from Schopenhauer.

What is most opposed to the discovery of truth is not the false appearance that proceeds from things and leads to error, nor even directly a weakness of the intellect. On the contrary, it is preconceived opinion, the prejudice, which as a spurious *a priori*, is opposed to truth. It is then like a contrary wind that drives the ship back from the direction in which the wind lies, so that rudder and sail now work to no purpose. (Cupitt 1984: 254)

What Cupitt fails to observe is that liberals, no less than conservatives, can be prejudiced about what it is and is not reasonable to believe; a spurious *a priori* can just as easily be at work in their unquestioned assumption that the 'supernatural' cannot be real, and that the Gospels cannot be construed (if only in part) as history properly so called. Indeed, a large part of my purpose in this book is to identify and contest those points in contemporary thought at which just such liberal prejudice is at its most striking and its most powerful. As Francis Watson notes:

a genuine and valuable hermeneutical insight is converted into a more questionable hermeneutical dogma. The insight that 'meaning' is more than the transference of a given content from the mind of the author to the mind of the reader is incorporated into a radical hermeneutic that proclaims the death of the author and the openness of texts to an unlimited plurality of readings. (Watson 1997: 96)

Actually, even this dogma is untrue to itself and disguises a shift in historical attention. In view of their actual practice

[i]t is difficult to avoid supposing that those who no longer think it possible to use the Gospels to reconstruct the historical Jesus compensate for this loss by using them to reconstruct the communities that produced the Gospels. All the historical specificity for which historical critics long is transferred from the historical Jesus to the evangelist's community. (Bauckham 1996: 20)

Still, however this may be, in explanation (if not justification) of both the liberal and the conservative reactions to nineteenth century advances in science and history, it has to be admitted that, on the surface at any rate, after Strauss biblical scholarship did indeed become subject to a bewildering multiplicity of 'approaches' – hermeneutics, form criticism, redaction criticism, literary interpretation, socio-linguistic inquiry, comparative anthropology and several more. In short, study of the Gospels became a sort of 'open season' for those impressed by the relatively recent disciplines of scientific history, comparative literature and social anthropology with the result that an 'enlightened' approach to the Scriptures seemed, to the liberals, to licence a strong anti-metaphysics. Conversely, to the conservatives the very same process seemed to usher in an era of anarchic unbelief.

All these new approaches included the study of people and texts 'in context', the only point at issue being the scope of the context. Was it simply the history of the specific tradition, or the much larger context of human anthropology? In confirmation of the conservatives' fears, the conclusions that were drawn from these innovative approaches tended to be negative, in the sense that each of the new methods threw increasing doubt upon received religious understanding. As a result, religious scepticism was given a powerful fillip by the new socio-historical-cum-literary study of Scripture. It seemed that 'scientific' study of the Gospels revealed them to be historically less and less reliable, thereby underlining the suspicion that 'scientific history' generated among traditionally minded Christians. In this way, biblical scholarship served to strengthen the division between 'liberals' and 'conservatives', the first seeking to accommodate 'science', the second seeking to oppose it. This is a division that has shaped the history of Christianity (and not just theology) through the larger part of the twentieth century. It is one that persists, and can be found expressly exemplified in a recent volume by Marcus Borg and N. T. Wright, *The Meaning of Jesus*.

Among the many studies of the Gospels which followed upon Strauss, one of the most notable was *Vie de Jesus* by the Frenchman Ernest Renan (1823–92). Renan's book differs from

Strauss's in that it was written at the outset from the point of view of non-belief. Whatever its deficiencies, which are now widely acknowledged, as well as sharing the aim of distinguishing between the natural and the supernatural, *Vie de Jesus* introduced an important new element, one that has continued to influence scholarship. Renan represented (and studied) Jesus as primarily a first-century Palestinian, a man of his own time, to be understood contextually. From this point on, New Testament scholarship had an aim as well as a method – to discover Jesus the Palestinian Jew. It hardly needs to be said that almost built into this aim was the elimination of the eternal, credal, Christ existing 'before the foundations of the earth'. A question of immense importance, and one with which I shall be much concerned, is whether, as has been widely supposed, there is indeed a conflict here.

Damaging though this focus on Jesus the Palestinian was thought to be to the formerly (largely) unquestioned authority of the Gospels, and hence to the credibility of the Christian religion, worse was to come, and once more from the pen of a scholar whom many supposed to be in the Christian mainstream, the German, William Wrede (1859–1906), though he himself would have regarded academic scholarship as above, or beyond, religious affiliation. Wrede turned his attention to the Gospel of Mark which had generally been regarded (as it still is in some quarters) as the least theological and most historical of the four. Read in a relatively straightforward and perhaps uncritical way, the Gospel of Mark has the most obvious claim to be unvarnished 'history'. What Wrede questioned in particular was the conception of the 'Messianic secret'. It had long been noticed that in Mark Jesus is forever asking his followers and others, not to broadcast the evident (usually miraculous) signs of his Messiahship, but to keep them 'secret'. The idea of the Messianic secret has a double function; it explains both how Jesus could believe himself to be the Messiah and why at the same time his claim to Messiahship was not acknowledged earlier than it was. By raising doubts about the Messianic secret, Wrede raised doubts about Jesus' self-understanding. If, in fact, by Wrede's account Jesus probably did not believe that he was the traditional Messiah long-expected by Judaism, two consequences seem to follow. First, Jesus thought of himself as a (relatively) ordinary Palestinian and his role as no more than that of the Prophets. Second, the attribution of Messiahship was a later accretion by the early Church, an acclamation of 'faith' not a record of 'history'.

Following Renan and Wrede, the next most significant work (of very many) is undoubtedly a book by Albert Schweitzer (1875–1965). The German title of this book signifies a self-conscious continuation of the history just recounted – *Von Reimarus zu Wrede*. The title of the English translation by which it is better known, *The Quest of the Historical Jesus*, can be taken as describing the agenda which has overshadowed all subsequent New Testament scholarship. In fact, Schweitzer's *Quest* was to some extent a self-acknowledged failure; the liberal Protestant attempt to replace the iconic Christ with a real Jesus drew it further away from, not closer to, the religious beliefs of ordinary Christianity, though Schweitzer himself remained a faithful Protestant (of a special sort) to the end of his long life. But the thrust of his *Quest* was that the more we know of the historical Jesus the further he becomes removed from the eternal Christ of popular religion. This is because the Jesus who emerges from Schweitzer's study is a confirmed 'eschatologist', which is to say, a Palestinian Jew of the first-century wholly convinced of the immanent end of the world, an outcome which, as we know, did not materialise. Amongst other conclusions he draws is the suggestion that the relative importance of Jesus and John the Baptist may have been rather different to what has normally been thought, and that perhaps Jesus is not to be identified with 'the One who is to come' at all. In any event, Jesus the first century Palestinian was firmly locked into the eschatology of traditional Judaism which expected an early end to the space–time world of history.

If this is true, if, that is to say, the message of Jesus the Jew was essentially messianic, and if, as we can hardly fail to admit, the end of the world did not arrive in his time, has not arrived, and shows no sign of arriving, there is reason both to regard the real Jesus as a creature of his time and the Christ of faith as a creation, if not entirely an invention, of Christians faced with the task of continuing their religion in the light of a striking refutation of its central doctrine. Jesus their Lord predicted the end of the world; the world did not end; now what? Should such have been the case it is no surprise that an alternative and quite different theological superstructure came to be raised on historical foundations which, in reality, provided it with little real support. As other commentators put it, what we find in the early Church is a transformation of 'the Son of God', a relatively lightweight theological conception, into the much more heavyweight conception of 'God the Son'.

There thus arises the suspicion that the whole of the Christian religion, with its doctrines of the Incarnation and the Trinity, is a construct that has floated free of the historical events which were its genesis. Jesus the Jew is real history; Christ the Second Person of the Trinity is theological myth. The identification of the two is the remarkable work of the early Christians, remarkable because it survived very many centuries, until the advent of scientific history, in fact. The story of biblical scholarship over the nineteenth century is that Strauss, Wrede, Renan and Schweitzer finally opened our eyes.

This result, interestingly, is one which challenged the liberal no less than the conservative, theology of the nineteenth century. Don Cupitt summarises the implication of Schweitzer's conclusions in this respect as follows.

The Kingdom of God in liberal Christianity. . . lay within the present historical order. It was the present dwelling of God in Christ in men's hearts inspiring their actions, and it was the future goal of social development to be brought about by human endeavour. But Schweitzer, together with a number of other scholars of his generation, argued that the original Jesus had been very different from the Jesus of Liberal Protestantism. He had been imbued with the ideas of late ancient Jewish eschatology. . . and all his words and deeds were governed by one dominant thought, that an entirely supernatural Kingdom of God would arrive very shortly whether men wished for it or not. (Cupitt 1984: 105)

And of course, it didn't. Yet the credulous found other ways of going on believing the literal version.

Or so postmodernist, anti-realist theologians (and others) contend. It is a thesis that derives not inconsiderable support from recordable phenomena in the history of religions. In the course of the last two millennia there have been many messianic movements, some of them quite modern. Generally they have predicted the end of the world, often giving quite specific dates. When these dates come and go and the world, despite the prediction, continues in its normal form, one would expect the messianic movement to fade away. But in fact this is not (or not always) so. The Buchanites, who took their cue from the activities of the colourful eighteenth century Scottish adventist Mother Buchan, almost all dispersed shortly after the spectacular failure of her predictions.[1] By contrast, both Jehovah's Witnesses and Seventh Day Adventists are adherents of movements that began with precise eschatological predictions. Yet, when those predictions, no less than Mother Buchan's, proved false, contrary to reasonable expectation the movements in question did not die, but found other doctrines and forms of expression which sustained them in existence. The questioning mind may find this puzzling, but in the end it has no choice but to record the fact that human beings are capable (who knows for what reason) of these extraordinary voltes-face. Why should this not be true of Christianity in general? Why should it not be the case that its founding inspiration was a messianic prediction which proved false but which, notwithstanding this proven failure, produced no diminution in the enthusiasm of its adherents, but merely caused them to re-interpret its message in other, less falsifiable, terms?

If this is indeed the case, is all lost for the Christian religion? Can someone who wishes to be intellectually serious, accepting the advances of both the natural and the historical sciences, at the same time be a conscientious Christian? This was Strauss's problem, a problem shared by very many since. Some, like Strauss, in the end answer 'No'. Others answer with a qualified 'Yes'; it is possible to be both a Christian and intellectually serious, *if* we re-interpret both the Scriptures and the central

---

[1] For an informative and entertaining account of this extraordinary movement see H. V. Morton, *In Scotland Again* (London, 1933) pp. 27–35.

elements of traditional Christian theology. Marcus Borg is a good example of this position in his contribution to the book already cited – *The Meaning of Jesus.*

In effect this is also the answer given by the next, and in some ways last, significant figure in the post-Straussian phase of New Testament scholarship, Rudolf Bultmann (1884–1976). Bultmann shares the ambition of retaining the essence of Christianity while abandoning much of the theology and all of the metaphysics which traditionally have been thought to be its essentials. It is to Bultmann that we owe the term 'demythologising', that is, the task of re-interpreting both the Gospels and the theological constructions that have been based upon them in ways undistorted by myth. But the point of demythologising is not to explain the religious away, as an irrational aberration of the human mind. Rather, to demythologise the Scriptures is to uncover their real meaning. Bultmann combined the history-of-traditions method of scholarship with the existentialist philosophy which had its religious origins in the Danish Lutheran thinker Søren Kierkegaard. As I observed in the previous chapter, at the heart of Kierkegaard's rather prolix writings is the basic thought that human beings are faced with fundamental choices, which is to say, choices that cannot be determined by any external reality or authority, but have to be *made.* One such choice is whether or not to be a Christian, and it is this thought that Bultmann follows. On his interpretation the Jesus of history called upon his disciples to make a choice, and the Christ of faith goes on issuing the same call. The point of connection between the two is pared down to an historical minimum – the Crucifixion – and demythologising, by eliminating great tracts of mistaken cosmology, far from undermining the heart of the Christian religion actually serves its purposes by allowing the fundamental religious demand – Do you say yes or no to Christ? – to be heard by the modern mind with the same sort of stark clarity that the first century Palestinians heard it. To quote Watson again, summarising Bultmann:

To try to prove that we encounter God's word in the gospel of the crucified Jesus indicates simply that one has failed to hear this word; for the word is a radical question directed towards our self-understanding rather than an invitation to reflect on its own credentials . . . [I]n its true being, the church is not an empirical inner-historical reality, but the empty space within which the event of salvation must again and again take place. (Watson 1997: 154–5)

Bultmann's account of the role of the historical Christ is theologically driven. In accord with the spirit of Lutheranism, Christianity must be theocentric, not Christocentric. The essential element is the place of the individual's response to the perception of being under the judgement of God, and from this point of view undue concern with the historical Christ is distracting. What matters, theologically speaking, is not the Jesus of history, about whom our knowledge will always be relative to sources and evidence, but the absolute demand of God to His creation. It is for this reason, rather than any generated by historical scepticism, that the 'Christ of faith', in any and every age must displace the 'Jesus of history'.

Now an important difficulty with this timeless and hence 'modernity relevant' existentialist version of Christianity is that it is not immediately clear what precisely the 'call' is to, if not to belief in the truth of some doctrine. The answer many have given, though it is not altogether in keeping with Bultmann's own, is that the call is to the Christian 'way of life'. Unfortunately, as I argued in the last chapter, whatever may have been true of first century Palestine, two thousand years later there is no one, nor even any very distinctive, 'Christian way of life' to be called to. The second difficulty is, if anything, more troubling. An important element in the story is that demythologising uncovers the same essential religious call that Jesus issued to his first disciples. But if their understanding of the world was structured around conceptions that it is impossible for the modern mind to deploy, what reason could there be to think that it is indeed the same call? If the differences are deep and numerous enough, as the history-of-traditions tended to claim, surely it is more plausible to think in terms of a complete rupture than an underlying continuity?

This brings us to a closely related question, and one that both conservative Christians and modern secularists have pressed: what exactly is the difference between a demythologised religion and atheism? To put the matter simply: how does the claim that there is no God 'out there' differ from the claim that there is no God at all?

III

The suggestion that 'religionless Christianity' (an expression of Bonhoeffer's not Bultmann's of course) and simple irreligion amount to much the same thing is not new, and may be illustrated to good effect by comparing the positions of Hume and Kierkegaard on religion. Hume being the great religious sceptic and Kierkegaard the great Christian fideist, one would expect their views to be at the opposite ends of some spectrum or other. Yet the fact is that their accounts of religious belief come strikingly close. Hume, at the end of the *Essay on Miracles* says this:

> The Christian religion not only was at first attended with miracles, but even at this day cannot be believed by any reasonable person without one. And whoever is moved by Faith to assent to it, is conscious of a continued miracle in his own person, which subverts all the principles of his understanding, and gives him a determination to believe what is most contrary to custom and experience. (Hume 1902: 131)

Compare this with Kierkegaard, who approvingly quotes Kant's German contemporary, the religious thinker J. G. Hamann, who regarded this passage from Hume as a proof, no less, that 'one can preach the truth in jest and without knowing or desiring to do so'. Kierkegaard himself says that 'to see God, or see miracles happen by virtue of the absurd . . . reason must stand aside' (*Journals* trans. A. Dru, p. 498). In short, what Hume offers as a sceptical thesis, Kierkegaard regards as confirming the fideistic point of view. But if both have succeeded in formulating their views correctly, the result is the disappearance of any real or substantial difference between faith and scepticism, between belief and unbelief.

Hume's philosophical doubts (which he gave expression to long before Darwin or Strauss of course) are to be found in his *Dialogues Concerning Natural Religion*, but of more immediate relevance here is the position he advances in his *Natural History of Religion*. Hume was a sceptic but a humanist also. It is with a kind of fondness that he records the absurd lengths to which human credulity can go, an absurdity illustrated in his view by the Christian religion writ large, and not merely in its more extravagant versions. Religious doctrines and stories are false and fantastical. It is a fact about human beings that they have a tendency to believe them, but as the passage just quoted remarks, it requires a miracle which subverts all the normal principles of the understanding for the serious thinker to endorse them.

There is an honesty about Hume's position which many have found lacking in those who happily deploy the category of myth to discount theological doctrine and yet continue to proclaim the relevance of Christianity. Are they not trying to eat their cake and have it, to abandon the intellectual credentials of the Christian religion and yet continue with the liturgies they like? Don Cupitt is one familiar figure against whom this charge has been laid. Certainly, in *The Sea of Faith* he appears to embrace enthusiastically a position even more radical than Hume's profound humanism, an anthropocentrism that makes man the measure of all things.

We have come to see that there can be for us nothing but the worlds that are constituted for us by our own languages and activities. All meaning and truth and value are man-made and could not be otherwise. The flux of experience is continuous and has no structure of its own. It is we who impose shape upon it to make of it a world to live in. (Cupitt 1984: 20)

Yet Cupitt, in contrast to Hume, finds this contention compatible with the continuing practice of religion. This is because he does not think 'that the practice of religion has to depend upon the acceptance of a body of dogmatic beliefs. Of course it commonly does so depend; but it need not do so, and indeed it ought not to do so' (257). In this he simply repeats what he had said earlier in a book significantly entitled *Taking Leave of God*: 'There cannot and must not be any religious interest in any extra-religious existence of God; such a thing would be a frivolous distraction' (Cupitt 1980: 9). As these quotations indicate, Cupitt in fact thinks that the abandonment of dogma is religiously liberating, a liberation in which the mystic is freed from the theologian.

The mystic attempts to overcome dogma, insisting that God, Christ and heaven are not 'up there' but are to be found in the heart by desire, by love, by the will; that is by a path of inner purification. (Cupitt 1984: 259)

A person who has become fully a Christian no longer experiences any kind of metaphysical yearning after any Absolute that lies 'beyond', for he possess all things now. It is misleading to speak of him as 'anti-metaphysical', or of his faith as 'non-cognitive', as if he were some kind of rejecter who holds a reduced faith and denies the metaphysical dogmas that are so precious to others. The truth is rather the other way round: one who has truly become a Christian no longer feels himself to be alienated from religious realities, and therefore no longer needs any credal convictions to connect himself to them. He does not need any beliefs when his whole mode of existence has become pure and absolute affirmation, a Yes now. (Cupitt 1984: 263)

To my mind, though I shall not at this moment argue the point, the 'pure and absolute affirmation' of which Cupitt makes so much, is indistinguishable from the spirit of humanism which sees itself (and generally has been seen as) arising from the honest abandonment of religion. There may even be something unpleasantly disrespectful here in a line of thought which identifies humanism, often a position hard won, with the very religion from which it has tried to struggle free. Humanism is a topic to which I shall return (in the final chapter), but for the purposes of this chapter, the passages just quoted contain more interesting material.

As the first passage makes clear, Cupitt certainly shares with humanists a profound anthropocentrism – humankind is both the source and the final purpose of human experience. But what the subsequent quotations make clear is that he interprets this anthropocentrism in a radically *subjective* way. That is to say, the source and final purpose of belief is human *desire*. Thus, the purified mystic is said to be freed from the 'yearning' for metaphysical beliefs that the conservative continues to hanker after, and is described as finding that he 'does not need' any credal convictions. What this whole way of thinking rules out, however, is the idea that whether anyone feels a need for such beliefs and creeds or not, the belief in question could still be *true*.

Now those who take a strongly anthropocentric line have a general difficulty with the idea of truth. It is a topic which warrants much further consideration. However, a more modest position in relation to metaphysical theology is that its propositions *cannot* be true, because they are not meaningful. In the passages just quoted it is striking how the expressions 'beyond' and 'up there' are put in scare quotes. This signals, I think, a doubt that even their denial can be given any meaning at all, and of course if it can't, then their denial does not amount to any real loss. In ceasing to believe the meaningless we are no worse off. But consider a similar sounding phrase – 'back then'. Surely I can hold meaningful beliefs about what was and was not true 'back then'? If so, I can hold meaningful beliefs about what was true of Jesus (or any one else) 'back then', and if such beliefs figure in credal formulations, the reasonableness or otherwise of believing them is open to assessment. Take the proposition 'Jesus never existed.' There seems no obstacle to my asking whether it is reasonable to believe this or not, and this is a question independent of the question whether anyone needs to or wants to believe it. In short, we seem to have made one small and easy move back in the direction of an objectivity independent of human needs and desires.

At this point anti-realists and postmodernists will be inclined to declare, of course, that there is no such thing as objectivity, or else, more sophisticatedly, that the idea of objectivity must in the end be given a subjective analysis. The first observation to be made here must be that this itself is a dogma. Why close your mind to the possibility of its being false? Is this not precisely one of those spurious *a prioris* described by Schopenhauer? However, I do not propose to tackle postmodernist or anti-realist epistemology directly, but to adopt a far more limited approach, the one suggested by the comparison between the phrases 'up there' and 'back then', namely, can *historical* beliefs be true or false? This brings us to a new range of topics, though importantly related to those with which we have been so far concerned.

Historiography, by which I mean a self-conscious attention to the aims and methods of historical inquiry, is a relative newcomer to the intellectual firmament. This is not to deny that those who have sought to write history, from the time of Herodotus indeed, have often turned their minds to the question of how best it is to be done. Nevertheless, an express and close attention to the 'scientific' basis and credentials of history is largely a product of the nineteenth century. It arose first from the development of hermeneutics, the belief that we can only understand the utterances and evidence of the past by setting them in a wider context, the social and historical context in which they were made. The crucial mistake of so much hitherto history, according to this way of thinking, was that it (unconsciously) interpreted the verbal evidence of the past as though it were the testimony of contemporaries, and was insufficiently reflective about the preconceptions that it brought to the study of the past. In *The Idea of History* R. G. Collingwood, perhaps the most significant philosopher of history of the twentieth century, provides a sustained attempt to distinguish (and discredit) this 'scissors and paste' conception of historical study from that exercise of properly critical thought which alone can result in historical understanding properly so called.

Collingwood is both insightful and convincing in his account of the difference between the 'scissors and paste' conception and (what I shall henceforth refer to as) critical history. But this distinction has become confused with another, to the detriment of thinking clearly about historical method. 'Scissors and paste' versus 'critical history' should not be confused with the distinction between 'mere chronicle' and 'historical interpretation'. To understand the difference and the implications it has for the study of the historical Jesus, it is necessary to make a short excursion into the philosophy of history. Accordingly, this section of the chapter will be devoted to historiography before returning in the next to the question of what we can know about the real Jesus and how we can know it.

The past is not present; we cannot now see it or hear it. This truism may not be as empty as it sounds. At the very least it should alert us to the fact that our knowledge of the past cannot be arrived at in quite the way our knowledge of the present is, but must be acquired in some other fashion. One commonplace explanation of the difference is generated by empiricism, a philosophical doctrine that has dominated a good deal of epistemology, which is to say, the theory of knowledge. Empiricism holds, very broadly, that the ultimate ground of all knowledge must be immediate sense experience – what we see and hear and feel. Now if this is correct, knowledge of the past presents an immediate difficulty because, since the past is not available for present inspection, if we are to have any knowledge of it, we have to obtain it in some other way. One natural line of thought appeals to memory, which it regards as a sort of substitute sense experience, less 'vivid', if we follow Hume, the high priest of empiricism, than our experience of the present. Memory is nonetheless a 'direct' connection between the present mind and past experience. We cannot see what is in the past, but we can remember having seen it. Even if this is the right way to think about historical knowledge, however, it is evident that memory can take us only as far back as our own experience goes. What about the time *before* that, when we were not yet around to witness anything? Here again the spirit of empiricism has a natural answer: we must gather the reports of those who *were* around. It is in this way that the concept of scissors and paste history comes about. If we want to know what happened in the past, empiricism implies, we must scour the recorded observations of those who were around then, clip out the testimony of these contemporaries, and paste it together into a continuous narrative of how the past was.

There are so many things wrong with this conception that it is difficult to know where to begin. Perhaps the most important observation to make is that the scissors-and-paste 'method', if it can be graced with such a designation, is deeply uncritical. It assumes that all the statements of past observers are true. Indeed it *must* make this assumption because the empiricism on which it rests allows the present historian no other knowledge of the past than the witness of those who were then present, and hence no basis on which to question their reports. Yet we know that people lie, and are deceived, and falsely imagine. How could it be reasonable to take past testimony at face value, therefore? The rational approach, rather, is to subject it to criticism. Is the avowed testimony of those who were there to be relied upon? Unless we can answer this question, we have no solid ground on which to proceed and the problem for empiricism, of course, is that it can in principle supply us with nothing against which the declarations of contemporary witnesses can be checked. This is why we must declare it to be uncritical.

A second major flaw is that the simple 'scissors-and-paste' conception excludes a vast amount of material that can be (and is) usefully deployed by historians. This other material includes not only archaeological discoveries like ruins, coins and potsherds, but a vast amount of documentation – bills of sale (the earliest recorded documentary evidence in fact), taxation records, political proclamations and such like – all of which is not observer's testimony. Collingwood was himself a noted historian of Roman Britain and saw at a glance how worthless the common conception of historical method is as a description of what any good ancient historian is actually doing.

A third objection to 'scissors and paste' is that it is silent on the question of how our clippings from the scrap book of the past are best organised into a continuous account. Faced with such a collection of clippings, what should guide our organisation of them? Without this, they remain a mere collection. In short, and combining these three points, scissors-and-paste history first of all relies exclusively on unsubstantiated *testimony* when it ought to be deploying *evidence*. Secondly, it mistakenly regards eye witness accounts as something special, when they should be regarded as merely yet more evidence. Thirdly, it has no methodology for the use of its much-prized testimony in the construction of historical narrative and explanation.

The identification of these deficiencies allows us to say something about the features *critical* history must have, and it does so without requiring us to launch into quite general epistemological questions or explore the philosophical foundations of empiricism. If history is to be critical it must view everything, including contemporary testimony, as nothing more than evidence; it must offer an interpretation of all the relevant evidence which allows the construction of an account of what happened; at the same time it must use coherence in the account as a test of its interpretation of the evidence. In other words, evidence and account must be made compatible in such a way that the evidence lends rational support to the account, while the account adequately explains the evidence.

It is true, no doubt, that this brief sketch prompts many further questions. What is coherence exactly? How are we to identify *relevant* evidence? What counts as an *adequate* explanation? It is not so very difficult to formulate plausible general answers to these questions in my view, but it would divert us too much from the subject in hand to go into them here, though we will return to versions of them in a more concrete application, when we consider the issue of New Testament history. For the moment, however, it is necessary to turn to the other distinction which (I contend) ought not to be confused with the one we have just been discussing. It is a distinction that has been very influential in the business of reflecting on historical method, the distinction between 'fact' and 'interpretation'.

Ask almost any contemporary historians and they will say, in my experience, that there is no such thing as an unvarnished, purely factual, historical account of the past. More than this, they will say that even if such were possible, it would not constitute history, for history proper begins *after* we have gathered the basic facts and begun to frame an interpretation of them. A familiar way of putting the point is to say that although bare 'chronicle' may be possible, the listing of names and dates in chronological order say, chronicle is not history. The important point about histories, on this account, is that they differ in the alternative interpretations they give of the same material, and although we can judge rival interpretations in terms of scope and plausibility, there is no such thing as 'the' true interpretation of the material, anymore than there is just one interpretation of a poem or a painting. Indeed, historians tend to rejoice in this fact, and to speak as though the intellectual interest in historical inquiry lies precisely in its scope for alternative interpretations.

This view of history is so firmly entrenched among historians (and many others) that it is almost impossible to dislodge it, another of Schopenhauer's spurious *a prioris*, perhaps. Yet it is relatively easy to point up difficulties in it. Moreover, so serious are these difficulties, in my view, that however obvious it may appear, and however orthodox amongst practising historians, we have no choice but to abandon it and start thinking again. We can begin the process of doing so by noting that it is not at all obvious where, or how, the line between fact and interpretation is to be drawn. Presumably it is a basic historical 'fact' that John F. Kennedy was assassinated. Now it is certainly true that history proper cannot rest content with the simple recording of this fact. We want to know why he was killed. What is the explanation of his assassination? But does this question usher in the level of 'interpretation'? Consider the suggestion that Lee Harvey Oswald, the assassin, was an agent of the CIA and that Jack Ruby, who in turn shot Oswald, was commissioned to make sure that the CIA's involvement did not come out. This is a putative, and not implausible, explanation. But why construe it as a shift from 'fact' to 'interpretation'? Isn't it equally in the realm of fact as to whether Oswald and Ruby were hired by the CIA, and for these purposes? Perhaps it will be said by the proponents of the fact/interpretation distinction that this is not a good example, that the explanation hypothesised does not amount to interpretation. If this really is a difficulty, however, we need only change the example. A great many Jews died in concentration camps. This is a fact, even if the precise number is disputed. But did they die as a result of Hitler's determination to bring about a genocide, the intended elimination of an entire people, or from some other combination of causes? Again, as it seems to me, the reality (and efficacy) of Hitler's intention either was or was not a fact. Of course, it is open to the advocate of the 'interpretation' view of history always to deny that I have hit upon an adequate example. Perhaps so. Nevertheless, it still seems to fall within the province of historical inquiry to wonder whether the Holocaust was a deliberate attempt at genocide on Hitler's part, or some hideous combination of malevolent forces that had no guiding intention.

Examples like this may be multiplied without difficulty. Did Lincoln fight the American Civil War to defend the Union or to end slavery? Or did changing circumstances bring the two aims together? Was the triumph of Oliver Cromwell a result of his strength of purpose, or the weakness of Charles I, or some combination of the two? It is hard to see why these are not to be construed as matters of fact. Either Cromwell had strength of purpose or he did not; either Charles I was strikingly weak or he was not. The resolution of such questions is a complex issue of course, but then why should we suppose purely factual matters are simple? It is not simplicity that is the mark of the factual, but answerability to realities. This is not just true of history and the past. Take a contemporary example from science. Is global warming a reality, and if it is, are greenhouse gases its main cause? These are complex and difficult questions upon which even the very expert may reasonably disagree. Yet it seems clear that the law of the excluded middle still applies: either global warming is occurring or it is not; either greenhouse gases are the principal cause of it or they are not. There is plenty of scope for differences of opinion, certainly, but these are differences of opinion *about* the facts, and there is nothing about the existence of reasonable dispute which supports the contention that the issue is not one of fact at all, but of something called 'interpretation'.

This example points us to an important difference between the commonplace account of history which separates 'fact' and 'interpretation' and Collingwood's account of critical history. By Collingwood's account interpretation ranges not over fact at all, but over *evidence* for the fact, and thus the point of attempting to interpret the evidence is precisely to arrive at the facts. One of his main contentions is that the simple appeal to testimony overlooks the possibility of intentional deception. There is, let us say, no dispute that x *said* y; but *why* did he say y? Was it to inform us that y, or to mislead us into thinking y? The answer to this question is not a matter of higher level interpretation of the fact, which is that he did indeed say it. It is, rather, a matter of establishing an additional fact; did he say it in order to inform his readers, or in order to deceive them?

A second difficulty with the 'interpretation' view of history is that it gives no account of the role of evidence at all. Is evidence involved in the establishment of the basic 'facts' over which interpretation ranges, or is evidence able to adjudicate between interpretations? If it is the latter, why should we not regard an 'interpretation' which cannot properly accommodate the evidence as effectively refuted, which is to say 'false'. In this case the distinction between fact and interpretation again collapses; the refuted interpretation turns out to be factually incorrect. If this is not the case, what *does* constrain interpretations? We need some account of the constraints upon interpretation because no one, I think, supposes that historical interpretation is a matter of the free play of the imagination, making of the evidence whatever you fancy. If it were, historical narrative would leave the realms of inquiry and enter the realms of imaginative fiction. There is nothing wrong with fiction, but there is a difference between history and historical romance. Each has its place. This does not make them the same. Of course, imagination does have an important part to play in history proper, as it does in every other form of intellectual inquiry including the 'hardest' of natural sciences, but its role is one of putting us on to the truth, not one of 'playing upon' truths already established.

We can draw a few modest, but important, conclusions from these reflections. Whatever may be the case for the higher flights of historical 'interpretation', it is the proper business of historical inquiry to ask such questions as these. Did Hitler intentionally aim at the genocide of the Jews? Did Lincoln go to war in order to end slavery? Was the CIA involved in the assassination of President Kennedy? In attempting to answer them, historians must adduce evidence. In adducing the evidence, they are not confined to contemporary testimony, the unquestioned word of those who were present when it happened. The evidence that is appealed to, both testimony and non-testimony, has to be interpreted certainly, but such interpretation is best understood as itself aspiring to factual accuracy, to getting it right – this eyewitness lied, that document was forged. These are not 'interpretations' in any interesting sense but merely claims about what actually happened, albeit claims that are more difficult to establish than the simpler facts upon which they must be based. Interpretation ranges over evidence. Explanation of the evidence must hang together, and nothing must be left out that can be shown to be significant. The resulting account of past events must be internally coherent and compatible not only with the evidence, but with general knowledge. All this is true, but none of it shows that there is a categorical, or even determinable difference between the 'facts' of history and their explanation. A good historical explanation is nothing more than a convincing claim about a more complex and inclusive realm of fact. And nothing less of course.

These modest conclusions, it seems to me, are incontestable, and perhaps they are not likely to be contested. What will certainly be disputed, however, is that they are sufficient to undermine the fact/interpretation distinction. Now, though I think that this distinction is neither valid nor interesting, for my purposes it is not necessary to show that the fact/interpretation distinction in general is redundant. For one thing, there is a useful pragmatic distinction to be drawn between historical hypotheses that are widely accepted (which we might think to be taken as 'fact') and those that are still widely contended (and hence have the more disputable status of 'interpretation'), and perhaps this pragmatic difference is all that many who employ the distinction mean to imply. But in any case, to advance the present argument it is sufficient to demonstrate that explanations with a purely factual character have a proper place in historical inquiry and that they can be sought in the study of the New Testament also. On this second point it is some encouragement to find the same conception of historical inquiry expressly endorsed by a leading New Testament scholar – E. P. Sanders:

[t]he only way to proceed in the search for the historical Jesus is to offer hypotheses based on the evidence and to evaluate them in light of how satisfactorily they account for the material in the Gospels, while making Jesus a believable figure in first-century Palestine and

the founder of a movement which eventuated in the church. (Sanders 1994: 166–7)

Sanders's contention (and mine) will be vindicated to a considerable extent if it can be shown that a good deal is to be achieved at this level without the invocation of anything more arcane by way of 'interpretation'. Furthermore, some of these (complex) factual questions bring us very close to both the central events and the cardinal doctrines of Christian history and theology. If this is so, then we can, without theological presupposition (including of course naturalistic presuppositions), begin the business of finding out about the real Jesus and at the same time, perhaps, something about his religious significance.

Here is one such question. There is good reason to take it as fact that Jesus was crucified. So far as I know, no one of even the most Straussian persuasion has been inclined to deny this. So why was he killed? To ask why Jesus was killed is to ask a question that is evidently historical, but which, I shall argue, does not obviously rule out something called 'the supernatural'.

v

Why *was* Jesus killed? This is the question on which some of the most interesting work in New Testament history of late has focussed. It provides the basic orientation of E. P. Sanders's *Jesus and Judaism*, and figures even more prominently in N. T. Wright's monumental study of the real Jesus (the two volumes to date being *The New Testament and the People of God* and *Jesus and the Victory of God*). Wright has invented the title 'the third quest' to refer to this new, deliberately historical phase in biblical scholarship, and though there are important differences between Sanders and Wright, it is a term I shall adopt.[2] 'The third quest' is one particular version of a wider movement in fact, – the revival of biblical theology. To appreciate the nature and implication of this third quest, and of biblical theology more generally, some further background first needs to be filled in.

---

[2] The 'first' quest began with Schweitzer, obviously. The 'second' quest was that launched by John Robinson in *A New Quest of the Historical Jesus* (London, 1959).

This returns us briefly to the concerns of an earlier section, and only then will we be properly placed to consider its historical results.

It will be recalled that the thrust of that phase of New Testament scholarship which began with Schleiermacher and D. F. Strauss was brought to what is perhaps its clearest focus in Albert Schweitzer's *Quest of the Historical Jesus*. The result of this quest was a picture of Jesus as a first-century Palestinian Jew, much taken up with eschatological prediction and quite different, therefore, from the Christ of faith beloved and believed in by Christians many centuries on. The outcome of a more rigorously historical approach to the Gospels accordingly seemed to be this: Look for the historical Jesus and what emerges is a figure less and less in keeping with the divine being who is worshipped in churches across the Christian world and more and more a creature of his own time. In short, serious historical investigation appears to show that there is relatively little connection between 'God the Son' to whom most Christians pray and the rural Jew who walked beside the Sea of Galilee uttering apocalyptic warnings which never came to be.

What then explains the common identification of the two? Here too post-Straussian biblical criticism has a story to tell, a story which appeals both to the mythological mindset of the pre-scientific world, and the additions the early Church made to the original story. An important part of this explanation is the claim that contemporary Christianity often fails to appreciate the depth of difference between a modern world view and the world view of twenty centuries ago. This, it is alleged, is a failure which non-believers can make no less than believers. Both have a tendency to approach the ancient writings they hope to understand with categories drawn inappropriately from the modern world. They insist that the events related in the New Testament are either (real) history or (fabricated) myth, and do not appreciate that the original authors and auditors simply did not work within these categories or think it important to do so.

This is a very familiar line of thought and a widely accepted one, though serious questions can be raised about its plausibility. Richard Burridge, for instance, has argued (convincingly to my mind) that contemporary commentators have overlooked the prominent genre of *bioi* which was common in the writings of the ancient world.[3] For the moment, however, it is enough to note that contemporary configurations of Christian opinion tend to mirror that of the nineteenth century and fall into two camps. There are those who enter into the spirit of historical inquiry and accordingly come to doubt the perpetual theological relevance of the real Jesus. If as a result, they do not cease to be Christians altogether, then they reckon his continuing significance to be of a (literally) much more mundane kind – as a political/social/moral visionary, at most a source of inspiration. On the opposite side are those who, precisely because they affirm the continuing theological relevance of Jesus, express grave reservations about the wisdom, and even relevance, of the historical quest. Their primary concern is with the Christ of faith, 'Jesus in the experience of men' to quote the title of a once well known book by T. R. Glover, and precisely because of this they seek a deeper faith not from the investigations of history but in being part of the living 'body of Christ', whether this means obedience to the authority of Rome, belonging to the fellowship of like-minded evangelical Christians or participating in the unchanging liturgies of the Orthodox Church. (The mirror image of this response on the part of 'the faithful', illustrated in Michael Grant's *Jesus: an Historian's Review of the Gospels*, is that of the agnostic who simply declines to consider certain questions – the historicity of the resurrection for instance.)

Now this opposition rests upon a disjunction that is rarely questioned; either we engage in the careful explorations of critical history and accordingly disengage ourselves from theological questions, or we make theological and religious significance our principal concern and largely disregard the findings of critical history. It is a distinction expressly endorsed by Sanders who says:

[3] See Burridge (1992).

I am interested in the debate about the significance of the historical Jesus for theology in the way one is interested in something he once found fascinating. The present work [*Jesus and Judaism*] is written without that question in mind, however, and those who wish a book written on that topic may put this book down and proceed further along the shelf. (Sanders 1994: 2)

It is here that a fundamental difference between Sanders and Wright is to be detected. To assess its significance we need to ask: Is this disjunction, characteristic of Bultmann and endorsed by Sanders, truly exclusive? An alternative position, one that is rather more rarely (though increasingly) canvassed, holds the two to be consonant; it is precisely by entering the spirit of the historical quest that we will better come to understand the theological significance of the historical Jesus. This third, unusual, but agreeably novel approach was expounded and defined with great skill and plausibility by D. M. Baillie in a once highly acclaimed work on Incarnation and Atonement – *God Was in Christ*. Baillie's discussion of the relation between the 'Jesus of history' school and the claims of High Christology is one of the most cogent I have encountered, and makes a compelling case for the indispensability of biblical theology, that is to say, the integration of historical inquiry into the life of the real Jesus with theological inquiry into the nature of God in Christ. Though he makes no mention of Baillie, it is the same approach that has been adopted, and revitalised, by Wright.

Is there any reason to believe that this is the right approach to follow? It is worth noting that *both* the Strauss/Schweitzer approach and that of their conservative opponents have tended, with varying degrees of sophistication, to adopt the methodology of 'scissors and paste'. That is to say, despite all the protestations of 'contextualism', both parties take the *basic* material for their studies to be the writings of contemporaries of Jesus (broadly speaking). This is more obvious on the conservative side perhaps, where the text is construed as valuable testimony of what 'actually' happened, and the task, consequently, is one of ironing out conflicts between the four Gospels and Acts and giving a unitary account of the events recorded in the New Testament. However, those who have adopted the more sophisticated stance of Strauss and his successors can also be seen to be tied somewhat slavishly to the text. Quite often, proponents of the *Sitz im Leben* school, whose watchword is contextualising, have actually failed to take proper account of the historical context they so applaud, and may be seen instead to have deduced the *Sitz im Leben* from the text. This is the conclusion, convincingly arrived at in my estimation, of an important collections of essays by Richard Bauckham and others – *The Gospels for All Christians*. The main thrust of these essays is to refute the view, so central to redaction criticism, that each of the Gospels was written for a distinctive audience – the Matthean community, the Markan community and so on. Bauckham's own essay reveals just how tenuous the evidential base for this contention is while Michael B. Thompson, by studying the seemingly independent topic of travel in the ancient world, impressively assembles extra-textual evidence which throws the question of the compositions of the Gospels and their audience in quite a different light.

The conservative approach seems naive in comparison with the sophistications of textual criticism, source criticism, form criticism, redaction criticism. Yet these other approaches no less than the former assume without sufficient critical reflection both that the scriptural canon is a collection of texts relevantly considered together, and that the textual evidence is that upon which much else is to be based and understood.

In addition to this erroneously limited focus on 'the texts', however, these two broad schools of thought share another underlying assumption, this time a metaphysical one. The 'historical school' from Reimarus to Bultmann was founded on a resolve to discount all 'supernatural' elements as genuine history; in response, conservative approaches to the Scriptures make regular attempts to defend 'the supernatural'. But both of them suppose that we are clear about just what this distinction is. Those who, like successors of Strauss and Schleiermacher such as Cupitt, believe that 'Man come of age' cannot any longer accept many passages in the New Testament at face value, have a choice. They can become sceptics (like Hume, for whom face value is all there is), abandon the supernatural and thus in effect abandon the Bible. Or they can become Kierke-gaardian fideists, like Bultmann, and hold that the 'super-natural' language of the Bible cloaks in 'mythology' the real religious meaning of the things related there.

The two assumptions both these positions share are well worth questioning.[4] Let us begin with the latter, and take a specific example – the temptation in the wilderness. As the Gospels of both Matthew and Luke have it, in preparation for his ministry, Jesus retreated to 'the wilderness' for 'forty days' where he ate 'nothing'. At the end of this time he was tempted by 'the devil' who, amongst other things, 'took him up and showed him all the kingdoms of the world in a moment of time'. Can 'Man come of age' credit any of this?

In a book to which reference has already been made T. R. Glover writes:

For the primitive peoples of today and for some not so primitive, the whole universe is full of daemon powers, more real than we can imagine. In an Indian temple I have seen women undergoing the process of having devils driven out of them. I have seen men of education bowing in these temples to avert the anger of such spirits. To the stranger from the West, with his modern science, they are nothing. To the ancient world they were more real than the men and women in the streets . . . All this dim world has passed from our minds; this tale of war in the spirit sphere is for us the merest mythology – 'as much a dream as Milton's hierarchies' . . . (Glover 1921: 2–4, the quote is from Keats)

Glover's general view of a radically changed mentality between the ancient and the modern worlds, which I take to be common, is one to be explored at greater length in a later chapter. The point here is to consider its implications for such stories as that of the temptation in the wilderness. And the implication seems to be that while the New Testament writers could, and did, believe in the literal truth of Satanic temptation, we, if we are to find anything at all in it, must look for other meanings. Stating the matter like this, however, supposes that we have a clear grasp of what 'literal' means, and it is not

---

[4] In light of my quotation from Sanders, it should be observed, perhaps, that his work has been a major stimulus to prompting such questions.

evident to me that we do. Consider the forty days. It is widely acknowledged that this number is not to be taken 'literally' but is a familiar *façon de parler* signifying a considerable period of time. Suppose this is true. Should we now say that this episode 'literally' lasted a considerable period of time? The same sort of point can be made about 'in the wilderness' and 'ate nothing'. These are all ways of speaking which taken together are to be interpreted as saying that Jesus withdrew from everyday life for a considerable period of time during which he led a very Spartan existence. I do not think it much matters whether we term this interpretation the 'literal' description or not. The point is that it has all the hallmarks of a claim about what actually happened, and is cloaked in nothing mythological. Effectively the same point has been made at greater length (and appropriately greater expertise) by Francis Watson in an interpretation of Mark 1.9 (Watson 1997: 103–6).

Now more importantly for present purposes, precisely the same move can be made about the encounter with Satan. There is no reason to hold that the New Testament authors thought that Jesus met up with a visible being something like the depictions of painters in the Middle Ages. To hold to this interpretation (as of course many do) is to be crudely insensitive to styles of writing, and anachronistically read later conceptions into earlier ones. As Walter Wink says, on just this topic:

[O]ur approach to interpretation must avoid all attempts to 'modernize' insofar as this means ignoring the mythic dimension of the text and transferring it in an unmediated way into modern (mythic) categories. It may be that the principalities and powers have been neglected as much as they have since the Enlightenment precisely because they were not easily reducible to modern themes . . . [The task is] to treat the data in all their alienness and . . . to let the categories and concerns implicit in the language arise out of its own matrix of meanings. (Wink 1984: 102)

On the strength of the story of the temptation in the wilderness *properly* read there is reason to hold that those who wrote in this way believed (i) that Jesus was powerfully, and not just mildly, tempted to abandon his mission for endeavours likely to be more successful in worldly terms, and (ii) that these temptations sprang not from within the *psyche* of Jesus himself, but from an external spiritual agent whose purposes were evil. The first of these claims, I take it, has nothing 'supernatural' about it at which a 'scientific' historian might balk. It is not in essence different from similar claims that might be made about a contemporary politician. The second claim about an 'external spiritual agent' does conflict with certain strands of modern thinking, but it is not an easy target for them in the way that, say, fairies at the bottom of the garden are. Indeed, as I hope to show in a later chapter, the idea of an evil agency external to self-generated human action can actually be made quite plausible in the context of attempting to explain phenomena that are as much a part of our experience as that of the ancient world. What needs to be stressed here is that the Straussian determination to purge New Testament history of 'hobgoblins and foul fiends' (so to speak) does not obviously replace 'the mythical' with 'the literal', and that those who wish to resist its naturalising tendencies are not thereby required to defend the idea that real spiritual powers of good and evil were, in those distant days, 'literally' encountered in the form of white-robed angels and cloven-hoofed creatures dressed in black. In short, in order to discover whether serious historical investigation of the real Jesus can uncover and illuminate a theological cosmology we must set aside all preconceptions about the natural *versus* the supernatural, the literal versus the mythological and the explanatory *versus* the symbolic. This is not, it should be emphasised, because there are no such distinctions to be drawn, another familiar dogma of (some) contemporary thought, but because drawing them must follow rather than determine our investigations into and discoveries about the past.

This remark returns us to the first of the two assumptions which I said both liberal and conservative approaches to the New Testament have tended to share, namely their focus upon the text. We have now uncovered at least one good reason to question a largely textual scrutiny, even one that is hermeneutically well informed. If we are to study the events of the New Testament in truly historical fashion, if we are to understand what the original authors 'really' meant, and/or if we are to appreciate what early Christians were attempting to do, we must look beyond the text of the New Testament itself and assemble as wide a body of evidence as we can about first century Judaism and early Christianity, evidence of the kind that ancient history more generally regularly deploys (as Thompson does in the Bauchkam volume). Once this attempt is made, we not only pass beyond the sophisticated version of 'scissors and paste', but we also, as it seems to me, begin to uncover a truly critical understanding of the 'testimony' of the Gospels, Acts and Epistles, and to see that the division between the Jesus of history and the Christ of faith is itself historically questionable. The two conceptions are essentially interconnected, a point C. Stephen Evans makes with the choice of title for his book – *The Historical Christ and the Jesus of Faith* – and on which he expands at length. A properly critical, properly historical approach aims to take seriously Schweitzer's original insight that the life and work of Jesus should be interpreted in the context of first century Palestine, while at the same time leaving quite open the possibility that this historical understanding may increase rather than diminish its theological significance. In other words, attempts to understand the Second Person of the Trinity may well be enhanced by what we can actually know of the historical Jesus. Indeed, in accordance with the conception of biblical theology and by Wright's account, the two enterprises are inextricable.

[T]here is simply no point in using the word 'Jesus' at all within theology unless one intends to refer to the Jesus who lived and died as a Jew in the first century . . . The Christian reader of the New Testament is committed to a task which includes within itself 'early Christian history' and 'New Testament theology', while showing that neither of these tasks . . . can be self-sufficient. (Wright 1996b: 139)

The evident truth of this first sentence, it seems to me, lends his enterprise very great credibility as well as interest.

VI

If it is agreed that Christian theology has to know about 'the Jesus who lived and died as a Jew in the first century', what *can* we actually know? On this point there appears to be considerable dispute among the equally expert. Sanders, Watson, Wright, and Bauckham *et al.* give grounds for thinking that our historical knowledge can be substantial; Borg, Crossan, Downing, Riches present a rather different view. In the face of these disputes, my own expertise runs out, of course. Yet there is wider intellectual reason to adopt, even prefer, the conclusions of the first group. I am not in a position to declare that the interpretation Wright gives of the evidence is better grounded than Borg's, say (though this is indeed my impression on reading *The Meaning of Jesus*). But I can say that the more robustly historical approach provides substantial material for an interesting and I hope re-invigorated consideration of the philosophical and moral issues which are the main subject of this book, and that this is a good reason to adopt it.

To this end, then, let us return to the question 'Why was Jesus killed?' On first appearances, it seems that we can canvass at least two quite distinct sorts of explanation. One refers to the social, cultural and political circumstances of the time, and the other invokes the divine economy of salvation. An explanation of the first sort might, for example, construe his activities as representing an act of rebellion in the eyes of the occupying Roman forces, or a threat to the Jewish establishment. An example of the second sort would construe his killers as (unintentional) agents of Satan who, ironically, made themselves instruments of a higher divine purpose and thus secured the Atonement of God and man. Categorising alternatives in this way appears to confirm the familiar distinction between the historical and the theological, the natural and the supernatural. What Wright aims to do is merge these categories by an historical exploration of the theological.

But let us start at an uncontentiously historical level. In answering the question 'Why was Jesus killed?' it is clearly necessary that we assemble evidence which will reveal how contemporaries thought of Jesus, how he himself conceived of his mission, and how the disciples (and other early Christians) responded to his death. Wright's method (following Sanders) is to construct a wide-ranging picture of first-century, Second-

Temple, Judaism, and an equally wide-ranging account of the early Church. He then deploys an amended version of a familiar methodological principle which he describes as 'double similarity and double difference'.[5] He starts, in other words, not with the evidence drawn from the text of the (synoptic) Gospels so much as general historical evidence of the periods before and after Jesus. The purpose of this methodological principle is to identify a conception of Jesus and his work that is both similar to and different from Second-Temple conceptions, and at the same time both similar to and different from the most plausible picture we can construct of the early Christians. Thus, separating out the common core, we can look for evidence in support of it in the three Gospels. By this method there emerges a picture of Jesus and his work which we have good reason to suppose was his own – like and unlike that of the Jews, like and unlike that of the early Christians. The resulting picture, however, though substantially validated by historical evidence, is not produced by sifting the 'historical' from the 'theological'. Rather, it explores questions about the real Jesus in terms of the Jewish theological conceptions which structured the historical context in which he worked, and it construes his historical distinctiveness in terms that we can infer in part from his theological reception among the early Christians.

Broadly speaking, and summarising drastically (the first two volumes of Wright's projected five run to approximately 1,200 pages, Sanders two major studies come to about 900) a number of specially important conclusions emerge. To begin with, first-century Judaism, in contrast to post-exilic Judaism, was a Temple-centred, not to say Temple-dominated, religion. At that time, everything focussed on the Temple in Jerusalem and there were an estimated 20,000 priests spread across the country who took part in the constant round of service and sacrifice there. Today, in very sharp contrast, Judaism has no temple, not a single priest, and no practice of ritual sacrifice. This simple observation gives us some idea of the importance of the Temple

---

[5] The more common version is simply 'similarity and difference' without the 'double'.

cult in the Judaism of Jesus' day and the dramatic change it underwent after AD 70.

Second, Jewish theology was and had long been messianic and apocalyptic, but the deliverance it expected and the end to which it looked was not the collapse of the space–time world (a wholly anachronistic conception drawn from far more modern times), but the restoration of Israel, an end to her troubles and the defeat of her enemy. The Kingdom of God which the Jews longed for was not something to be achieved in a celestial hereafter or in some extra-mundane reality yet to be ushered in, but in the course of the history of Israel itself. It cannot be stressed too much, perhaps, that Judaism (and therefore Christianity) was and is a deeply historical religion, albeit one informed by a theological (rather than, say, a political) history.

Third, the Jews (or many of them) had become deflected from more traditional conceptions. They no longer perceived where the true enemy of Israel lay, but mistakenly supposed it to be embodied in the Roman occupiers, a false supposition that had led to a nationalist zealotry which Jesus was at pains to counter. Rather, on his understanding the real enemy of Israel was what it had always been supposed to be – Satan, The Accuser, The Adversary, a subtle spiritual enemy, not an obvious temporal one. By Wright's account, Jesus, as both his followers and the Pharisees in their different ways eventually came to realise, was warning of a double error widespread among the Jews of his time – that rebellion against Rome would be both a political and a religious disaster. The political character of the disaster lay in the fact that it would result in the final destruction of the Temple and the dispersion of the Jews (which he predicted and which it did), and the religious error was a singular failure to see that the real battle lay, and would be won, elsewhere, in the person of Jesus himself.

Fourth, this was because, extraordinary though it may sound, Jesus was in his own person the replacement of the Temple, the deliverer of Israel, the instrument of victory over Satan, death and evil. This self-conception of what it meant to be the Messiah finds expression in many recorded utterances, but more dramatically and significantly in an *action*, the overturning of the tables, a demonstrative statement the meaning of which simply could not be mistaken by devout Jews who witnessed or heard of it. It is this which led ultimately to the Crucifixion.

[T]he Temple had become in Jesus' day, as in Jeremiah's, the talisman of nationalist violence, the guarantee that YHWH would act for Israel and defend her against her enemies . . . Jesus' action in the temple was intended as a dramatic symbol of its imminent destruction . . . [the] specific actions of overturning the tables, forbidding the use of the Temple as a short-cut, and the cursing of the fig tree, were likewise all designed as prophetic and eschatological symbolism, indicating both the arrival of the kingdom and the doom of the city and Temple that refused it . . . Jesus saw himself, and perhaps his followers with him, as the new Temple. (Wright 1996a: 420, 424–426)

To his orthodox contemporaries, the message Jesus symbolically enacted was plainly blasphemous, not to say absurd. Unchecked it meant not only the undermining of the centrality of the Temple and all that that symbolised, but even more dramatically the end of the special, God-given status of Israel and the Jews. As another New Testament scholar says:

To evoke, even conditionally, the destruction of 'this temple' was to touch not just stone and gold and not only the general well-being but history and hope, national identity, self-understanding and pride. (Meyer quoted in Wright 1996a: 425)

On Jesus' interpretation, the vindication of Israel in the victory of the Messiah opened the promises of the Covenant to all, Jew and Gentile, an implication that St Paul grasped suddenly on the road to Damascus and which he repeats insistently even in the face of some opposition among the Apostles. The victory of God in Jesus, by securing the final defeat of Satan, brought to an end the peculiar role of Israel. It is of the first importance to stress, however, that, though the destruction of the Temple was a part of this defeat, the death and resurrection of Jesus brought the peculiar role of Israel to an end not by replacing, but by *fulfilling* its essential purpose, to be a light to lighten the Gentiles (a claim of some significance in any consideration of the rather vexed topic of 'supersession'). This theme of fulfilment is, of course, repeated again and again both in the Gospels and the letters of Paul. Because of his proclaimed and perceived religious significance, Jesus was killed. Save for a short treatment in *The Meaning of Jesus*, Wright has not, as yet, completed his account of the real Jesus with the further, necessary, historical-cum-theological exploration of the Resurrection. But even without broaching this essential topic (except to say that it must somehow figure as the *sign* of victory), we can observe that to represent the Crucifixion as the *means* of victory is, to say the least, extraordinary since, to any eyes – those of contemporary Jews, early Christians, the modern mind and Jesus himself – it must have the far more obvious appearance of an ignominious defeat.

VII

To summarise: if the argument of the previous section is sound, it follows that we can only grasp the theological meaning of Jesus' death by a properly historical understanding of the whole period of time in which it took place. The theological cannot be separated from the historical in the way that post-Bultmannians suppose. That is to say, it cannot be reduced to a single point of connection – the Crucifixion – upon which an existentialist theology can then fasten, precisely because seriously informed historical inquiry cannot help expanding the theology of just this event; it cannot help elaborating upon the question of what the crucifixion amounted to, what it meant. Now it might be said on behalf of proponents of 'the historical quest' that all this, even if true, is nonetheless compatible with a (broadly) naturalistic interpretation. Can we not recount the 'Third Quest' version of the life of Christ in terms of the *beliefs* of Jesus and his contemporaries without inquiring into their truth? In other words, even if the architects of the Third Quest are anxious to draw from it the implications for contemporary theology, their story of the real Jesus *could* be confined within the theological meaning Jesus' words and deeds had *then*, and fail (or refuse) to wonder what meaning they might have *now*.

This is not quite right, however. It is true that the story of which elements have just been retailed does not forge the historical and theological into an indiscernible unity. This is not what we want in any case. Theology is not history, nor history theology. But it does link the two in an essential way. The theological question – is the message Jesus preached in parable and symbolic action true? – can only be answered if first we know what that message actually was, and we can only know *this* by historical investigation. Otherwise, to defend it, or attempt to demolish it, would be to promote or attack a straw man. Thus 'was Jesus indeed the Messiah?' is a question within which historical and theological elements, though conceptually distinguishable, are inextricably interconnected.

The naturalist critic might claim in response that the *inter*connection of history and theology has not been satisfactorily demonstrated. That there is a *connection* is not to be disputed perhaps, but it is essentially one way; the truth of Christian theology does depend upon historical fact; for example, Jesus can hardly have been the Messiah if, as a matter of history, no such person ever existed. But the truth of history does not equally depend upon theological adequacy. In fact, it is possible to establish the historical without any appeal whatever to the theological; for example, we can determine whether or not Jesus was widely *reputed* to have been the Jewish Messiah without inquiring into the metaphysics of the messianic.

But once again this is not quite right. To understand what it is to *be* the Messiah (and not merely to be held to be) is certainly to grasp and articulate a theological conception. Such a conception does not arise from an exercise of the pure intellect, however. It must, rather, be derived from some actual religious-cum-theological tradition. Otherwise it is a quite idle invention, not without point perhaps, but without real religious/cultural content. In this sense messiahship is *itself* an historical, as well as a theological notion. Even so, a critic might persist, if it is to be a properly theological conception *for us*, we have to have some reason to appropriate it. Such a reason cannot properly be founded in past history; it must make some appeal to our present experience, understanding 'experience' here in a broad rather than a narrow way. In other words, we must have reason to hail Jesus as *our* Messiah, and the fact that an illuminating and convincing historical account can be given which both shows that people in the past so hailed him and uncovers what they meant by this, still falls short of giving us reason to do likewise.

There is an important presupposition at work in this rejoinder. Why should we think that the grounds upon which they hailed him as Messiah are not grounds for us as much as for them? Here we return to the general question of the modern reception of the Scriptures. The familiar answer, already canvassed, is that their mind set and understanding differed radically from ours. Beliefs about Jesus that were plausible in the ancient world are not even possible in the modern. Why so? Because, it may be replied, the ancients believed, assumed indeed, that the world was populated by spiritual beings – angels and daemons – which play no part in ours. The first part of this claim is unquestionably true. The most cursory reading of the Gospels confirms it. Jesus is for ever encountering, confronting, and battling with daemons, powers and principalities, so much so that it is surprising it is as little remarked upon as it is. These spiritual powers are to be found at work in the sickness and madness and wickedness with which he contends, and an important part of his commission to the disciples is empowering them to cast out devils. Angels make regular appearances as well – to bring important messages, to tend to his needs, to guard the empty tomb. What are we, now, in the modern age, to make of these? Such beings long since passed from our ontology. Or so it seems.

The first point to be observed is that we need to understand these conceptions aright. To put it simply, it is easy to fall into the mistake of supposing that the ancient belief in daemons is rather like a childish belief in fairies or Santa Claus, and the corresponding mistake that there is not much to choose between miracles and magic. To counter such mistakes, an historically informed understanding is required, and this will show that whatever we make of it in the end, as Walter Wink has argued persuasively in his three volume study of *The Powers*, the belief in daemons was part of a serious explanatory enterprise. It will also show that there is an important difference between the miraculous and the magical. Indeed, Keith Thomas's famous book *Religion and the Decline of Magic* amply demonstrates that, until recently the great enemy of magic was not naturalistic science, but the Christian religion. This hardly makes sense if religion and magic are metaphysical bedfellows.

A second point, if anything of even greater importance, is that the impossibility of daemons and angels playing any part in contemporary understanding is generally *assumed* rather than *shown*. It is a twofold assumption for it presupposes *both* that the existence of daemons and angels is ruled out by modern naturalistic science *and* that naturalistic science is adequate to the explanation of our own experience. These two suppositions, the first about the nature of the ancient belief in spirits and the second about adequacy of scientific understanding, are connected. We can only legitimately suppose that the naturalistic explanation of our experience does not need to appeal to daemons and the like if we are clear what they are, and we can only declare the belief in daemons to be worthless if we know what they were intended to explain.

I propose to question whether these suppositions are correct. Indeed, though it will take most of the rest of this book to do so, I shall suggest that they are not. If this aim is to be accomplished with any degree of plausibility, however, it is first necessary to provide some intellectual motivation for entertaining what must seem a very strange idea. Why should we bother even to consider the postulation of daemons, still less lend it any credence? The aim of the next chapter is to lay the foundations for this motivation, but in order to do so, we must turn away from both the issue of the real Jesus and the ontology of spiritual powers, and only after a considerable journey that begins elsewhere will we converge once more on the topics that have comprised the subject matter of these first two chapters. For the moment, however, it will be useful to summarise their principal conclusions, for it is these the ensuing argument will eventually employ.

VIII

In chapter one I argued that the belief in a distinctively Christian ethic, though common, is in fact illusory. There is no code or moral doctrine which can be said to be distinctively Christian either in the sense of being shared by all Christians or being exclusive to Christians. This claim is troubling only if we suppose that Christianity's relation to morality is to be construed in terms of doctrine. In fact, the absence of an identifiable Christian ethic still leaves open the possibility of a distinctively Christian moral theology, whose concern is with the meaning or significance, rather than the content, of morality.

In chapter two I have been arguing that my claim about a lack of any Christian ethic is further borne out by the text of the New Testament. This contains no express teaching on the vast majority of those moral issues which concern contemporary society. Moreover, even if this were not so, the history of New Testament scholarship would raise a different, and more damaging, difficulty because it suggests that all knowledge of the real Jesus, including knowledge of what he taught, is historically uncertain. Assessing the basis and justification of such scepticism is a complex matter, discussed at length in this chapter, but in so far as there is reason to reject it, firm historical foundation seems to attach far more easily to claims about what Jesus uniquely was and did than to what he taught either by way of theology or ethics, though to say this is not to deny that the nature of his existence and action can only be adequately recounted, and understood, in terms of the religious conceptions he employed, and in this way, in terms of what he said.

In short, what these two chapters show is that Christianity, if it is to have anything distinctive to say about morality, must offer us an account of its meaning, not a set of moral rules or principles, and it must do so by connecting morality with Jesus as an agent of cosmic history rather than a teacher of precepts.

CHAPTER 3

Evil and action

The set of issues with which this book aims to deal are interrelated in complex ways. As a result it is necessary to suspend the topics of the opening chapters and turn to two other, rather more philosophical issues – the justificatory basis of morality and the problem of evil. These two issues are themselves not very obviously related, and so the chapter naturally falls into three parts (each with several sections), the first concerned with morality, the second with evil, and the third with connecting these two apparently disparate subjects. The stage will then be set for returning to the suspended topics of the first two chapters.

I

We can begin by returning to the issue of moral motivation. 'Why should I be moral?' This is a question that has occupied philosophers for a very long time, arguably since Plato, though it is doubtful whether the concept of the 'moral' as we understand it nowadays is to be found at work in Greek ethics. Indeed, as we shall see, the abandonment of 'the moral' is sometimes made the occasion for the resurrection of an alternative Greek conception. But at any rate the question 'why should I be moral?' provides an important starting point, though to understand it properly, there is a good deal of scene setting to be done.

What is the subject matter of morality? Over what does it range? A common answer is: 'Right and wrong'. This cannot be correct, however. There is a right and wrong way to sew on a button, set a fracture, solve a crossword puzzle, write a research proposal, bring a case to court, accelerate away from the traffic lights, fill in an application form, etc., etc. None of these presents us with a *moral* problem, and yet, since there is nothing either unusual or improper about describing them in terms of right and wrong, it seems plain that judgements of right and wrong extend far beyond anything that can plausibly be thought of as 'the ethical'. From this it follows that morality must at most be concerned with some subset of right and wrong in general. But how do we distinguish this subset? Obviously it accomplishes nothing to say that the subset is 'the *morally* right and wrong' for this leaves unexplained precisely what we want to uncover – the distinguishing mark of the moral.

One familiar answer in the history of moral philosophy is that morality concerns the *overridingly* or *categorically* right and wrong. It is an answer that received its greatest philosophical elaboration at the hands of Immanuel Kant, whose conception of morality will provide the subject matter of a large part of this chapter. The basic idea is easy enough to set out. Faced with a range of choices, and desirous of acting rationally, we often have to take into account not merely the alternative courses of action open to us, but different kinds of consideration which favour one over another. An action might, for instance, be profitable but inconvenient, cheaper but less effective, enjoyable but expensive, and so on. How are we to adjudicate between these competing considerations? One strategy is to seek a common denominator, some underlying value in terms of which the competing considerations are commensurable, and to most people's minds there is an obvious candidate – the desirable. Which of a range of options open to us do we *most want* to do – make money or avoid inconvenience, save money or have fun? Once this question has been settled the answer is plain; choose the course of action which accords with your strongest desires. I shall call this conception 'egoism'.

Utilitarianism, one of the most influential philosophical doctrines of the modern period, deploys a similar strategy. It bids us consider every choice under the aspect of its capacity to generate pleasure (according to earlier versions) or happiness (according to later ones). Having determined which action will maximise happiness (or pleasure), it is plain which there is most reason to perform. Or is it? Utilitarianism is not an egoistic doctrine. It does not hold that one's *own* desires provide the sole criterion by which choices are to be made. Famously, it holds rather that the happiness of each, including the agent in question, counts for one and not for more than one. In other words, when it comes to deciding what to do, other people's happiness counts as much (though no more) than one's own.

But though utilitarianism and egoism deploy a similar strategy with respect to decision making, egoism appears to enjoy an advantage. It seems evident that my own happiness (or more generally the fulfilment of my own desires) gives me a reason to act. What better reason could I have to do something than that I want to? By contrast, it is much less evident that the happiness of others (or what others want) generates reasons for action just as readily. Why *must* the happiness of others count with me? Of course, it may well be that their happiness *does* matter to me, as well as to them. This is generally true of friendships and family relationships. In this case I have good reason to take the happiness of others into account – but for entirely egoistic reasons. Their happiness (or desire) does not *directly* provide me with reason for action, only indirectly, by way of *my* desire that they get what they want.

Stating the matter this way reveals, I think, the principal philosophical problem of moral motivation. We think that morality is by its nature altruistic and we also think that people are moved to action primarily by their own interests and desires. How then can the altruistic requirements of morality – the wants, needs, desires and well being of others – give *me* an immediate reason to act, and not merely a mediated one, one mediated by my own desires? It is in response to this question that the idea of morality being distinguished by the *overridingly* or *categorically* right and wrong becomes relevant.

Egoism and utilitarianism, in their different ways, seek a common denominator by which the respective merits of alternative courses of action can be assessed. An alternative strategy appeals to a hierarchy of reasons, and puts moral reasons at the top. The appearance of moral considerations at the top of the hierarchy is what it means to call them overriding; they 'trump' all other considerations, and are not merely to be traded off against them in some more general calculus.

This view of the nature of moral reasons gathers a good measure of support from ordinary ways of thinking. For instance, someone engaged in commerce might be presented with a course of action which is highly profitable but at the same time dishonest. Most people would say that in deliberating about what to do, profitability and honesty are not on a par, that the requirements of honesty override considerations of profit. Examples like this can be multiplied without difficulty – loyalty *versus* career advancement, truthfulness *versus* convenience, for instance – and in every case, many will suppose, the morally right course of action must take precedence over all other possibilities, however personally advantageous they may be. Indeed, most people will also think that they should take precedence over the *generally* advantageous, and this is the ground upon which doubts about the acceptability of Utilitarianism are usually based; utilitarian calculations about the general welfare can quickly seem to conflict with, say, doing justice to the individual and respecting human rights.

Now even if we assume that this way of thinking about morality is broadly correct (though it is a matter to be considered further), an important question arises: on what is the overridingness of morality based? Why should moral reasons come at the top of the hierarchy? Unless we can give a satisfactory answer on this point, we have made no real progress in the matter of moral motivation. This is because someone could both acknowledge that overridingness is the *mark* of the moral, and still ask 'Why should I *be* moral?' What makes the moral overriding *for me*?

To answer just this point, Kant employs the concept of 'pure practical reason'. The overridingness of morality derives from the categorical character of moral imperatives, 'imperatives' being instructions to act – 'do this', 'don't do that'. 'Categorical' here is to be contrasted with 'hypothetical'. Hypothetical imperatives take the form 'do x, *if* y' and they thus lose their action guiding force, if it is the case that *not* x. The formulation of hypothetical imperatives is an exercise of practical reason, but not of *pure* practical reason. This is because they have an 'empirical' as well as a 'rational' part. That is to say, their force rests upon a contingency. For example, the hypothetical imperative, 'Take another qualification if you want to get a better job', applies only if as a matter of fact you do want a better job. If you are quite content with the one you have, there is no reason for you to take another qualification; the imperative loses its force.

The basic insight in Kant's moral philosophy is that morality cannot be made to rest upon contingencies such as these. The obligation to be honest applies irrespective of whether or not you want to be honest; the duty to help others in danger is incumbent upon you whether you care about them or not. Another way of putting the point is to say that requirements like these hold 'absolutely', not 'relatively', and in accordance with such terminology, this understanding of the distinctively moral is sometimes said to be an 'absolute conception'. In other words, it construes moral requirements upon individual action as applicable irrespective of inclination, in contrast to those other practical requirements that apply only relative to the desires and purposes we happen to have. If this were not so, then we could avoid the demands of morality simply by refusing to accept them, and this seems absurd.

Even so, the absolute conception of morality faces at least three important difficulties. The first, which has already been alluded to, concerns what I shall call the 'authority' of morality. Where exactly does its normative connection with motivation lie? Second, how long can the requirements of morality withstand conflict with personal and public disaster? It is all very well to say 'Let justice be done, though the heavens fall', but what if the price of doing justice really were global destruction? Third, even if we can find satisfactory solutions to these first two problems there is a third, more radical still. Ought we to deploy an absolute conception of morality at all? This is Nietzsche's challenge – to have the courage to go 'beyond good and evil'. In the next three sections I consider each of these problems in turn.

II

Wherein does the authority of morality lie? Kant's answer is that it lies within the limits of reason alone. The moral law is derivable from the exercise of pure practical reason, and its claim upon us, accordingly, is exactly the same as the claim of logic upon the reasoner, a general requirement upon rational beings to follow the laws of reason. One difficulty with Kant's explanation of the basis of morality, as elaborated in the *Groundwork to the Metaphysics of Morals*, is that the reason to which he appeals appears to be purely formal. In the end, it requires us only to be consistent in the moral maxims we endorse, and it is therefore equally satisfiable by mutually exclusive moral principles, provided only that each is held consistently. Kant himself believes that from pure practical reason we can derive substantive duties, the duty to improve one's talents, tell the truth and eschew suicide, for instance. No one, I think, has ever been very convinced by his derivations, and in fact it is not difficult to amend the maxims upon which these examples are constructed to arrive at rival but equally consistent conclusions. In other words, the most Kant succeeds in doing is to provide us with *formal* principles of practical rationality. But without *material* principles, we are no further forward.

This is a very well-rehearsed objection, and a telling one in my view, but it is not one I propose to dwell on here. This is because more relevant to present purposes (and more interesting perhaps) are those problems that remain *even if* Kant were successful in generating substantial moral principles that could be shown to be the demonstrable dictates of pure practical reason. The first of these problems relates to a gap between reason and action which still seems to need some bridging. Suppose it is true, as Kant believed, that it is categorically wrong to make a lying promise. However advantageous, profitable, convenient, life-saving, beneficial, sensible or understandable, to make such a promise is to act wrongly *tout court*. Suppose further that this can be *proved* by pure practical reason. There still seems to be logical space for this question: why should I follow the dictates of pure practical reason? Kant himself was aware of the gap. By his account it is a gap that arises from our double nature. To perfectly rational beings, such as we may suppose angels to be, the laws of reason are like laws of nature to physical objects; whatever reason dictates they invariably (though freely) do. Human beings, however, are not angels and are imperfectly rational. They have an empirical as well as a rational part to their nature. That is to say, they are moved by feeling and desire (what Kant calls inclination) as well as reason, and it is an inescapable feature of human experience that the empirical and the rational parts can and often do come into conflict. What then?

Kant resolves such conflicts, and bridges the gap between reason and action, by appealing to a 'reverence for the law'. As a solution, this is not very satisfactory, however. Either, this 'reverence for the law' is a sentiment, and hence part of our empirical nature, in which case its involvement as a determinant of action sullies the purity of pure practical reason, or (though this is hard to see) it is itself a rational constraint, in which case the gap between reason and action simply opens up again in a slightly different place; why should I do what reverence for the law requires?

This problem is not one for Kantian moral philosophy alone. It arises for any conception which wishes to apply *objective* constraints upon action irrespective of the *subjective* desires of the individual whose action it is. It applies, for instance, to Utilitarianism. Suppose it is true that, objectively speaking, the best course of action is that which maximises the greatest happiness of the greatest number. This fact can come in conflict (and often does) with what I myself want, with, indeed, my own pursuit of happiness. When this is the case, why should I prefer objective good to subjective happiness? The problem of moral motivation can thus be stated most succinctly in this way: how can the subjective and the objective be unified? If they cannot be unified in some way, then moralism – the belief that there is an objective, reason-generating moral order – has no response to egoism – the belief that only personal satisfaction of some kind (including, let it be noted, the taking of satisfaction in what is commonly thought of as moral endeavour) can plausibly be held to motivate human action.

This conflict between egoism and moralism is sometimes mistakenly represented as a clash between egoism in the sense of 'love of self' and altruism or 'love of others'. To construe it in this way is to misinterpret what is at issue, however. Philosophical egoism is quite compatible with love of others. It holds, certainly, that the ultimate spring of action must be subjective desire. But there is no reason why that desire cannot be a desire for the welfare and happiness of others. What philosophical egoism denies is that such desires can be rationally or causally overridden by purely objective considerations. For example, events might bring about the circumstances in which there is a conflict between the interests of my children and the well-being of the world at large. To prefer the interests of my children on the grounds that I want the best for them is egoistic, but it is not selfish. The best in view is my children's, not my own. It is true that there can be cases in which the apparent love of children is actually a kind of self-love, but this is not the standard case. I may give preference to the interests of my children because they are *my* children, but it is still *their* interests I give preference to, even over my own perhaps.

In short, it is not common selfishness that presents morality with a serious theoretical difficulty, but the much more subtle requirement that the claims of morality be made to speak to the motivating factors of the human mind. Kant holds that the most fundamental maxim of right action is to prefer duty to inclination, and that the contrasting evil maxim is that which prefers inclination to duty. What we have still to discover, however, is what it is in the springs of action that gives the first precedence over the second?

III

The tendency to suppose that the alternative to moralism is simple self-centredness (a tendency no doubt encouraged by Kant's contrast between duty and inclination) can also deflect us from a second major difficulty that the idea of the overridingness of morality encounters, namely the possibility of its leading to disaster. Once more, this difficulty may be linked to a prominent feature of Kant's conception of morality, for he holds that the requirements of duty must be acted upon irrespective of consequences. Like the contrast with egoism, this too accords with a common belief – that people may *do* badly while *meaning* well, and that they are not to be blamed for any lack of success a 'step-motherly nature' (as Kant puts it) may have denied them. What they *can* be blamed for is wrongful intention; actual consequences are not to be held to their account because they are only imperfectly under their control.

Thus stated, there seems little to dissent from. We generally believe that fault can be imputed only with respect to those things which fall within the sphere of our immediate control, and it is not hard to move from this familiar belief to the more ambitious philosophical claim that this must make the *will* rather than the *outcome* of our actions the proper object of moral judgement. Still, there is a larger problem here that neither the common-sense view nor its Kantian expansion expressly allows. Frequently the requirement to tell the truth, or to act in accordance with justice, for instance, can be predicted to have widespread consequences of a highly undesirable nature, not just for ourselves but for all those who will be affected by our actions. It is not difficult to imagine examples, partly because they seem such a regular feature of our experience. Suppose an employee is faced with a clear moral responsibility to 'blow the whistle'. The predictable result of doing so, let us say, is almost certain dismissal with all the consequences this has for family and other dependants. Similarly, justice is 'blind', we are told, but this blindness may require it to discount social ramifications of dramatic proportions. To be blind to the fact that, in the particular political circumstances prevailing, punishment justly merited by a violent revolutionary will be widely interpreted by supporters of the cause as martyrdom may well be to run the risk of civil war. Is it obvious that justice and integrity should *always* prevail? The force of this question lies in the fact that in all such cases an issue arises about the *wisdom* of morality. The sharpest conflict facing a determination to do what morality requires, come what may, need not lie with personal inclination to the contrary, but with the general welfare and interests of ourselves and other people at large. Moral action, in short, can be imprudent, and it seems right to regard those who give precedence to moral scruple over every other countervailing consideration in the same class as fanatics.[1]

Two observations are specially worth making on this point. It is sometimes supposed that the possibility we are here discussing is a difficulty peculiar to the Kantian conception of morality, and hence one which gives us reason to prefer utilitarian (or other consequentialist) conceptions. This is not so. If we take the fundamental utilitarian principle to be the maximisation of general happiness, this principle is itself an overriding one, and hence one which can come into conflict with personal prudence. Again, this is not a matter of its flying in the face of personal inclination. The accurate calculation of general utility can in theory require me to sacrifice job, family, friends and reputation, in short, to do a lot of damage to the ties that bind me.

In other words, it is not just the Kantian conception that can put in jeopardy what we might call my 'life plan', thereby undoing all (the good things) that I have striven for. *Any* conception structured round the idea of a fundamental and overriding principle can be made to generate this implication. All such conceptions, it seems evident, aim to capture that feature of morality which makes it distinctive – its overriding importance. But if morality so conceived has the potentiality to unravel my life, and thus make the pursuit of moral integrity deeply imprudent, this (in contrast to the first difficulty) raises a question not about motivation but about rationality. How could it be *rational* to pursue the moral life so conceived? After all, prudence is *also* a form of practical rationality, which is to say, a deliberative disposition that tempers our inclinations in the light of experience and foresight.

This second point is the more important one of the two to stress. Kant claims for morality the high ground of reason over

[1] On this see Wolf (1984).

inclination. Yet prudence too may be contrasted with inclination and therefore rightly regarded as a form of reason. Nor is it correct to suppose that prudential considerations always act upon existing desires in the manner of hypothetical imperatives. Prudence, by which I mean deliberation conducted in the light of reflection on our own experience and that of others, can lead to both the formation and the abandonment of desires. I might, for instance, relinquish a deeply desired ambition in the light of greater self-knowledge and the advice of others more experienced than I. I come to see that my ambition is not a *sensible* one to have, something that is worth learning only if I already have that ambition.

We might summarise the problem outlined in this section in a similar way to that in which we summarised the problem outlined in the last. Just as we can ask how (and whether) the subjectively desired and objectively required can be unified, so we can ask how the claims of morality and prudence are to be integrated.

IV

One response to this question is to deny that they are to be integrated at all. From this point of view, the difficulties we have been discussing are intrinsic to, and inescapable from, the pursuit of *any* absolute conception of right and wrong, which is to say they arise from the very idea of 'morality' itself. In other words, the two problems we have identified are intractable, and instead of fruitlessly pursuing impossible 'solutions', we ought to abandon the way of thinking which gives rise to them. This is the response we find, partly explicitly and partly implicitly, in Nietzsche. It would not be apposite here to enter into the complex arena of Nietzschean exegesis and criticism, but we can usefully begin examining the suggestion that the idea of morality should be abandoned by returning to a contrast drawn in the first chapter, one which Nietzsche himself draws. This is the contrast between 'good and bad' and 'good and evil'.

In an earlier section of this chapter we saw that one way of trying to characterise the moral is to seek the distinguishing mark of the *morally* right and wrong as opposed to all those other sorts of right and wrong with which we are thoroughly familiar in ordinary life. So, too, we might try to pick out from all the ways in which we use the terms good and bad – a good essay, a bad attack of bronchitis and so on – those that mark out the morally good and bad. It is this imagined subset that Nietzsche marks with the pair 'good and evil'. The evil, on this understanding, is not merely the bad; it is the *absolutely* bad, and though we do not have a single word for it, its opposite may be said to be the *absolutely* good.

Nietzsche thinks that the 'genealogy' or history of morals shows 'morality' in this sense to be an historically recordable human invention, and something quite alien to the ancient world of the Greeks. Further he thinks that it is an invention (in part) sustained by the concept of the Judeo-Christian God, and that with the death of God (thanks largely to Darwin) any persistence with the idea of 'morality' is a mistake on the part of even those who profess to believe in it. What the world requires is a 'Revaluation of All Values' (the title of a projected but unwritten book) that would take its cue from a reconsideration of the aristocratic virtues of the ancient world. It is not the detail of this genealogy with which I am concerned but with certain general ideas that animate it, ideas that we can find in other, older, thinkers.

One alternative to seeking a distinctive 'moral' right and wrong, good and bad, is to formulate a principle of rational action which does not require us to classify these evaluative terms into different kinds – the ethical, the aesthetic and so on. For instance, consider what is sometimes called 'the synderesis rule' – 'always prefer the better to the worse'. Although it may sound somewhat platitudinous, this is in fact a very powerful principle of practical deliberation. Whether we are deliberating about what to choose from the dinner menu, which concert to attend, what bicycle to buy, what book to read, or which foreign policy to follow, the principle can be relied upon to give us an answer, or to identify a number of equally good answers. Of course, the rule itself does not tell us what the good consists in; this will vary from case to case, is something to be learned from

investigation and experience, and calls for a measure of judgement. Nevertheless, once, in the light of information and
judgement, we have placed all available choices on a spectrum
from the best to the worst (allowing that more than one may
occupy the same place), the rule gives us a clear decision
procedure. Moreover, it is a rule whose rationality is hard to
deny. Who could suppose that it is more (or as) reasonable to
prefer the worse to the better than to prefer the better to the
worse?

What the synderesis rule excludes, however, is any absolute
requirement or absolute prohibition. There is no action or state
of affairs that cannot in principle accord with it. No action is so
bad that there cannot be a worse, and hence no action is so bad
that it can never be right to choose it. Conversely, no course of
action is so good that there cannot be a better, from which it
follows that no course of action is ever absolutely required. In
short, though there is good and bad in the choices with which
experience presents us, there is no choice we face which can be
described as *evil*, that is to say so bad that we could never be
justified in making it, and no course of action so good (or
unquestionably right) that we would never be justified in failing
to take it.

It is important that this rival, non-moral, conception of
practical deliberation be properly understood if we are to
appreciate its strengths. It is not, for instance, to be dismissed as
a licence for the evil-doer. It cannot be, precisely since its
purpose (at least as I have introduced it here) is to stop us
thinking in these terms. Nietzsche was acutely aware just how
powerful the idea of 'morality' is in the modern mind, and how
deeply the conception structures our thought. This is why he
uses a battery of rhetorical devices as well as analysis and
argument to advance the alternative. At times this may lead
him to extremes both of thought and expression. But the
protagonist of the synderesis rule need not follow him in this.
Faced with an action that according to common consciousness
would be impossibly abhorrent, advocates of this rule can
consistently maintain *both* that it would be much better if we did
not have to perform it, *and* that given this is the (unfortunate)

best of the available choices, it is right so to do. Thus, they can hold that as a general rule it is certainly better not to lie, to steal or to murder. And just because it is generally better, we should generally strive to avoid such things. But an unhappy combination of circumstances may nevertheless bring it about that it is best to perform an action accurately so described – to tell the lie that saves a life, to steal the secrets of an aggressive foreign power, to murder a tyrant, domestic or political. Similarly, nothing in the rule bids us discount, still less ignore, 'moral' considerations, but it holds that these are simply considerations amongst others, and have no special 'absolute' status. Telling the truth is important, but not so important that it overrules every eventuality. It may be best, for instance, to give truth second place to beauty, as when the preservation of a valuable artwork requires us deliberately to mislead those who are indifferent to its destruction.

In order to spell out the synderesis rule convincingly, a great deal more would have to be said about commensurability and judgement, about how comparative estimates of the better over the worse, all things considered, are to be made. This is a large and important task, and perhaps it cannot be accomplished satisfactorily. But whether it can or not is not directly to the point here. For present purposes we need only observe that the great strength of this alternative conception is that it offers us a unified conception of practical rationality. There is no in-built conflict between one dimension of practical reason – morality – and another – prudence. Moreover there is reason to think that it overcomes the tension between egoism and altruism also. I shall not defend this claim, except to observe that if, for example, your musical talents mean that money would be better spent on lessons for you than for me, the rule 'always prefer the better to the worse' gives me reason to prefer its being spent on you rather than me. If I am truly set on preferring 'the better' there is no reason to think this will lead me, in general, to give priority to my own desires or aptitudes.

If this is correct, if the non-moral synderesis rule can overcome the problems the idea of 'the moral' encounters, should we then abandon our conception of morality altogether? The answer depends, I think, on what view we take of the implications the rule has for our view of human beings. Kant, who has so far largely come in for criticism, reformulates his first version of the categorical imperative into two further versions. There is considerable debate about whether these second two versions are really formulations of the first, but this need not concern us here. What does concern us is that the third – the requirement to treat other persons as ends in themselves and never as mere means – expresses an ideal (usually called 'respect for persons') that has a powerful hold on post-Enlightenment thinking and underlies a very great deal that characterises the modern world – a strong emphasis on human rights, political liberty, democracy and equality before the law, to name just some of the most important features of our culture. Now whatever logical failures we may find in the detail of Kant's text, there does seem to be sufficient consonance between this ideal and his conception of morality. Respect for persons, it is plausible to think, must imply that there are ways in which we are *never* justified in treating others. If so, to abandon the absolute conception of morality is to raise a serious question about the ideal on which it rests.

So serious is this question, it is imperative that we be clear about the implications of abandoning the idea of morality, and with it the contrast between good and evil. In the next section my aim is to spell out these implications and thus motivate a reconsideration of the two conflicts I have identified, moralism versus egoism and morality versus prudence. This will provide the context in which to turn in the direction of some of the theological concepts which are the main concern of this book.

v

Whatever conceptual difficulties the idea of 'morality' may encounter, it is a fact that the modern world universally believes there to be *some* ways of treating human beings that are indeed absolutely forbidden. One of the most obvious is slavery. Torture might be thought to be another, and the knowing punishment of the innocent a third, but there are hardened political 'realists' who will allow that under certain circumstances both of these may not only be permissible but right. By contrast, even occasional slavery will not find any defenders, in the main because enslavement is so clearly and unmistakably contrary to the ideal of respect for persons. To make people slaves – the property of another – is to treat them not as an end in themselves, but as a mere means to the ends of others, their owners. Moreover, as Hegel contends in his famous master/slave dialectic, the dehumanising nature of the relationship extends to slave owners as well.

But from the point of view of the philosophy of morality one clear example is enough and slavery will do as well as any, better than most, in fact, just because it is so uncontroversial. This claim needs some expansion. As I observed in the first chapter, it is unhappily, but nonetheless certainly, true that more than a century after its world wide abolition there are still people in slavery, a fact regularly confirmed by anti-slavery organisations. More importantly perhaps, there can be (and are) widely accepted forms of social organisation, even in the modern world, that are in many respects morally indistinguishable from slavery, though they do not go by the name. Romanies, Aboriginal children in Australia, certain immigrant groups have all been subject to laws and practices that are indifferent to family ties and confining to certain social roles in just the ways characteristic of slavery. Does it matter much if they are not given the same name?

I think it does. What shows anti-slavery to be morally uncontroversial, is the fact that this description is always denied, and hidden, by those who perpetuate it, and in so far as the surrogate conditions described are acknowledged to be indistinguishable from slavery their existence too will be denied. By contrast, in the past there were people who not only denied the wrongness of slavery, but positively endorsed it as a useful social institution. Nowadays the *cause* of slavery is dead; no one does, or could, *advocate* it, however much they may secretly connive in its continuance, or in the perpetuation of social relationships that are horribly close to it. This is what lets us say that, actual practice notwithstanding, the absolute wrongness of slavery is uncontroversial.

In any event, no one reading this book, I imagine, will have the slightest inclination to query the wrongness of slavery, or expect me to do so, even if the semblance of an argument could be mustered to this effect. The 'evil' of slavery is thus a datum upon which something of substance can be erected. A further important observation is that practical deliberation which relied on the synderesis rule alone could not support this contention. Though it might support the suggestion that *in general* slavery is the worse option to all others available, it cannot rule out the advent of circumstances in which the best, if unfortunate, choice would be to enslave people. Taking these two points together – the existence of at least one thing that can be regarded as absolutely forbidden *and* the fact that the synderesis rule cannot accommodate it – it follows that we have good reason to look again at the difficulties said to attend 'morality'.

These, it will be recalled, related to the conflict between inclination and duty, and the possibility that the pursuit of morality could lead to personal and social disaster. Consider the first of these. Philosophical egoism rests crucially on the idea that whereas objective good lacks immediate motivating power, subjective inclination is directly motivating. As I put it earlier, what better motivating reason could I have to choose a course of action than that I want to? Is this true, however? We know from common experience that what I undoubtedly want can be bad for me, that is, contrary to my interests more broadly considered. The addict, to take a crude but instructive case, wants another fix. Yet a reflective addict might see that he would be better off without this desire. If this is the right way to put it, we can see that there can be conflicts *within* egoism, conflicts which arise from a competition we might describe as that between inclination and interest. Moreover, this competition can exist independently of the individual's perception of it. An unreflective addict could have the very same reason to free himself of his destructive desires as the reflective addict does; he simply does not know this.

Now already this introduces an objective dimension to practical deliberation. As a matter of subjective experience the addict wants a fix, but as a matter of objective fact, this is not a desire which it is in his interests to accede to. A determined egoist might insist that the 'objective' character of this consideration is only apparent. In the end, the motivating power of interests is as egoistic, in the philosophical sense, as the power of felt desire; it appeals to (and in the case of ignorance reveals) what is good *for me*, a claim that gains additional support from the idea of 'prudential desires'.[2]

I do not know that it is necessary to contest this point. It is sufficient that the following propositions hold. First, I can have reason to do something (what is in my interests) whether I want to or not. Second, I can be ignorant of what is in my interests. All sorts of factors can generate this ignorance, and not just wilful blindness arising from strong immediate felt desire. What is truly in my interests can be hard to discern, even, sometimes, beyond the power of my unaided intelligence, which is why there is scope for taking advice and learning from others. Drawing these limited implications is sufficient to rebut a certain sort of egoism. However, it is not sufficient to establish pure moralism as such on a firm foundation. What *pure* moralism requires is that moral right and wrong, good and bad be shown to have an objective character *wholly* independent of the egoistic motivations of the individual, that is to say, motivations of self-interest as well as immediate inclination. It is the ambition of the meta-ethical theory known as 'moral realism' to do this,[3] but it is also a matter of great philosophical dispute as to whether it can in fact be done.

Because of the intractability of the issues surrounding moral realism I propose to settle for something less. In response to the question with which this chapter began, 'Why should I be moral?', the realist must answer that the reason lies in an objective moral order constituted by moral 'facts', and that these facts have motivating power built into them, so to speak. To demonstrate this satisfactorily is a major undertaking, a

[2] See Nagel (1970).   [3] See Brink (1989).

topic to which we will have occasion to return, in fact. For present purposes, however, a rather less ambitious answer to the question is available. It is this: it is in my interests to observe and abide by the constraints of morality, even if I do not know precisely why (or how) my best interests are furthered by moral endeavour and rectitude. It should be admitted at once, though, that even if the greater modesty of this answer avoids certain difficulties, there are serious problems facing this answer too. These need to be addressed, but for the moment I shall suspend their consideration and turn to the question of morality *versus* prudence.

It is easy to imagine circumstances in which to do justly would result in the heavens falling. The sort of example philosophers regularly deploy is that in which, by a somewhat complex narrative route, torturing an innocent child (say) is the only way to prevent a nuclear holocaust. Students (and others) commonly object to the fancifulness of such examples – 'that would never happen'. Often this is not a pertinent objection; good philosophical moves can be made by the judicious use of far-fetched examples. Nevertheless, it is worth observing that it is much easier to invent examples like this than to find real cases. Moral extremity of the sort imagined is very rare, and may even be non-existent. If so, this throws a different light on the clash between morality and prudence. In principle the two *can* come into serious conflict; in reality this need not (and perhaps never does) happen. So, for example, the refusal ever to enslave another, however sensible as well as right it might appear on the surface, *could* result in the collapse of the social order. It is an eventuality that defenders of slavery often anticipated in the past. In fact, it did not happen then, and there is no special reason to think that it would happen in the future. Of course, its happening is a logical possibility. But mere logical possibility is not itself a reason to abandon the absolute prohibition on slavery.

If we generalise this point we can say that while any absolute requirement or prohibition *could* court total disaster for us and the world around us, there is plainly no necessity that it does so. The 'workability' of morality is thus a contingent matter. Now this is a fact of some consequence in assessing the conflict between morality and prudence. To see this it is worth stating the problem one more time, in a slightly different fashion. To abide by the constraints of an absolute morality is to insist on acting in a certain way whatever the consequences. Faced with the possibility of disastrous consequences, absolute morality seems contrary to reason, because deeply imprudent. Its actually being contrary to reason, however, depends on the *prospect* of disaster and not merely its *possibility*. So long as there is no prospect of disaster, the rationality of morality is not actually called into question. An obvious objection arises at this point. Whatever about global disaster (the heavens falling) isn't the prospect of personal disaster as a result of moral rectitude – death as the price of moral integrity, for instance – a familiar fact of experience? The answer to this objection, I shall argue, as well as the answer to difficulties about squaring morality and interest, is to be found in the concept of moral faith. This new and important topic is the subject of the next section.

VI

I shall characterise moral faith as the faith required if absolute morality is to be both motivating and rational. What is it faith in? Initially at any rate, it is faith in the truth of two propositions: (i) acting morally is in my interests even when I do not and cannot know this; (ii) morality will not ultimately conflict with personal or social well-being, appearances to the contrary notwithstanding. If both these propositions are true, then we have good reason to endorse the constraints and requirements of morality despite the moral psychology of the egoist and the reservations of the prudentialist. If the first proposition is true there is no fundamental conflict between moralism and egoism; what is right and what is in my interests ultimately coincide. If the second is true there is no real conflict between morality and prudence; the wisest course, in the end, will be that which morality requires. The question, of course, is whether these propositions *are* true, or better, whether we have any grounds on which to believe them to be true.

Moral faith plays an important part in Kant's moral philosophy, though I have to some extent adapted the concept to my purposes here. He uses it partly to fill what John E. Hare calls 'the moral gap', that is, the gap between our actual rational powers and the ideal rationality which moral deliberation requires. *The Moral Gap* is the title of Hare's unusual and illuminating book, but his concern is primarily with a gap between the requirements of morality and our ability to meet them, a gap which he thinks traditional theological conceptions of atonement and redemption may be shown to bridge. It is not my intention to deny the existence of such a gap, or to dispute the claim that there is a good account to be given of how the saving work of God in Christ supplies our deficiency in this respect. These are not topics that concern me here. My concern, rather, is with another (if in many ways similar) gap – the gap between moral rectitude and prudence. Kant, as it seems to me, has things to say about moral faith with respect to this gap also. In fact he also deploys the idea of moral faith in his celebrated moral argument for the existence of God. This argument has been misunderstood and misrepresented. At its crudest, the misrepresentation alleges that Kant thinks that morality is the way to benefit in the end because it gets us to heaven. In fact Kant does not claim that the motive to act morally lies in the pursuit of benefits. On the contrary he holds that moral action proper arises from a disposition to act in accordance with duty for duty's sake and for no other reason, including hopes of heaven. My purpose, however, is neither the careful exposition nor the textual defence of Kant. Rather, I want simply to deploy some such conception of moral faith as a way of enabling us to make some headway with the topics of this book.

The concept of moral faith understood as an adherence to the two propositions with which this section began, is in effect a trusting belief that the conditions which make morality possible do actually hold. Lack of moral faith, conversely, renders morality an impossible ideal. Why would we think that such conditions do prevail? We have reason to think so (and this it seems to me is at the heart of Kant's moral argument for the existence of

God) if these contingent conditions result from the way the world is constructed. That is to say, moral faith would be well grounded if the world in which we live is indeed the creation of an omnipotent and benevolent God, who, despite appearances no doubt, ensures that acting morally is in our best interest and that morality and prudence do not in the end conflict. (According to Kant this requires the further presupposition of human immortality.) It is here, finally, that the connection between the philosophical questions with which we have been concerned in this chapter and more general theological issues lies.

However, it is essential that this connection be stated correctly. It is plainly insufficient to make the possibility of morality rely upon wishful thinking. It is no use to argue thus:

> Morality is possible only if God exists.
> So let us assume that God exists.

Nor will an argument of this form (though valid) achieve much:

> Morality is possible only if God exists.
> Morality is possible.
> Therefore,
> God exists.

Such an argument rests upon the assertion that morality *is* possible, and this is precisely what is under dispute. Kant's argument (or something like it) is this, rather.

> Morality is possible only if God exists.
> If the engagement in morality is to be rational,
> therefore,
> it must presuppose the existence of God.

Clearly a counter argument of this form can also be mounted.

> Morality is possible only if God exists.
> There is no God,
> therefore,
> the engagement in morality is irrational.

This is one interpretation of Nietzsche's position. How are we to adjudicate between the two arguments? There is no simple decision procedure here, it seems to me, no clear demonstration that will favour one over the other. What we can do, however, is explore a rather more diffuse line of thought by asking this question. What could motivate us to accept one rather than the other, as, so to speak, a working hypothesis?

Let us return to the example of slavery. I claimed that universal agreement about the wrongness of slavery gives us a datum upon which something of substance may be built. To hold that slavery is absolutely wrong is to adopt a 'moral' stance. It is one which everyone reading this book, I imagine, will have a deep reluctance to abandon. Now nothing in this life is certain, and that is why all practically significant argument must be built upon foundations that fall short of certainty but are as firm as we can reasonably hope. The wrongness of slavery, it seems to me, is one such foundation. If we are to abandon our belief on this matter, we will need an even surer ground upon which to do so, and it is not obvious that there is any; the absolute wrongness of slavery is as firmly held a conviction as any, and far more firmly held than a great many 'scientific' beliefs, for instance. If this is granted, then we seem launched upon the following chain of reasoning.

There is at least one absolute evil. Therefore we must make our conception of practical reason accord with its possibility. To do this we must presuppose that the conditions of its possibility prevail, and that to abhor this evil is better for us as agents and for the world in general than to accommodate it. We can only reasonably suppose this, however, if we hold that there exists some sort of Providence which makes the maintenance of these conditions its purpose. To believe coherently in the existence of absolute evil therefore requires us to believe in a providential God. Our conviction about slavery is the foundation upon which we believe in the existence of absolute evil. It is upon this conviction, then, that we have reason to believe in the existence of God.

This is what is known as a 'transcendental argument'. Like other such arguments it does not purport to prove its conclusion, but to establish reason for *presupposing* the truth of the conclusion. Kant makes a similar transcendental move in his argument for the freedom of the subject (as elaborated in the closing section of the *Groundwork*). Given that people are not only subjects but material objects and that material objects are governed by (broadly) deterministic laws, there seems reason to hold that our actions must be determined in the same way that the behaviour of all material objects is. Confronted by this argument for determinism, Kant does not think that he can prove to the contrary, but he thinks that the falsity of determinism (and hence the reality of freedom) is nonetheless a necessary presupposition of the practice of choosing and deliberating. To put the point simply, but I think effectively, faced with a dinner menu, the conviction that determinism is true will not enable us to make a choice. We *have* to presuppose our freedom; this is the only rational presupposition to the business of choosing. Let all that we know about the material world and the laws that govern it be called into play, even so, there is a *choice* to be made. So too, faced with the reality of absolute evil, the pull of egoistic motivation and the (seeming) conflict between morality and prudence, the only rational presupposition is that these competing features of experience, like choice and causation, are at some point in accordance with each other. Since we know that we cannot ourselves secure this accord, we must presuppose that there is an agent both omnipotent and morally motivated who can and will.

Now, all such transcendental arguments rest upon antinomies. That is to say, they are produced, and can only be effective, in the face of equally incontrovertible chains of reasoning which, in so far as we can tell, lead to contradictory conclusions. It is precisely because there is a seemingly conclusive argument for determinism and at the same time an argument no less strong in favour of freewill, that the transcendental deduction cuts some ice. This raises an important question in the present context. Is the existence/non-existence of God, considered independently of a moral argument like Kant's, a genuine antinomy? Most will agree, I imagine, that the position in this case is somewhat different. It is not that the existence and the non-existence of God can both be proved. Rather, *neither* can be proved, and it is the absence of proof either way which generates the thought that if there is to be any resolution of the question it must proceed transcendentally. To put the matter this way however reveals an important difference of philosophical opinion. Very few people, if any, believe that the existence of God can be proved; but many believe that it can be disproved, and that this disproof (somewhat ironically, given the line of argument we have been pursuing in this section) is to be derived from the very thing we have been trading on – the existence of evil. Does this disproof work? This is the topic of the next few sections.

VII

The existence of evil, both moral and natural, forms the basis for one of the oldest and most persistently troubling arguments against Judeo-Christianity. Anyone who holds that there exists a God who is both all powerful and wholly good owes us an explanation of how it can be that there is evil in the world He has created and continues to sustain. This is because it seems an easy business to turn the fact of evil against such a contention. The argument may be set out as follows:

> God is benevolent.
> God is omnipotent (which should be taken to include omniscience).
> There is evil in the world.
>
> If the first two propositions are true, the third cannot be.
>
> However the third is true as a matter of observable fact.
> From this it follows that one (or both) of the first two premises must be false.
> But if either is false, there is no God as Judeo-Christianity portrays Him.

Set out in this way, the argument is clearly intended to be deductive and supposes that the first three propositions taken together are contradictory. Plainly this is not so. There is no contradiction between the propositions *as they stand*. What has to be shown, then, is that they *contain* a contradiction, and this can only be shown if they are expanded in some way. Purported expansions are not far to seek. Here is one.

> If God is benevolent, then He *will* prevent evil.
> If God is omnipotent, then He *is able* to prevent evil.
> Since there is evil, either God does not will its elimination,
> in which case He is not benevolent,
> Or, He is unable to eliminate it,
> in which case He is not omnipotent.

Expanded in this way, however, a proposition of a much more contentious kind comes into play. What grounds have we for thinking that a benevolent God is under an obligation to prevent evil? Some people think that this is logic chopping. Perhaps it is, but logic chopping is enough, in fact, to undermine any argument that purports to be deductive. At a minimum, the argument from evil to the non-existence of God is not what it seems. Of course, the epithet 'logic chopping' sometimes implies the invocation of a logical distinction that is not worth making. Suppose this is true of the present case. Let us agree, in acknowledgement of this contention, that we have every reason to suppose, even if we cannot strictly prove, that a wholly good God would prevent evil. Even so, there is another, more substantial logical gap that opens up. God is not any the less good if the evil that exists is not evil for which He is responsible. God's goodness can only be found deficient if there is evil for which He is responsible and which He has not prevented. To deny this is to assert an even more contentious principle – that an agent is to be blamed not merely for the evil actions he performs, but for all the evil actions performed by others that he could have prevented. We do not apply this principle to the moral agents with whom we are most familiar – ourselves – so why should we think it applies to God?

This is the gap into which the famous Free Will Defence steps. According to this defence, the argument from evil should actually run as follows:

> If God is benevolent, then He ought to prevent evil.
> If God is omnipotent, then He can prevent evil.
> The evil in the world is evil that He can prevent.

Only if we hold this version of the third proposition can we generate the sceptic's conclusion. But, if some of the evil in the world is *freely* committed by other agents, then God cannot prevent it without impugning their freedom. Since 'ought' implies 'can', it follows that the undoubted fact of the existence of evil cannot be made to generate the conclusion the first version draws from it; the evil in the world may not be evil that God can prevent, in which case He cannot be held to violate the obligations of his benevolence. In order to plug *this* gap we would have to say that God ought not to allow other moral agents the freedom that He does allow them, but this is an even more substantial proposition and one that we certainly have no reason to suppose follows simply from God's benevolence. If God values the freedom of His creatures, we cannot say on grounds of His benevolence alone that He should not.

There is often thought to be a special difficulty here about what are called natural evils. If we include in the list of evils that the world contains such things as congenital illnesses, earthquakes and volcanic eruptions, which are not in any obvious way the outcome of human activity, have we not uncovered a body of evil for which God alone can be held responsible? If so, it seems the argument still works, albeit not in the way that the sceptic may at first have supposed. Strictly, however, there is still a gap. In order to make the revised argument watertight we have to suppose that there are only two possible classes of free agent – God and human beings. Traditionally, of course, Christian theology has denied this. The conception of Satan (and his agents) introduces the possibility that natural evils are the outcome of the free actions of purposeful agents other than God or human beings, and even if the idea carries little weight today, its supposition is enough to undermine the certainty of the proposition that the natural evil in the world is evil God can, and hence ought to, prevent.

The *existence* of such agents will be thought by most people to be fanciful. It is a subject which will be taken up in the next chapter. For the moment, however, the point does not have to be pressed either way. The mere *possibility* of Satanic powers is enough to undermine the deductive version of the problem of evil. It breaks the logical chain by which the non-existence of God is supposed to have been proved. We may conclude, therefore, that the 'proof' from evil does not work. There are, certainly, other manoeuvres that the proponent of the argument can make, and these are to be found in the vast quantity of literature that there is on this subject. I shall not consider them here, however, because I do not think that they are crucial (or of very special interest) to either side in the debate. This is because, even if the *deductive* version does not work, there is a closely related, and powerful, *inductive* version which remains unscathed by this failure.

VIII

Broadly speaking, the inductive version of the problem of evil holds that while the mere existence of evil may not refute the existence of a good, all powerful God, the *amount* of evil that there is does constitute a refutation. In short, there is *too much* evil in the world to be consistent with the existence of such a Being.

To see the basis and appreciate the force of this claim, consider a parallel. Imagine that a schoolteacher is on play-ground duty. Two children are squabbling and, predictably, one hits the other, sufficient to hurt him and make him cry. As a result of the first child's action a little bit of evil (pain and distress) is brought into existence, evil which the teacher with his greater power and foresight could have prevented. Now despite the truth of this, there is still an important moral distinction to be drawn between this case and that in which it is the teacher herself who hits the child, a distinction it is relevant to draw even if the amount of evil in both cases is the same. In the first case it is the other child who is to be held responsible for the extra evil in the world, and not the teacher. The significance of the difference lies chiefly in the fact that there is a justification at hand for the teacher's non-intervention. She can (plausibly) claim that if children are to learn to get on, some such incidents must be allowed to happen from time to time, and furthermore that, taking the larger view, it is actually *better* that they do. In short, even a well-meaning and more powerful teacher could be justified in allowing the level of pain and distress in the world to rise in this way in the wider interests of both children. But suppose we amend the case to one in which the more aggressive child takes out a knife and starts to stab her playground rival. In this case the same excuse and explanation could hardly be given. Here the teacher *is* to be held responsible for not using her superior strength to prevent the injuries which ensue. In other words, whether we think the teacher's behaviour justifiable or not depends upon *how much* suffering and distress she permits.

The application of this parallel to God seems plain. God may decently permit lesser free beings to bring about certain amounts of evil, but only up to a point. Past that point He must be held morally responsible for the evil that exists because, even if others (including non-human agents if such there be) were the primary agents, He ought to have stopped them. Of course the crucial question is: how much is too much? Here, it seems to me, we are speedily reduced to appealing to intuitions. We might hold, for instance, that God acted rightly when He permitted (in the sense of staying His hand) the Crimean War, but not when He permitted the colossal slaughter of World War I; or that he acted rightly when He tolerated the Inquisition's expulsion of the Jews from Spain (in 1492), but not when He permitted the Nazi Holocaust. And so on.

But this appeal to intuitions about what a good God would and would not be right to allow, however powerfully they may strike us, cannot ever be conclusive. Even the case of the Holocaust will not settle the question. Someone determined to 'justify the ways of God to Man' can always claim that God *did* stop the Holocaust. It did not go on to the completion of genocide after all, and could, for all we know, have been even worse if God had not, in ways unknown to us, brought it to a halt. Of course, if examples such as the Holocaust cannot settle the matter logically, to many minds they nonetheless carry sufficient weight to be wholly persuasive. Wilful slaughter of the innocent on the scale of the Holocaust, Stalin's 'harvest of sorrow' or Pol Pot's 'killing fields' is too much by *anyone's* reckoning surely? Most will say 'yes', I imagine; some will say (more modestly) 'I don't know'. It seems that we must simply take our stand.

Yet, though it may be true that the appeal to intuitions cannot supply conclusive proof, and that each side in the debate is free to take its stand, it does not automatically follow that we have reached a complete impasse over the inductive argument from evil. There is a further line of thought to be explored. It will not lead to a demonstrable conclusion, certainly, but then few lines of thought on any matter do. What further reflection can do is show that there is more to be done here than simply taking a stand. We can cast the debate about evil into a larger frame, one which reveals that the full implications of accepting the Holocaust (and similarly unspeakable episodes) as sufficient evidence against the existence of a good God are not as straightforward, or as easily accepted, as might at first appear.

To begin this further line of thought, consider this question. Why should anyone resist the claim that the Holocaust is a degree too far? What could reasonably motivate anyone, in the face of such evil, to persist with the idea that the world as we know it is governed by an omnipotent, benevolent, divine Providence? The short answer, I think, is that this is a necessary presupposition of hopeful moral endeavour in the face of just such evils. In other words, it is moral faith and not empirical evidence that provides a rational basis for belief in God.

Thus succinctly stated I do not suppose this claim will carry much weight. Nor will it stand any chance of becoming more persuasive until a great deal more has been said, as much in fact, as is contained within all the projected topics of this book. Even so, it is helpful to set out plainly the point that the ensuing arguments are supposed to reach – that a certain theology is the necessary ground of moral hope. All the topics covered up to this point, in fact, are of importance chiefly as an essential context against which to explain and defend this thesis.

IX

Let us suppose that in the light of the Holocaust, and innumerably many other events both human and natural, the inductive argument from evil works. If so, the unavoidable conclusion is that the world as we know it contains more evil than is consistent with the existence of a benevolent and omnipotent being such as Christianity represents God to be. It is a world, in short, which such a God ought neither to have created nor to sustain in existence. Ignoring for the moment the possibility of angels and devils, this inductive proof of the non-existence of God means that human beings are the only moral agents that there are. Where then does this leave *us*? What ought our attitude to the world be, if we are to act as we ought? If it is as bad as the inductive argument from evil makes it out to be, should we not endeavour to destroy it? It might be thought that the fact that we are not omnipotent is of special relevance here. We cannot be held responsible for the great evils in the world because we are powerless to prevent them, even collectively. This is not so obvious, in fact, in a nuclear age. Humankind has invented an effective means of destroying the world and thus putting an end to the evil that it contains. Why does a campaign to use nuclear weapons to this end not seem morally acceptable?

One obvious answer is that such terrible destruction would be worse than letting things be. Now obvious though such an answer may appear to be, it is not clear that it will serve the present purpose. Taken at face value it implies that in the calculation of good over evil, the good comes out on top. But if this is true, then the conclusion we have drawn from the inductive argument from evil is itself undermined. What is good enough for us as moral agents is good enough for God (though not the other way about of course). If the world, however awful, is sufficiently good that morally responsible agents such as ourselves should not work for its destruction, than it is sufficiently good for a moral agent such as God to sustain. It is tempting to reply that this calculation excludes the nature of its destruction. A nuclear holocaust itself would be such a huge evil that we ought not to contemplate it, whatever the outcome. But this will not do. We are, reluctantly or not, engaged in a calculation of good over evil and however bad the process of destruction might be, we can be confident that it will be outweighed by the indefinitely many future wars, earthquakes, plagues, floods and famines that will not now happen.

There will, I imagine, be strong resistance to this line of argument by many readers on the grounds that equating our responsibilities with those of a (putative) God overlooks differences of the greatest importance. This is a natural thought. But what are these differences exactly? God, it might be said, is not faced with a straightforward choice between sustaining or destroying the world. He has it in his power to improve the world. This is no doubt correct, but it works against us at least as much and possibly more than it does against God. If we interpret it to mean that we, unlike God, do not have the power to make the world a significantly better place (minor and temporary improvements will not do), then we are faced even more markedly with the choice of continuing the world or destroying it. Indeed, even if we do not think ourselves in a position to bring about its total destruction, the implications are hardly comfortable. If the world is as bad a place as the inductive argument whose cogency we are assuming assesses it, then we are acting irresponsibly when we bring new children into existence or save the lives of those to whom death promises an escape. The alternative, of course, is to claim that our moral duty, faced with evil, is to work for the improvement of the world. But have we any real hope of bringing this about, except in temporary, partial and hence ultimately insignificant ways? Have we any real reason to engage in *hopeful* moral endeavour?

Putting the point in this way begins to make some sense of the claim I made that the existence of an omnipotent, benevolent, divine Providence is a necessary presupposition of hopeful moral endeavour in the face of evil. It only *begins* to do so, however, because for all that has been said so far, it is open to us to conclude that moral endeavour, our moral endeavour, is indeed hopeless, which is to say, based upon the false belief that a world such as ours can be significantly improved by merely human moral agents. Still, the desirability of rejecting such pessimism seems a powerful starting point.

The line of thought I have been pursuing may seem fantastical, and there is more work to be done in making it less so. For the moment, however, there is greater philosophical illumination to be gained by *increasing* the degree of fantasy. Imagine that the world is the creation not of a good but an evil God, whom in the traditional fashion I shall call Satan. Clearly, if this is the case the evils we see about us are not there as a result of default or impotence, but as part of his (or her!) deliberate intention. So too are the good things, however. In order to promote his evil designs, Satan has good reason to keep the world in existence; its destruction would put an end to suffering and distress after all, which is what he is committed to maximising. Nor would he be wise to make life an intolerable hell. There will only be people (and animals) to torture if there is enough that is good about their lives for them to persist (foolishly) in trying to survive. The outcome could well be that the mix of good and evil is pretty much as we encounter it. Yet, should we come to know that Satan is in charge, we will know that kindness, decency, courage and so on, will always be thwarted and that any seeming triumph of good over evil will at best be temporary, and allowed to persist only in so far as its persistence serves evil ends. Given this knowledge, together with a belief in our own moral agency, would we not have a clear obligation to refuse to co-operate in whatever way we could (such as failing to have children) and to seize whatever chance that might present itself (such as nuclear weapons) to bring about the destruction of the world?

The answer seems to me to be plainly 'yes'. But if this is correct, a further thought arises. As far as our responsibilities are concerned, does this (let us hope) imaginary scenario really differ from the position with which the inductive argument from evil presents us if it is taken to be successful? By that argument the world in which we find ourselves has more evil in it than good, and it is one which we cannot hope to mend or improve significantly. In this respect it is no different to one that arises from evil intent. It follows that the character of the world implied by the inductive argument from evil, combined with a sense of our own moral agency, should lead us to react in the same way as we would to a Satanic creation – refusing to co-operate as far as possible, and seeking its destruction if and when we can.

X

How are we to escape this unhappy conclusion? One way, as I have been hinting, is by questioning the supposition with which the last section began – that phenomena such as the Holocaust provide sufficient support for the inductive argument from evil to sustain the contention that the world as we know it is incompatible with the existence of the Christian God. But before embracing this strategy, which many will still think implausible and still poorly motivated, we should look at the humanistic alternative. There are a number of writers who have recognised that there is, as they put it, a 'secular problem of evil' no less than a religious one. This is the problem of making moral endeavour intelligible given the often catastrophic nature of human existence and our relative powerlessness to render it otherwise.

One such writer is John Kekes, in a book expressly entitled *Facing Evil*. Kekes disavows any theological or religious aids to the solution of the difficulty with which he is concerned. His version of the difficulty may be said to be another analysis of 'the moral gap', that is, the gap between moral aspiration and its realisation, and his aim is to give us reason to continue as moral agents nonetheless.

Kekes is concerned to elaborate and defend a conception of 'character-morality' over conceptions based primarily on principles of action, or estimations of outcomes, but for present purposes the difference between his and other accounts of morality does not specially signify, since what we want to know, whichever conception we employ, is what reason we have to persist with moral endeavour. In reply to our main question he says this:

As a response to the secular problem of evil, I have proposed character-morality. The guiding ideal of character-morality is that people should get what they deserve. And what that is depends on the good and evil they have caused, or, in short, on their moral merit. But the achievement of this ideal is impossible because of the essential conditions of life, the scarcity of our resources, and the difficulty of establishing proportionality between merit and desert. These obstacles cannot be removed; they can only be made less formidable. Yet making them so is necessary for good lives; consequently, we have no reasonable alternative to doing what we can to approximate the ideal. (Kekes 1990: 223)

In the previous section I argued that *pace* this last sentence, we *do* have a reasonable (in the sense of rational) alternative – putting paid to the world. This is not a possibility that Kekes considers and let us suppose, if only for the sake of argument, that I am wrong about it. There is nevertheless another part of this same sentence with which there is reason to take issue – his claim that moral endeavour as he characterises it is 'necessary for good lives'. Recalling the earlier parts of this chapter, it is important to note that there is an ambiguity here. Are we to take this as meaning *morally* good lives? If not, if it means generally good lives, then there is the Nietzschean alternative. On the other hand, if it does mean morally good, the egoist still awaits an answer to the question 'But why should I be moral?' Why should I want a *morally* good life, as opposed to a subjectively satisfying one? On this point Kekes is, in the philosophical sense, a moral realist, a believer in the factual nature of moral considerations. This is not a position he expressly defends, but he does assert it with vigour – 'Evil is undeserved harm, and some occurrences of it are as hard, factual, observable, and empirical as other items in the furniture of the world' (Kekes 1990: 150–1). The story seems to be, then, that evil is a fact and, by implication presumably, the goodness of minimising it in our lives is a fact also. What, though, makes goodness (and evil) factual? Just as the moralist faces a challenge from the egoist, so the moral realist faces a challenge from the subjectivist.

I shall take subjectivism to be the view that for something to matter, there must be someone to whom it matters, that there is no 'mattering' in the abstract. The 'someone' need not be anyone in particular, however; it can be a class of people, perhaps the class of human beings in general. Now if (as humanists in general and Kekes in particular contend) there are no subjects or agents other than human beings (let us leave other animals aside), then anything that matters, must matter to some or all human beings. This might be said to be the fundamental tenet of humanism, in fact; 'mattering' begins and ends with human beings. Note that this position is not necessarily egoistic. I can hold that the fact that something matters *to others* makes it matter, whether or not I myself care very much about it. If I do hold this then other people's disadvantage or discomfort matters (full stop, we might say) just because it matters to them and not because it matters to me. Subjective humanism in this sense is compatible with altruism and can consistently maintain that the fact that something matters to others gives me reason to act. In itself such a view contends only that there must be some human subject to whom an action or state of affairs matters; it does not (need to) contend, as egoism does, that it is only actions or states of affairs that matter to the acting subject that can generate reasons for that subject to act.

Humanism, then, is a restricted version of subjectivism. It believes, in an ancient phrase, that 'man is the measure of all things', that the valuable is the *humanly* valuable. Consequently, a moral realist such as Kekes, who is also a humanist, must address this issue. Be evil and good as 'hard, factual, observable, and empirical' as you like, there nonetheless appears to be an important difference between them and other 'observable, and empirical' facts – namely, that they can move to action. The fact that $E = MC^2$ carries no implications for action; the 'fact' that slavery is wrong does. The difference is this: the wrongness of slavery matters to us in a way that $E = MC^2$ does not. Unfortunately for moral realists, however, this difference makes all the difference, for it is this difference between one kind of fact and another (whatever it is) that converts the 'fact' into a morally relevant one. Without it, the wrongness of slavery is indeed just like 'other items in the furniture of the world'. But that is not enough. The point is one which J. L. Mackie made famous in his widely discussed book *Ethics*, significantly subtitled *Inventing Right and Wrong*. Mackie alleged that anyone who tries to construe moral and/or evaluative descriptions as the record of 'factual' properties brings into existence some very 'queer' properties indeed. For unlike all the other properties with which we are familiar, these must somehow induce or move to action. The only alternative to this 'queerness' is to suppose that there is, in addition to the factual element which resides in a judgement like 'slavery is wrong', a projected subjective element, of feeling, emotion, will, desire or whatever. Without this, the factual element, as Hume claimed long ago, is 'inert'.

If this analysis is correct, humanism faces a huge difficulty, one which I shall express by saying that it cannot take evil seriously. Why is this? Consider any great evil – child abuse say. To most minds child abuse is a problem, and to seek to make the world a better place is to try to do something about the problem. This is normally thought to imply only one thing – the reduction of instances of child abuse. But if the humanistic explanation of value is correct there is an alternative strategy – to work for the condition in which its existence does not matter to any one. Bring it about that no one *cares* if there is child abuse in the world, that it does not matter to anyone, and the 'problem' has been eliminated.

One response to this extraordinary implication would be to say that the world simply is not manipulable in this way, that human beings care deeply about some things and cannot be brought to be otherwise. This seems to me an unsatisfactory response in at least two ways. First, it is not obviously true. To begin with, it is a recordable fact that general attitudes can change enormously. Pictures and stories that would have appeared to almost everyone as grossly pornographic fifty years ago, can now be found with regularity on prime-time television and in supermarket news-stands. Furthermore, it just is the case that some human beings do *not* care about those things which most think to be of great importance; they are, as we say, callously indifferent. Why should all human beings not reach this condition? Indeed, such an alarming possibility was more than hinted at some years ago in Colin Turnbull's anthropological study of *The Mountain People*. Turnbull claimed to have found a tribe, the Ik, who had been reduced by a combination of material and social factors to what most of us would regard as an exceptional degree of inhumanity, one in which most if not all of the normal range of feelings and affections had been corrupted or eliminated. There was much discussion then as to whether his observations were accurate and as to what, if they were, this implied. But whatever the truth of the actual case, Turnbull's book made horribly plausible the possibility of drastic alteration in what we normally take to be 'human nature'.

It might be replied that there is an ambiguity at work here. Some human beings are indeed callously indifferent to what happens to others, but they do not show the same indifference to what happens to themselves. The Ik, by all accounts, continued to seek individual advantage. Now it certainly seems that there is built into almost everyone a natural basis of unreflective reaction to certain things. When, say, someone carelessly treads on my toe, my resentment at their carelessness is automatic, not something mediated by deliberation. The same sort of point could be made about a range of reactions, many of them relating me to the things that happen to others. A mother's care about her children, grief at the death of friends and relatives, anger at unfair treatment – all these might be said to be built into the human frame. Yet it does not follow from this that such reactions are ineliminable, and the mere logical possibility that the problem of, say, child abuse, would be 'solved' if only human attitudes changed is sufficient to show that the implication which I claim to have detected in humanist explanations of value still holds. Depending on what we mean by 'built in', this 'solution' may well be more impracticable than the normal one, and therefore to be rejected on pragmatic grounds. The trouble is that to make this move is to concede that the two 'solutions' are in principle on a par, and it is in this equation, not in their equal practicability, that the second objection to the humanist response we are considering lies.

The same point can be made in another context. Some versions of Buddhist thought (and Eastern thought more generally perhaps) hold that the root cause of suffering is desire or 'craving'. The pain of an experience lies not merely in what it is but in our desiring its elimination. Consequently, when once we cease so to desire, the painful element disappears and the experience becomes simply what it is – mere appearance. The Stoics, or some of them, had a similar view. Both views, in my terminology, fail to take evil seriously. They hold that evil is not itself a reality, but a function of our apprehension of reality, and in so far as we can control and amend that apprehension evil comes to be seen for what it really is – an illusion. So too with all humanistic explanations of evil, and of good. If positive and negative value lies, so to speak, in the eye of the beholder, we, the beholders, are free to look away.

I do not propose to argue further on this point. It is difficult to see how such deep differences of thought and conception as lie between Eastern and Western religious outlooks could be resolved. My point rather is that humanistic conceptions of morality cling to the reality of evil when their abandonment of underlying theological conceptions gives them no basis for doing so. This assertion will no doubt merely prompt a further inquiry. In what way does theology make up the difference? This question, in fact, provides us with the starting point on which the twin themes of this chapter, morality and evil, can be related to the theological themes of the first two chapters. But first, a summary of the position we have reached may be useful.

XI

In the first part of this chapter I argued that if we are to characterise 'morality' we have to be able to distinguish moral uses of the terms 'good' and 'bad', 'right' and 'wrong' from the much more general and very widespread uses that all these words have. One way of doing so – Kant's broadly speaking – is to distinguish them as overriding, which is to say, considerations that take precedent over all other evaluative assessments. The morally right, we might say, 'trumps' the rest. The trouble with this suggestion is that it has great difficulty in explaining from whence such overridingness might arise. It cannot easily demonstrate that moral considerations have a claim upon the egoist, and it cannot demonstrate the rationality of an absolute morality in the face of a radical conflict with prudence. One way round both these difficulties is to abandon the idea of morality altogether, to employ the synderesis rule as the sole foundation of practical deliberation and, with Nietzsche, go beyond good and evil.

The trouble with doing so, however, is that there appears to be at least one candidate for the description 'absolute evil', namely human slavery, and while we could boldly drop the idea that slavery is overridingly wrong, our conviction in this matter seems as solid as any basis on which we might try to defend its rejection. Our choice, then, would appear to be to stick with the idea of (at least some) forbiddens and persist in attempting to overcome the difficulties that lie in the way of 'absolute morality'. One solution lies in an appeal to 'moral faith', the belief that conditions do as a matter of fact prevail which will ensure that neither self-interest nor prudence ultimately conflicts with the requirements of morality. We can reasonably hold such a faith if we presuppose that there is a God who has the moral interest and the power to guarantee the truth of such a belief.

A transcendental argument may be mounted in defence of this presupposition, but however cogent, by the nature of the case it cannot withstand a positive disproof. This is where evil makes a second appearance in the argument, for the traditional problem of evil is potentially just such a disproof. Yet all is not what it seems with the argument from evil. A strictly deductive version, one which logically disproves the existence of a good God, cannot be formulated convincingly and while a strong inductive case can be mounted for saying that God's existence, given the evidence of evil in the world, seems very unlikely, this version has an unpleasant sting in the tail. Its strength lies in the proposition that the world as we find it is not the sort that a morally responsible agent would create or sustain. If, on these grounds, we conclude that God does not exist, however, this has the effect of passing such responsibility on to us. How could we, any more than God, be justified in sustaining a morally monstrous world? Our only choice, if we are to avoid this unfortunate implication is to return to moral faith, the belief that despite appearances to the contrary, there is a God who supplies the conditions under which we can intelligibly engage in morality. This conclusion is further strengthened by the examination of humanistic alternatives which, it turns out, cannot explain adequately the seriousness of evil, and, as Stephen Clark says, 'Can we seriously choose not to take the evils of this world as seriously real?' (Clark 1984: 43). We are thus brought to the point at which we have very good reason to ask how exactly the existence of God, if He does exist, might help.

XII

There is an ancient problem, dating back at least to Plato's dialogue *Euthyphro*, about how the appeal to God could underwrite morality. Couched in modern terms rather than the terms he himself employs, Plato in effect presents us with this dilemma. Either God declares things to be good because they *are* good, or they are good *because* he declares them to be so. If the former, then the good is good independently of God. If the latter, the good is nothing better than what God arbitrarily elects to choose as such; had he chosen those things which we normally hold to be evil, we would have to accept this. Pain is bad because he says so. If he said to the contrary, it would be good. More importantly, if all turns on God's dictate, we cannot hold that the goodness or badness of an action or state of affairs lies in its nature. There is nothing about painful experiences that makes them bad. Their negative value is something simply 'attached' to them by the will of God. How could this be? How could pain cease to be the bad thing it is if God should choose to change His mind? The consequence is that neither horn of the dilemma seems attractive. Whichever we opt for we have no adequate ground upon which to base morality (or the good more generally perhaps).

Let it be said at the outset that the literature on the *Euthyphro* dilemma is very large. I cannot hope to review it, therefore, and must rest content with exploring a line of thought which to my mind has considerable plausibility. To state the conclusion in advance, its upshot is to provide reason for thinking that the second horn of the dilemma is not as objectionable as it looks. How is this result to be achieved?

The first step involves, perhaps a little unusually in defences of theological ethics, endorsing a subjectivist meta-ethic. Subjectivism as I characterised it is the view that to say that something is good or bad implies that there is someone to whom it matters. Where a theological interpretation of this doctrine parts company from humanism is in its contention that human beings are not the only caring subjects there are. God too is a subject, and what matters, ultimately, is what matters to Him. How can this make a difference? It makes a difference not because of properties in the object upon which this care is based (which would return us to the first horn of the dilemma), but because of the person doing the caring. Return for a moment to the human case, and consider a non-moral example. Which pieces of music are worth valuing? It is a mistake to suppose that philosophical subjectivism must make the act of valuing consist in the (rather) whimsical application of immediate likes and dislikes. In exploring the world of music I can take valuable advice from those who have a great deal of knowledge and sensibility. They have listened to a lot of music and have a proven aptitude for hearing all the dimensions upon which musical compositions have something to offer. It is for these reasons that it makes sense to seek their opinion and guidance. The evident truth of this possibility, however, does not of itself imply that we must go beyond the bounds of human interest and into the realms of the 'objectively valuable' construed on a realist interpretation of objectivity. What musical experts have to offer me is not, as it were, a factual report from a different level or order of experience, accessible to them but not to me, but the means to arrive at informed preferences. In short, what is on offer is the education of taste.

How does this help the appeal to God as the basis of morality? One of the problems which Kant's conception of pure practical reason encounters is its seeming to present us with an unattainable ideal. It makes the possibility of morality depend upon full information and perfect rationality, neither of which fallible human beings can reasonably aspire to. As I observed earlier, it is 'the moral gap' in this sense, rather the sense in which I have been concerned with it, that John E. Hare addresses in his book of that name. His question is how human beings are to fill it. But it should be evident that God, if He exists, does not experience this gap, for He is all knowing and all good. To apply the musical analogy, God is the possessor of the best possible informed preferences. No preferences could be better informed (or formed) than His.

So what? Even if this is true in principle, we are no better off if we cannot know what these preferences are. In this response, it seems to me, there hides an important mistake. The purpose of moral philosophy is not to tell us what things to choose, but to explain how it is that in pursuing the moral we are engaged in an intelligible enterprise. The moral as I have described it is concerned with absolutes, the limiting cases of the unqualifiedly good, the irredeemably bad, the absolutely required and the completely forbidden. The problem with which we have been concerned in one way or another throughout this chapter is to make sense of the very possibility of a limiting case in judgements of good and evil. The conception of God as wholly rational, omniscient, omnipotent and benevolent provides us with a theoretical underpinning for this idea of a limiting case, for the idea of the absolute in other words. Theoretically, then, we *are* better off, if there is such a God. If God requires something of us, we have reason to regard it as absolutely right or good; if He forbids or excoriates something, we have reason to regard it as evil. To choose the second horn of Plato's dilemma, therefore, is to solve *in principle* the philosophical problem of morality.

Maybe so but, it will undoubtedly be said, for all this we are still no better off *in practice*. This is an important observation which needs to be addressed. But it ought not to be confused with the different claim that the appeal to God accomplishes *nothing*. What can be said, though, at the practical level? The correct answer to this question will initially appear somewhat disappointing. In trying to discover not the basis but the content of morality, with one possible exception the religious moralist will do what everyone else does – seek information, reason critically, formulate general rules and principles, exercise judgement. The possible difference (to which I will turn shortly) is appeal to revelation. For the rest, the task of trying to discern good from evil will be just as complex and difficult for religious moralists as for any other moralists. The fundamental difference lies in their understanding of what it is they are trying to do when they engage in these inquiries; what *they*, in contrast to humanists, are trying to do is to discern the will of God. To repeat a remark of John Wester's, quoted in an earlier chapter, 'For Christian ethics, the world is a different place, and part of the Christian theory of morality, is a careful delineation of that difference.' The whole of moral theology, I should say, is the delineation of that difference.

Some religionists believe, of course, that the difficult process of discerning good from evil can, as it were, be short-circuited by appeal to the revealed will of God. Whatever may be said about this in general, I do not think that it can be a plausible recourse for Christian ethics. This is chiefly because of the argument I advanced in the first chapter. Scrutinise the Gospels as you will, there is not much guidance or instruction to be obtained on the wide range of moral issues which concern contemporary morality. But not much less important is the further consideration that to rely exclusively on revelation would be to ignore an important theological dimension – the creative action and historical purposes of God. It is only if we hold that God's creation – the world in which we find ourselves (including ourselves, of course) – and His actions in history, are both irrelevant to the discernment of His will that we could rest content with an exclusive reliance on revelation. And besides, unless we subscribe to a very narrow version of the inerrancy of Scripture, even in understanding and interpreting (purported) revelation, we also have no choice but to deploy our natural reason.

Christians, unlike humanists, will not dismiss the deliverances of Scripture or the accumulated religious experience of their tradition, of course. But it is to be understood as one more, if specially important, resource in the difficult task of determining how we should live. What it supplies is a general context within which the moral life is to be understood. Such a context is more than theoretical in the sense I identified, however, and may thus be made to have a more direct bearing upon moral endeavour. This claim, which remains to be expanded, returns us to and connects the topics of the present chapter with those of the previous two. Traditional Christianity holds that moral endeavour has a part to play in God's redeeming purpose and that this purpose is to be recounted in terms of a cosmic history. It further holds that God aids or assists humanity in this, both by revealing these purposes in human history and by making available a 'holy spirit' which supplies some of our deficiencies. To quote Clark again: 'The proper attitude to the world is not a reverent contemplation of whatever is, nor a fearful rejection of it, but willingness to be part of the solution' (Clark 1984: 53).

The claim that God assists us in this supposes that there exists (at least) one agent for good other than human beings. It is also consonant with the contention of chapter two – that the moral relevance of the historical Jesus, in so far as our best endeavours allow us to discern it, lies in what he was and did rather than what he taught. These two contentions can be brought together in a conception of history as a cosmic battle between forces of light and forces of darkness, one in which human beings are left free to make a choice about which side they will join.

Now to put the matter like this is picturesque and it may further prompt within us an agreeable and inspiring sense of purpose and destiny. But is it more than a pleasingly aggrandising metaphor? Are there *really* forces of light and forces of darkness engaged in a battle? This is the subject of the next chapter.

CHAPTER 4

Forces of light and forces of darkness

In the previous chapter I quoted John Kekes as a representative of the humanist explanation of value. This is allied, in *Facing Evil*, to the belief in naturalism which he also describes as part of 'our modern sensibility'.

> Western heirs of the Enlightenment [are] people whose sensibility is formed, negatively, by the rejection of all forms of supernaturalism and, positively, by the combined beliefs that whatever exists or happens is natural, that the best approach to understanding their causes is scientific, that while human beings are part of the natural world, we still have some control over our lives, and that one chief purpose for exercising the control we have is to make good lives for ourselves. I call this *our sensibility* to indicate that many people in contemporary Western societies and elsewhere share it . . . (Kekes 1990: 11, emphasis original)

Kekes thinks, correctly in my view, that evil presents a problem to such a mentality no less great than it does to the traditional Christian account of moral experience. There is, as he puts it, a 'secular problem of evil'. In the last chapter I was concerned to reveal the inadequacies of the humanistic element in 'our modern sensibility' in dealing satisfactorily with the reality of evil as a challenge to moral endeavour, despite Kekes's best efforts. But there is another dimension on which we must also deal with evil – namely its explanation: why it happens. Is it true that, faced with some of the appalling occurrences we find perpetuated against, and by, human beings, 'the best approach to understanding their causes is scientific'? 'Our modern sensibility' as described, accurately, by Kekes, has in fact two components, humanism and naturalism. In the previous

119

chapter my aim was to make plausible the contention that humanism cannot adequately account for the moral significance of evil; it cannot, that is to say, properly capture what we might call its evaluative darkness, and, consequently, cannot rationally justify moral aspiration in the face of it (I shall return to the topic of humanism in chapter six). My aim in this chapter is to show that there is another (though related) level on which 'our modern sensibility' fails – the 'scientific' explanation of the nature and occurrence of those things called evil. On this point it is the naturalism rather than the humanism inherent in our modern sensibility which proves inadequate. Or so I shall argue.

Just as we are inclined to rank the things that we ought and ought not to do on two spectra – from good to bad and from good to evil – so we apply a similar distinction to the things that happen. Life is full of unfortunate and regrettable events, but even to the relatively unreflective consciousness it must seem obvious that human experience also contains powerful and striking encounters with episodes that go beyond these relatively mild negative epithets and constitute great *evils*. Many people can testify to this personally, but in any event history provides more than sufficient evidence. Moreover, though we commonly refer to one period of the past as 'the Dark Ages', it may well be true that, compared to other times, the twentieth century was specially notable for the occurrence of a large number of horrors; the Nazi Holocaust, Stalin's Gulag Archipelago, Pol Pot's Cambodia, the Hutu genocide of Tutsis in Rwanda are just some of the most momentous. What explains such great evils? How did they come about? Why did they happen? In what way are we to understand them? So out of keeping do they appear to normal motivations and to the relatively humdrum course of human life, that they must surely require special explanation. How can seemingly ordinary human beings engage in such atrocities? Does the explanation of such occurrences lie with scientific causes, are the human beings who perpetrate them simply part of the natural world, as Kekes alleges? If so, it would seem that the explanation must lie in some conception of malfunctioning, the 'natural' going wrong. It is this suggestion I want to explore.

Actually, our attention need not be confined to evils on a dramatically large social scale. In addition to the horrors of the Holocaust and so on, there are other phenomena more individual but no less terrible. Though I shall return to these macro-phenomena, it is evil at the level of the individual upon which I shall first dwell at length – the phenomenon of the serial (or multiple) killer. When we look not at the excesses of the Nazis or the Khmer Rouge but at the behaviour of individuals such as Charles Manson, the Boston Strangler, Jeffery Dahmer or Dennis Nilson we seem also to be looking not merely at the bad, the undesirable or the unfortunate, but at the deeply evil. If so, how are we to comprehend and explain the occurrence of such things? This highly topical as well as troublesome question about contemporary human life, will lead us, I think, to question the contention of T. R. Glover quoted in an earlier chapter and which there is point in quoting again, somewhat more briefly.

For the primitive peoples of today and for some not so primitive, the whole universe is full of daemon powers, more real than we can imagine . . . this tale of war in the spirit sphere is for us the merest mythology. . . (Glover 1921:)[1]

Contrary to this assertion, my aim is to show that, whatever our modern sensibility may suppose, the 'tale of war in the spirit sphere' is rather more substantial than 'the merest mythology'. Indeed it was so for much later periods than those to which Glover refers. As another writer observes, 'The sharp smell of an invisible battle hung over the religious and intellectual life of Late Antique man' (Brown 1971: 53). So too, perhaps, we ought to think of ours.

---

[1] Quoted out of context this passage may suggest an erroneous interpretation of Glover's own view. A little later he goes on to say:

If [the modern psychologist] has disposed of the daemons and demigods by whom the ancient thinkers used to explain the existence of evil in the world, he has achieved a great stroke for mankind, in ridding men of the most paralysing terrors it has known; but he has neither eliminated evil from the world we know, nor explained its presence there.

I

The phenomenon of the mass murderer has become distress-
ingly familiar. The killings by Hamilton at Dunblane and
Bryant in Tasmania in a single year (1996) gave it a higher
world wide profile, but unhappily these are merely more names
in a long and continuing list. This is true even if we restrict
ourselves to very recent times. Whenever yet another case hits
the headlines, there are two immediate reactions. The first is to
condemn the perpetrators as evil; the second is to declare them
mad or mentally ill. This second reaction is confirmed, often,
when more details emerge about the killings, since these details
reveal actions that are readily described as 'sick'. How are the
two – evil and sickness – to be connected within the terms of
'our modern sensibility'? One obvious answer is that 'evil' is
'unnatural' in the sense of being the radical dysfunction of
normal psychological-cum-physiological processes. As the term
'mental illness' implies, on this account madness is a sort of
sickness. But it comes in degrees, and a natural system gone off
the rails *drastically* can for this reason be said to come within the
compass of those things called 'evil'. The parallel with physical
illness is evident; it too has a spectrum – from colds and 'flu at
one end to tuberculosis and bone cancer at the other. These
also call for a differing range of evaluative attitudes and in
expressing them here too ordinary language often invokes the
bad/evil distinction. Cancers are cases of the natural gone
wrong, not in any moral sense, but in the sense of radical
malfunction, so radical that, within the sphere of the physical, it
seems inadequate to describe them merely as 'bad'. Rather,
they strike us as great *evils*.

There is then some reason to employ the idea of a natural
process going badly wrong as an explanation of a certain sort of
evil. In line with this idea, and under the assumption that the
human mind is itself a naturalistic phenomenon, there is some
plausibility in the suggestion that multiple murder arises from a
psychology gone drastically wrong. Is this suggestion borne out
by the evidence? It is not uncommon for people to suppose that,
strictly, we need no evidence because the thing speaks for itself

– *res ipsa loquitur. Res ipsa loquitur* is in fact quite an old legal principle. Someone who invokes this principle is claiming that so abnormal are the actions, they are in themselves sufficient evidence of profound mental dysfunction. This *assumes*, of course, an essentially naturalistic explanation, one which seeks to explain the bizarre in terms of some aberrant natural process. But to approach the matter in a more critical spirit we have to leave open this question: Is this sort of explanation adequate to the phenomenon? It is worth noting at the outset that so perplexing is the subject matter under discussion, some writers who have studied it in detail have thought that science (even broadly understood) must give way to philosophy. Brian Masters, for example, in his study of the Milwaukee killer Jeffrey Dahmer, quotes the ethnologist Niko Tinberger: 'Man is the only species that is a mass murderer, the only misfit in his own society. Why should this be so?' Masters then comments:

This is obviously not a question that can be answered in a court of law, nor is it one, really, which the psychiatrist's definitions can cope with. It is primarily a philosophical question and, as such, capable of contemplation, if not resolution, . . . (Masters 1993: 16)

Whether the phenomenon of multiple murder really does push us from psychiatry (or some other science) to philosophy, is obviously of considerable relevance to the present inquiry, because if it does, this would in itself constitute an important breach in the claims of naturalism and represent a significant step in the return to a (revised) conception of another, and an older understanding. My strategy, in fact, will be first to disclose the inadequacy of contemporary scientific explanations, and second to consider the potential merits a different sort of explanation, one closer to that which Glover dismisses. This alternative type of explanation re-introduces the necessity of an appeal to the spiritual and while there are interpretations of 'the spiritual' that do not identify it with 'the supernatural', it is nevertheless a step in its direction.

Before the exploration proper begins two preliminary remarks are required. First, the terms 'mass murderer' and 'serial killer' are not always used interchangeably. When they are not, the difference is sometimes nothing more than the time period within which the killings took place. Human beings, rather curiously to my mind, are disposed to be impressed by concentrated events, to be more impressed, for example, by a single plane crash than a month of road accidents, even when the death and injury represented by the former are actually less than the latter. Whether there could be any rationale for this disposition is an interesting philosophical question, one related to the question philosophers know as 'discounting the future', but neither is a matter I shall inquire into here. Some writers think there is much more to the distinction between 'mass murderer' and 'serial killer' than this; Levin and Fox regard it as fundamental. Others, such as Elliot Leyton, hold it to be of relatively little consequence. Whether it is or not depends in part on the approach to the subject, but for present purposes I shall use the neutral term 'multiple murderer' and take no special interest in whether the killings of the multiple murderers to whom I refer took place serially (as in the case of the Boston Strangler) or all at once (as in the case of Hamilton).

Second, it needs to be emphasised that the question under discussion is this: Can multiple murder *always* be explained in terms of a pathological condition? Are multiple murderers *necessarily* mad? That at least some multiple murderers have been suffering from profound psychological disturbance seems incontestable. At any rate, I shall not contest it. (The 'Texas church killer' Larry Ashbrook, who shot seven churchgoers at a Forth Worth Baptist church in September 1999, seems to have been a plain instance.) All I contest is first, the suggestion that madness *must* be the explanation, and second, that, if it is, it provides us with an adequate account of what it is about their behaviour that is properly described as 'evil'.

It is useful to start considering these matters by characterising madness as an extreme form of mental disorder. This may sound rather an empty statement, one which accomplishes little since it says the same thing twice. But the point of making it is to stress that it is *mental* disorder that is to be explored. Modern philosophy of mind is strongly predisposed to physicalism (an application, or perhaps a version, of naturalism of course). Indeed, it might not be inaccurate or unjust to describe this as a prejudice. If it is, it is a prejudice shared in large measure by contemporary psychiatry and psychology. Consequently, it is widely believed that madness, along with other aberrations of mind, is in the end a matter of neurophysiology, whose remedy will finally lie with physical, biochemical or genetic treatments. This prejudice explains the somewhat desperate action of officials in California to have scientists dissect the brain of 1984 multiple murderer James Oliver Huberty in the hope of finding 'lesions' which would explain his conduct. Where else, they thought, could the explanation lie? Where indeed, if we are physicalists?

The attractions of such an explanation are evident if we are convinced of the virtues of naturalism, for it seems that from such a point of view the most satisfactory explanations will in the end be those of natural (understood as physical) science. For my own part I think there is reason to question the presuppositions of physicalism in the philosophy of mind. But whether there is or not, it is evident that, as a matter of fact, on most occasions physicalist accounts of mental phenomena amount to little more than dogma. The reality is that, though some headway has been made in effective drug treatment of depression and schizophrenia, there is virtually no theoretical understanding of the physical basis of these, and in almost all other types of mental disturbance (neuroses and phobias being specially striking examples) there is neither effective drug therapy nor even the beginnings of a neurophysiological explanation.

This fact alone cannot be used to undermine naturalism however, which can instead be couched in wholly mentalistic terms, provided only that we are still able to employ law-like generalisations and functional explanations. There can be naturalistic psychology which is not physicalist. For this reason, if no other, it is best in the present context not to hammer the deficiencies of an infant neurophysiology, but to stick to the much older language of mind (commonly called 'folk psychology') which by and large we understand, and ignore the search for an alternative set of physical/neurophysiological concepts which (for all we currently know) may never actually be forthcoming.

Accordingly (though the list is not meant to be exhaustive), I shall say that the mind is composed in the main of the following elements: sensation, belief, memory, desire, emotion and will, and that mental dysfunction is the condition in which some or all of these are disordered, sometimes radically, from their normal law-like functioning.

The least contentious application of these concepts is probably disordered sensation – usually referred to as hallucination – namely those cases in which visions and voices have no detectable causal counterpart in reality. People who exhibit susceptibility to hallucination are generally acknowledged to be mentally disturbed, however various or obscure the causes of this disturbance may be, because the pink rats (say) they claim to see are not actually present in their field of vision. The function of sight and sound, on this understanding, is to apprehend the world around us. Hallucinators have vivid but erroneous visual and aural sensations, so erroneous that we have reason to think there is serious malfunction somewhere in their psychological system, even if we cannot say where exactly. Disordered belief is also a reasonably uncontentious mark of mental malfunction. Obviously, though, disorder of this sort cannot be simply a matter of disconnection with reality in the way that sensation is. If it were, *every* false belief would be evidence of insanity since all false beliefs are misapprehensions of reality. Such an interpretation, I take it, is a *reductio ad absurdum* of itself, because the distinguishing feature of disordered belief must be, rather, the fact that normal checking procedures play little or no part in its formation. And in extreme cases such procedures are abandoned altogether. To put the point plainly, there is no reasoning with the man who believes himself to be the Queen of England because if there were any vestige of rationality about his belief formation in this matter, the belief would not be entertained at all. No person engaged in reasoning *could* think this.

Now importantly, it has been observed by very many writers that typically the multiple murderer is *not* of this kind. In few cases, if any, is there evidence of either hallucination or radically disordered belief. This explains why, when a man such as

Hamilton guns down large numbers of children, it is almost always (as in this particular case) greeted with astonishment by those who knew him, and when the gruesome activities of a serial killer such as Nilsen become known there are equally astonished witnesses to his normality. This apparent normality, in fact, is an important feature of the problem with which we are concerned. As Elliot Leyton puts it 'if the killers are merely insane, why do they in fact so rarely display the cluster of identifiable clinical symptoms . . . which psychiatrists agree mark mental illness?' (Leyton 1984: 11). If there is serious mental disorder, accordingly, it must lie rather deeper, and in the sphere of desire, emotion or will rather than belief or sensation, which for the most part is strikingly normal in such cases.

It might be said that the way in which I have categorised the life of the mind is misleadingly straightforward. It suggests separate, possibly exclusive functions. This is not so, let it be admitted. Desire, emotion and will are all elements in what philosophers know as the 'affective' aspects of mind, and the affective is in part revealed in belief. For instance in evaluative beliefs about the good and the bad, the desirable and the undesirable, there must be some combination between belief and attitude. The same truth is also revealed in what may be broadly described as '*cognitive* attitudes', that is to say reflective attitudes to emotion, power, danger and so on. I can only truly believe to be dangerous, for example, that which I actually fear (to some degree). Such beliefs and attitudes do not stand in relation to reality as straightforwardly factual or empirical beliefs do, and this is why 'believing' in a non-affective sense may be regarded as a distinguishable activity of mind. Thus, the exploration of desire and emotion and will inevitably include the exploration of beliefs and attitudes, and vice versa.

II

To understand what it means for the affective in this wide sense to be disordered, then, we have to deploy notions of belief and attitude, at least in so far as these are indicative of will, desire and evaluation. This evaluative component, however, introduces an important new dimension to the analysis. To see this, and by way of somewhat lighter relief, consider a quite different case to those with which we have been concerned so far. In his diaries *Writing Home*, Alan Bennet recounts the extraordinary case of Miss Shepherd, 'The Lady in the Van', a vagrant who lived in a van in his driveway for the best part of twenty years. There is much in the account that is interesting and amusing, but one episode in particular is striking and will serve as a discussion point. Moved by the fate of General Galtieri after the defeat of Argentina in the Falklands War (in 1982), Miss Shepherd composed the following letter.

To Someone in Charge of Argentina

Dear Sir,

I am writing to help mercy towards the poor general who led your forces in the war actually as a person of true knowledge more than might be. I was concerned with Justice, Love, and, in a manner of speaking, I was in the war, as it were, shaking hands with your then leader, welcoming him in spirit (it may have been to do with love of Catholic education for Malvinas for instance) greatly meaning kind negotiators etc... but I fear he may have thought it was Mrs Thatcher welcoming him in that way and it may hence have unduly influenced him.

Therefore I beg you to have mercy on him indeed. Let him go, reinstate him, if feasible. You may read publicly this letter if you wish to explain mercy, etc.

I remain, Yours Truly

A member of the Fidelis Party (Servants of Justice)

PS Translate into Argentinian if you should wish

In language which is no longer approved no doubt, but which was in its time almost a term of endearment, Miss Shepherd can best be described as 'batty'. The letter's crazy syntax and the evident falsity of some of its assumptions are indications of the mind that composed it. But it is not these that are most telling. As the signature indicates, Miss Shepherd had a 'mission', the mission of the Fidelis party of which, of course, she was the only member. This mission was not very consistently or vigorously pursued, though at another time it led to a short-lived plan to stand for Parliament. Nor was its precise nature very clear. As the letter 'To Someone in Charge of Argentina' implies, it had to do, vaguely, with Justice, Mercy, God and Roman Catholicism.

Now interestingly it is a recurrent (though not universal) characteristic of multiple murderers, that they too are engaged in a 'task' or a 'mission'. This is a notable feature of the famous cases of Edmund Kemper, Charles Manson, David Berkowitz and Peter Sutcliffe. However, there is an important difference between them and Miss Shepherd. In her case the peculiarity lies not with the *end* but with the *means* of the mission. There is nothing odd or unfamiliar about Justice, Mercy, God or even Roman Catholicism as the objects of missionary zeal. Rather, what is indicative of mental im-balance is the absurd evaluation Miss Shepherd places on the efficacy of her own agency to these ends, an agency which she puts on a par with that of Mrs Thatcher in fact. Miss Shepherd's sense of justice and mercy may have been mis-placed, but her ultimate ends were intelligible enough and even worthy, perhaps. It is the *means* by which she seeks to realise them that are so manifestly inadequate, and for this reason indicative of a disordered mind. No one in their right mind, we might say, could think that a letter from such a source, expressed in this fashion and directed in this way (even if translated into Argentinian!) was a rationally adequate move in securing mercy for General Galtieri. Still less could they think that the recipient might find opposition to such a step helpfully assuaged by the letter's being read out publicly.

By sharp contrast, the 'campaigns' of many multiple mur-derers are marked by the radical abnormality of the *ends*, to which efficient or at least intelligible means are carefully chosen. In fact there are several instances in which multiple murderers have admitted that their first steps were fearful and fumbling and they had to learn from experience how to conduct their gruesome activities with skill. For instance, Edmund Kemper, who killed ten people (both family and strangers), spoke of himself as engaged in a 'task' which required the killing, sexual assault and dismemberment of certain social types, and described how he had to master the techniques of killing required to accomplish this task. Even if the 'task' in hand has no element of social 'mission', but is simply the pursuit of a specific kind of desire or gratification, the relation between means and ends may well be that of rational agency. Jeffrey Dahmer, the Milwaukee homosexual multiple murderer whom Brian Masters has studied in depth, seems to have found a profound sexual satisfaction in handling and masturbating over the dismembered elements of those to whom he was most attracted. Given this *end*, their murder and dismemberment was a necessary, and hence wholly rational, *means* to its achievement. What is unnerving is the end.

We can explain the absurdity of Miss Shepherd's letter in a relatively straightforward way. The factual probabilities by which the rationality of her chosen means to her given end is to be assessed are easily ascertained, and yet have plainly been ignored (or gone unregistered, perhaps). This is what gives evidence of mental disorder. There is a dislocation between belief and reality here similar, though not the same, as there might be in the case of hallucination and delusion. But when the means to a given action, still more to a strategically organised plan, are rational so that it is only the end that can be thought bizarre, on what grounds can it be declared irrational (or dysfunctional) in such a way that we can question the mentality of the one who espouses it?

In exploring this question it is useful to look a little more closely at the case of Edmund Kemper, the multiple murderer operating in California in the early 1970s. Kemper's actions included not only the abduction, rape and murder of eight young women, but the murder of his own mother and the sexual abuse of her mutilated headless corpse. To most people this will seem the plainest possible case of *res ipse loquitur* – if these are not the actions of a sick mind nothing is. However, Kemper, in his confession, speaks of these as essential elements in the accomplishment of a task, and he further speaks of losing control only *after* the task was complete. Indeed, by his own account it was not until he found himself driving somewhat mindlessly from state to state that he came to think, *for the first time*, that things were getting out of control. It was because of this new sense of things going awry that he gave himself up (and might otherwise never have been caught, as a matter of fact, so well had he planned his activities).

Elliot Leyton makes a plausible case for putting the following construction on Kemper's actions. Kemper, who (despite the surface appearance of his actions) believed strongly in the conventional order and values of middle-class America, felt himself rejected by the very society to which he had given his loyalties and of which he wanted to be a part. This sense of exclusion was given particular focus when his application to join the police failed, and was further exacerbated by constant harsh criticism from his rather loathsome mother (a university administrator) who seems to have despised him for his failure to rise above the status of a Department of Highways flagman. Kemper believed he had been short changed, that handsome middle-class college women represented a specially striking symbol of society's indifference, and that he had it within him to make a mark, to be someone. His 'task' was to accomplish this, and the means consisted (in part) in destroying some of these symbols. Now the important point to notice is that he *did* make himself someone by these means. He successfully acted both on behalf of and at the same time contrary to society's most cherished norms. As a result he shed the status of nonentity and became someone of note, a fact confirmed by the considerable amount of attention (including that of scientists and psychologists) that he attracted while in prison. In short, his aim was to have people pay attention to him despite his personal and social disadvantages; and they did. In short, he succeeded in his chosen aim.

Of course, the identity he thus achieved was that of social monster; it is all very well to make your mark, we might say, but to make it in *this* way is grotesque. Let us agree for the moment that this is so. It is nonetheless the case that *given* that this was his aim, his conduct towards the end was perfectly rational. The same can be said of Jeffrey Dahmer. The details of his actions are hard to read about, so appalling are they. But given that he had insistent necrophiliac desires which could only be satisfied by killing the homosexual partners with whom he wished to have sexual congress, the steps he took and the success with which he managed to remain undetected, show to a remarkable degree the rational pursuit of desire. They also explain why it came as a complete surprise to those who knew him that he was engaged in such sordidness. Precisely the same point can be made about Dennis Nilsen.

The point to be emphasised is this. Unlike Miss Shepherd, many (probably the majority) of multiple murderers function *well* with respect to the formation of belief and the effective pursuit of desire satisfaction. They are able to discover what they need to know, to chose and pursue ends in a rational and effective way. They cook meals, drive cars, hold down jobs, read the newspapers, buy clothes, write letters just as everyone else does, and the same practical rationality, often of a very high order, is also displayed in their nefarious activities. This is true, sometimes, even of those multiple murderers who kill themselves after an orgy of slaughter. Consequently, if they are to be declared dysfunctional, possessed of deranged mental processes – it must be on the strength of the *ends* they espouse.

Now the attempt to detect malfunction at this level raises an interesting question. If the mark of madness is the inability of mind to track reality, what is the reality of ends with which there is a mismatch? There is a familiar, and naturalistic, account of mind and value which is built on the assumption that rationality consists in the pursuit of efficient means to desired ends. This conception is often known as 'internalist' because it identifies the end of action with internally generated desire. If this internalist account is correct, however, it makes no sense to suppose that the *ends* of action can be declared irrational. Where could their irrationality lie? Rather, only the means to realising them can be so described. But the implication of this way of thinking is that we have no ground upon which to declare the mind that pursues what most people would think of as wild and crazy ends irrational, still less mad.

The founding father of this account, or at least its most famous and influential exponent, was David Hume. Hume's largest and most important work is not entitled *A Treatise of Human Nature* by accident. The use of the term 'nature' here is significant, because the model of inquiry he has in mind is that of Bacon and Newton. In a sense the *Treatise* is not really a work of philosophy as traditionally conceived at all. It is rather, an exploration in what Hume (along with many others of his time) calls 'the science of mind'. The distinction between natural science and philosophy is (possibly) more marked now than it was in Hume's day, and his using the terms almost interchangeably may disguise what is in fact an important shift. In the modern sense Hume's investigation is scientific rather than philosophical, and his intention is to solve long-standing metaphysical problems by using the observational methods of Bacon and the mechanical conceptions of Newton. In his view, these had proved so productive in natural science that there was every reason to think they would prove profitable in the mental and moral sciences also. He makes this very plain in the Introduction to the *Treatise*, but it is made plainer still in the 'revised' version, namely the *Enquiries*. In the section 'Of Miracles' in the first *Enquiry* he expressly seeks additional authority for his argument by asserting that 'Lord Bacon seems to have embraced the same principles of reasoning' (Hume 1902: 129), and in the section 'on Justice' in the second *Enquiry* he claims that his argument is an application of 'Newton's chief rule of philosophizing' (Hume 1902: 204). Like several other major philosophers (Wittgenstein and Nietzsche are specially striking examples) Hume believed that the significance of his work and its claim to originality lay in the adoption of a method wholly new to philosophy, and that (in his case) this new method was the method employed by the natural scientists.

In his adoption of the 'scientific' method, however, Hume was not as novel as he supposed. In fact, the move to a 'science of mind' as the basis of moral philosophy is now recognised to be a distinguishing feature of the eighteenth century quite generally, and of writers belonging to the Scottish Enlightenment especially. Indeed the movement was so widespread that Pope could include the dictum 'account for the moral, as for natr'l things' in his *Essay on Man*. But the difference between Hume and many of his contemporaries is that, while *they* saw in the science of mind a new basis for moral philosophy, *he* develops it in a way that essentially divorces the two. Whereas

Alexander Gerard, for instance, thought that 'we must inquire what is the constitution & structure of human Nature' in order 'to discover whether Virtue has any foundation in the nature of man' (quoted in Wood 1990: 141), it is well known that on the basis of an empirical account of human nature Hume uncovers a logical gap between what is (nature) and what ought to be (virtue). Indeed, this is just one of several traditional philosophical positions that he undermines. Notably, he finds no logically conclusive basis for inductive reasoning, cannot find any ground for attributing necessity to causal relations, and argues that reason is necessarily inert with respect to action, which is always determined by desire or 'the passions'. The gaps that these conclusions seem to present to our customary ways of thinking are, in the end, to be bridged by recording that this is just how the human mind typically works. It is our brute nature, not logical intelligibility, which underlies the simple passage from one thought or belief to another. So, since we cannot prove that the future will be like the past, or that a cause must give rise to its effect, we must rest content with the observation that 'reason is nothing but a wonderful and *unintelligible* instinct in our souls which carries us along a certain train of ideas . . . [This] habit is nothing but one of the principles of nature, and derives all its force from that origin' (Hume 1967: 179, my emphasis).

The eighteenth century was the high point of the first great attempt at a science of mind. Then, as various kinds of intellectual dissatisfaction assailed it, the project was caused to fade, to be replaced in the course of the nineteenth century by Hegelian (which is to say, historical-cum-philosophical) conceptions of meaning and understanding. In the twentieth century, the pursuit of a science of mind returned. Though known variously as naturalism and physicalism, there is reason, as I noted earlier, for the naturalist to hold these two terms apart. However, in my view the modern account, as a new basis for moral philosophy, serves no better than the old. Hume was right and Gerard wrong; naturalism, if it works, in the end puts all human desires on a level. Some may be more or less common than others, and in the ordinary run of people, they may waken still further feelings, some of approval some of disapproval. In the light of this we can determine which of them accord with the feelings of the majority, but none can be declared right or wrong, good or bad, rational or irrational in any more substantial sense.

This implication of the naturalistic conception of mind that I am here pointing to was expressly conceded by Hume when he famously said:

Where a passion is neither founded on false suppositions, nor chuses means insufficient for the end, the understanding can neither justify nor condemn it. 'Tis not contrary to reason to prefer the destruction of the whole world to the scratching of my finger. (Hume 1967: 416)

If this is true, for the same reason the understanding can neither justify nor condemn Kemper's preference for notoriety over the degradation and destruction of young women, nor Dahmer's necrophiliac desire over the death and dismemberment of young homosexuals. The most that can be said is that such aims and desires are *abnormal*. But abnormality, within the Humean conception, can only have an uninteresting statistical sense. What is 'wrong' with multiple murderers, in the end, is that they are highly unusual. If this is the right way to think about it, then the evil that the ordinary mind finds in the Kempers and Dahmers of this world turns out to be nothing more than the unusual, albeit the highly unusual. It can also be said, certainly, that such mindsets are dangerous to others, and for this reason it is important for society (though only construed as a numerical majority) to check the people who possess them. It may further be true that individuals generally come to have such abnormal desires and aspirations as a result of atypical personal and psychological histories (though this is not altogether borne out by the evidence and in any case could be nothing more than a matter of statistics). It also seems to be the case that very many of them (not all) are 'loners', people largely cut off from ordinary, everyday social intercourse, a feature which may help to explain why their desires are uncommon. Even so, none of this shows that their mental condition is tantamount to madness in the sense of radical dysfunction, and none of it explains why we should think of them as evil. The same relative rarity might, for all I know, be recorded of devoted collectors of garden gnomes, with the happy difference that their statistically aberrant desires and behaviour constitute no risk to others. If avid collectors of gnomes, despite their statistical abnormality, are not mad, no less are multiple murderers. Both are simply odd.

It follows that multiple murderers, even of the grossest sort, cannot be declared mad, which is to say minds gone wrong, at least if Humean moral psychology is correct. This conclusion follows from Hume's internalist contention that human desires cannot themselves be in conflict with reality and hence with reason. They simply are what they are. In Hume's terms they are 'original existences', statistically unusual no doubt, but nothing more than this. It is a contention fully in accordance with naturalism, as it seems to me, for even a naturalistic psychology more sophisticated and better informed than Hume's, which invokes all the experimental data that modern psychology supplies, can, at bottom, only record what is found in nature. It has no grounds on which to judge it fundamentally *wrong*. Unusual, yes; wrong, no. The failure of this way of thinking to account for such casts of mind in terms that most people perceive them – evil – is sufficient to warrant this question: Could such an account be correct?

The idea that desires no less than beliefs can, so to speak, be 'out of sync' with reality is incompatible with naturalism, and hence unfashionable. Desires simply are what they are. The problem is that it is precisely the presence of some such desires that seems to put people like mass murderers into a radically different class. How is this to be explained? The fact appears to be that naturalistic ways of thinking *cannot* explain it. And this is why there is reason to look beyond them. Where then are we to look? In the longer history of human thought, longer than the Enlightenment that is to say, alternatives are not far to seek, nor even unfamiliar. Plato's moral psychology, for example, rests upon a variation of the theme that human beings may be divorced from reality with respect to ends no less than means, since for him the Good is as much a reality as the True. Aristotle too can give some account of the matter. Human beings have a natural *telos*, an *ergon*, which includes a range of desires, and in so far as they depart from these, they may be described as defective, just as the lion that (who knows why) will eat only grass is defective. More obviously still, Christian moral theology, which regards human will and desire as by its very nature sinfully self-destructive and in need of redemption by being brought into line with the will of God, clearly invokes a standard from which actual human desires can be more or less radically deviant. In the light of such conceptions it would be possible to say that Dahmer or Kemper or Ryan or Hamilton had desires as radically misplaced from rationality – the truly good, the natural, the God-given– as it is possible for means to be.

It is worth noting that, whatever may be true of Plato and Aristotle, to reject the Humean conception of mind in favour of the Christian alternative does not, importantly, generate the conclusion that such people are in need of some other sort of 'treatment'. Rather, it abandons such a way of speaking in favour of the view that the fundamental explanation lies not with malfunction, but with evil, and this, significantly, is just how ordinary people commonly describe them. In short, what they need is not to be *treated* but to be *redeemed*. At the same time, talk of 'redemption' in its fullest, theological sense is not fashionable either, just because of that very 'modern sensibility' which, as Kekes rightly observes, determines most of our thinking. This is not a simple prejudice, however. One objection to the idea of evil desires (as opposed to malfunctioning systems) and redemption (as opposed to cure) is that it seems to offer little in the way of *explanation*. All that is on offer in such ways of talking, it seems, is *redescription* or even simple *reclassification*. Serial murders of a gruesome kind or mass killings which display an utter heartlessness are (still) relatively small in number. If the best we can say of the desires that prompt them is that they are evil, whence comes this degree of evil?

A further objection is that simply classifying them as evil does not seem to take much account of an interesting feature – internal conflict of will – something that is present in many of these cases. Dahmer's is one such case. He appears to have believed throughout his gruesome career that his desires were contrary to right and wrong and ought not to have been acted upon, and indeed for a time he seems conscientiously to have struggled against them. But he speaks in terms of a sort of pull which in the end he could not resist, an urge that was too powerful for him, one that took him over and from which, at his arrest, he seems glad to have been relieved. Do we not need to return to the invocation of psychological causes and mental imbalance to explain this seeming subversion of choice and deliberation?

The answer is: perhaps we *could*, but we do not *need* to. In the past, as Glover observes, it is at this point that the language of daemonic possession would have been invoked, to explain both the degree of evil and the sense of compulsion. It is worth observing that even today something of the language of possession continues in common speech – 'I don't know what came over me', for instance. Such ways of speaking are rarely taken seriously, even by Christians, despite the fact (as we saw in chapter two) that references to supernatural powers, both angelic and daemonic, are extensive throughout the New Testament. Yet, given the failure of the naturalistic alternative we have been considering, there is reason to think that we should at least entertain a substantial reading of them, that we *should* take these ways of talking seriously. What we have to explain is the sense of psychological compulsion which some multiple murderers profess, even in those cases where we have found no reason to regard them (in modern terms) as mad. And also, perhaps more importantly, where we have reason to think (arguably in the case of Dahmer), that though they did evil things, they were not of unmistakably evil character. Both features are accommodated by the idea that they came under the influence of spiritual powers.

Now generally, the mere *possibility* of an alternative mode of explanation is, to all but philosophers, unpersuasive of anything. Most people are interested in its *plausibility*. Interestingly, so far as modern psychological studies go, even with respect to plausibility this alternative possibility cannot be wholly discounted. Some serious studies of serial killers – Brian Masters's books on

Nilsen and Dahmer are good examples – go some distance to showing how ideas of possession cannot be easily dismissed, and at the same time, the distinguished American psychiatrist Willard Gaylin has freely admitted 'most of us are aware how trivial, ephemeral, descriptive and meaningless are psychiatric diagnoses' (quoted in Leyton 1984: 140).

The plausibility of the radical alternative to explaining multiple murder depends upon making some sense of daemonic possession – a very large task. Yet, given the failure of naturalistic psychology, there is good reason to attempt it. This is the topic of the next section.

III

In her acclaimed novel *Scarlet Song*, the African writer Mariama Ba is concerned, on a number of levels, with the subject that interests us here, the conflict between the modern 'scientific' Western way of thinking and a traditional pre-scientific one. Towards the end of the novel, the second of these conflicting forces is powerfully captured in her description of a traditional invocation of miraculous spiritual powers.

Chanted incantations merged with the beat of the tom-toms . . . There rose up an ever increasing roar of exhortations, born in the night of time, from tormenting anguish and man's inability to find any rational explanation for certain events.

Among this crowd of onlookers, attentively following the proceedings, were certain persons to whom the duty of attending on the *rabs* and perpetuating offerings of flesh and blood, had been handed down by their ancestor, who had no doubt reddened the blue of the sea by festivals of sacrifice. The same ancestor who had doubtless shuddered with fear or thrilled with joy when the greedy waves licked at the blood shed at his feet. He had listened to the voices of the deep and found in their wise gravity balm for his sufferings. Had his anxieties then melted away in the surging waters, and had strong gusts of wind carried his wishes away to be fulfilled?

Arms jerked upward in supplication to heaven. Women and men conversed with the Invisible. Their eyes were fixed on the same point, and the smile on their lips bore witness to some dazzling experience. Every gesture, accompanied by a particular resonance of the tom-

tom, was a message. The Perceptible and the Invisible were in communion. Souls quivered in a trance of possession, inspired by their familiar. And the tom-tom muttered, muttered; the tom-tom muttered, muttered, the catalyst for the intermingling of two worlds, the living world and the world of the imagination. (Ba 1986: 142–3)

['*Rab*: a type of jinnee; invisible, supernatural creatures of either sex who can protect or harm mortals, particularly by 'possession' of those who neglect or displease them' – *Glossary*]

This compelling description brilliantly captures a common conception of daemons and the attempt to deal with them. It also contains the elements of analysis and explanation which sustain this conception. The motive to engage in such practices lies in 'tormenting anguish and man's inability to find any rational explanation for certain events'; the effect, and the attraction, is the inculcation of 'dazzling experience'; the re-sulting trance is an undiscriminating confusion of 'the living' with 'the world of the imagination'.

That such occasions and experiences have been recurrent in human societies, that they were once common but are now rare (at least in large parts of the world) and that their demise has much to do with the rise and success of science, especially medical science, are not claims that I propose to question. Nor is it my intention to suggest that ceremonies of this kind must be revived if we are to deal successfully with evil. Nevertheless, it is easy to identify, and dismiss them, as paradigmatic examples of a supernaturalism belonging to times past, and at best having a mere residual existence in the present. To begin with, as we have seen, there are phenomena connected with the dark and dangerous sides of the human mind which, so far at any rate, the alternative world of modern 'science' has failed to explain, and there is a certain arrogance about ruling out of considera-tion conceptions and beliefs that have been recurrent in almost every age and culture other than our own. Second, it may be that it is primarily the cultural context that makes the practices here described so alien and that there is nonetheless something important to be learned from the ideas embodied in them, once they are shorn of their atavistic overtones. Third, as I observed before, the New Testament, which contemporary Christians go

on reading, is replete with the language of powers and principalities, and must itself be given an interpretation of some sort,
therefore, if it is to have meaning for the contemporary reader.
In so doing the task, as Walter Wink has observed, is to
distinguish accurately between myth and mystification.

To do this, we have to return once again to that branch of
philosophy sometimes known as 'moral psychology'. There is a
constant tendency for philosophies of mind to be structured
around certain dualities. There is of course the fundamental
division between body and mind, of which René Descartes,
perhaps, was the most brilliant and influential exponent. But
there are other (usually interconnected) dichotomies too – the
internal *versus* the external, the logical versus the causal, the
rational versus the empirical. This last division is a notable
feature of the psychology underlying Kant's moral philosophy.
According to this way of thinking, as I noted earlier, human
beings have two natures; they are rational deliberators, and
they are physical objects. As physical objects they are subject to
the same laws of nature as everything else; the human body
conforms with the law of gravity and falls at 32 feet per second
per second no less than a lump of stone does. This is their
'empirical' part. But as rational deliberators, human beings are
subject to a different sort of law – the law of reason. Unlike laws
of nature, the laws of reason are normative rather than descriptive; they determine not what does happen, but what ought to,
and they address the subject's *will*. It is of course a major
philosophical task (not to say problem) to say just what the
relation between these two natures could be, but that is not our
problem here. In a more preliminary way, what we need to
know is how and whether this division between the empirical
and the rational can be applied to the contents of mind.

Let me here recall that at an earlier point in this chapter I
offered a list of the elements which commonly constitute the
mind – sensation, belief, memory, desire, emotion and will. It is
(reasonably) clear that in this list the first – sensation – can be
classified as 'empirical' (though there is the important difference
between 'looking' and 'seeing' to be accounted for) and let us
agree with Kant that will is an obvious candidate for the

'rational'. But what about emotion? Kant thinks of this as 'inclination', and places it in the sphere of the empirical. Most people, who know nothing of Kant of course, have a settled tendency to contrast emotion with reason, and if we do operate with Kant's radical division, it therefore seems that emotion must indeed be part of the empirical. Is this correct? The subject is such a difficult one that it is possible only to proceed in a very tentative way. However, I think that even a tentative exploration of emotion will make plausible the suggestion that we need some further, or different, classification, one that shows the rational/empirical bifurcation to be too simple, albeit attractively so.

Consider, for the purposes of this exploration, the case of falling in love. The emotion someone in love experiences is not merely passive. It is not something that merely happens to them in the same way that pain is a passive experience. It has an *object* as well as a cause – the person loved – and the relation between the object and the feeling is not like that between food and indigestion, say, where the first is simply the cause of the second. There is a causal element, certainly. It is true that my encounter with the object of my affection is (part of) its explanation; I could not have fallen in love had I not met them. But I can also be asked what I find attractive about the person I love, and the features I list are themselves part of the explanation of my being in love. What I *find* loveable about them partly explains *why* I love them. In this way, I am inclined to think, love is rather different from sexual attraction pure and simple. Asked what it is about the other person that I find sexually attractive, I do not know that there is anything to say. I just do. In the case of love, by contrast, even where this also involves sexual desire, the attraction is *mediated* in important ways. Whatever about 'love at first sight', in the standard case, love arises from conversations, shared experiences, the discovery of fellow feeling, and so on, and all of these involve the active exercise of mind and judge-ment, thus making falling in love something more than a passively experienced 'visitation' into our consciousness by the outside world. Being pierced by Cupid's arrow, we might say, is different from being pierced by a real one.

At the same time, it would be odd to locate love in the sphere of the rational, ordinarily understood. The things I find loveable about another person do not in any sense rationally *justify* my love for them. To think that the love I feel is an *inference* from my perception of their loveable characteristics is absurdly intellectual. To detail these characteristics, however, can make my love *intelligible*, or fail to do so. Suppose for instance I cite the way the other looks, or talks, or describe their curiously vulnerable shyness. Others may see and experience these things, yet not be in love, and they cannot be faulted for not being so. By contrast, they *could* be faulted for not arriving at a belief the evidence for which we all see, and evidence which implies the belief. Even so, though not constrained by rules of inference, individuals in love do not have altogether free rein here either. If I give, as a reason for being in love, the size of the other person's bank balance, I have made a joke, or a mistake.

Love, then, seems to straddle (and confound) Kant's divide. Something like sudden, unexpected anger may well fit his claim that emotion lies in 'the empirical part'. The error is to think that this is the nature of emotion in general. Indeed, even the relatively simple example of anger can be made to throw a different light on the subject. There is, people commonly believe, something identifiable as *irrational* anger. If Kant were right, how could this be? Anger is certainly something felt, something we undergo. At the same time, to claim it to be irrational suggests that it is out of step with the world, in something like the way a false belief is. But if it is something we simply undergo, how *could* it be out of step with reality? It simply is what it is, something which happens to us. (Curiously, this is the outcome of Kant's moral psychology no less than Hume's, despite the fact that Kant is consciously responding to Hume's sceptical challenge.)

How could feeling fit reality? The answer to this question lies in our seeing that, though an emotion, unlike a belief perhaps, has no representative function, and cannot therefore correspond or fail to correspond with 'the world out there', nevertheless, there can be a lack of 'fit' between the feeling and its object; the feeling (or its degree) is in some sense or other *inappropriate* to the object. The waiter's careless mistake in executing the order, say, *causes* but does not *warrant* the customer's wrath; his wilful neglect of his customers both causes *and* warrants their anger. There is a distinction between something's being merely the occasion of an emotion, and its also being its intelligible object. Irrational anger is the former but not the latter, and will, I imagine, be readily acknowledged as a familiar phenomenon.

Now the same lack of 'fit' can occur in the case of love, and it is this second example that throws a some light on the rather more obscure idea of daemonic 'possession'. Imagine that my daughter falls in love with someone I regard as highly unsuitable, and not on social or financial grounds. He is, I might contend, unworthy of her love. Or I may think that (as we say) 'there is no future' in the relationship, that only hurt and disappointment can arise from it. The two objections are not exclusive, of course. In many literary examples they both apply. Why on earth is she in love with him, then? There is no accounting for these things, people often suppose, and perhaps in many cases this is true. One interesting counter instance, however, is the case in which she has been seduced by his charm. Seduction (and I am not thinking of the simple act of taking sexual advantage) is a very interesting phenomenon. To put it plainly if bluntly: seducers are neither rapists nor kidnappers. One important difference is that they acknowledge the autonomous agency of the other. Unlike the rapist and the kidnapper, seducers do not override the will of those they seduce. Rather they work *through* it.

They might do this by means of simple falsehood. This is not, to my mind, the most interesting case. Certainly there are many recorded and imagined examples in which someone is induced to 'fall for' a completely false representation of the other person. However, this is not of any special significance to our present purpose precisely because it is so easily captured under the category of ignorance, a failure in the faculty of knowing, about which Hume and Kant are largely agreed. When deception is operating, the explanation of my daughter's falling for some rogue is that he has cleverly disguised his roguery. In other words, she does not really love *him* at all, but only the person she falsely believes him to be. More interesting is the case in which she is brought to see his failings and weaknesses under a certain aspect, as vulnerability rather than weakness say, or as aberrations rather than fixed characteristics. Such judgements can of course be interpreted as errors also, but if this is the right way to think of them, then they are errors of a more complex sort. The important point is that while in the first case she simply fails to perceive his defects, in the second case she is fully aware of his failings, but is brought to apprehend them differently. And the seduction lies in his having brought her to see them in this way.

Now here, I think, we have an appropriate model for understanding an important aspect of evil. The puzzle in many cases, perhaps all, is how seemingly intelligent and rational people can be moved to act by evil ends. The naturalism which plays such a central part in 'our modern sensibility' prompts us, contrary to the evidence, to interpret such actions as those of people who do not or cannot apprehend the evil. They are so sick, which is to say malfunctioning, that they do not perceive the real nature of what it is they do or desire. The problem with this interpretation is that in the most striking cases, this just does not seem to be true. Kemper and Dahmer are, as far as the best psychiatric classifications can tell, as sane and rational as you or I. It is only the unwarranted assumption of *res ipse loquitur* that suggests the contrary. An alternative explanation is that they have been seduced by evil. Before we can move to the further, metaphysically more ambitious, claim that in these cases no less than that of my (imaginary) unfortunate daughter, we have to show that there is not merely seduction, but a seducer. Only then will daemons have entered the account.

IV

I propose to approach this issue somewhat indirectly. The first step is to show that the analysis I have just offered does indeed offer insight and explanation in a real case. And the case I shall consider is the gruesome killing that took place in a Colorado school in April 1999.

The slaughter which occurred at Columbine High School, Littleton, Denver was, at the time of its occurrence, the worst school massacre in American history. Eric Harris and Dyland Klebold, aged eighteen and seventeen respectively, armed with four guns, thirty bombs and hundreds of rounds of ammunition arrived at the school at which they were themselves pupils and began killing classmates. For some time they strode along the corridors, through the canteen, the library and so on, shooting those they found there, and laughing with pleasure as they did so. By the end the dead amounted to twelve children and a teacher, at which point Harris and Klebold turned the guns on themselves. Even carnage on this scale, it seems, fell short of their ambitions, since police found a further armoury and documents outlining their original, larger, plan.

It is difficult to imagine anyone who, in the face of such an event, is not prompted to ask the following range of questions: why did they do it? How could a good education, a loving (and Christian) family, a stable childhood and all the advantages of prosperous circumstances result in attitudes and actions as drastically anti-social and evidently immoral as these? How should we react? What lessons are there to be learned from it all?

The answers that people attempted to give to these questions at the time are illuminating, not because they make sense of the Littleton massacre, but precisely because they so massively fail to do so. As usual, of course, *with hindsight* people saw tell-tale indicators in Harris and Klebold's previous behaviour. They were, it was claimed, the school misfits, deeply resentful 'out-siders', especially resentful/contemptuous of sporting success among their classmates (and it seems they did pay special attention to the school athletes in the course of their rampage). Now even supposing that hindsight was not doing all the work, it seems evident that such indicators fall very far short of the explanatory. Does not every high school in the world have teenagers who are resentful, envious and contemptuous, 'out-siders' who do not fit into the main currents of social life in the school? Even if all these things were true of Harris and Klebold to an exceptional degree, this would do little to throw light on their actions. 'Difficult' teenagers are part of the regular staple of human life; moral monsters are not.

It is true that subsequent investigation revealed some highly unusual aspects of behaviour on their part. It turned out that these two boys were part of a larger gang, the 'Trench-Coat Mafia', whose members evidently had both an inflated conception of their own sophistication, a love of pornographic violence, and a deep contempt for the activities, attainments and values of their contemporaries. In particular, the 'Trench Coats' devoted much time and effort to exploiting the resources of modern information technology. They made videos and constructed web sites whose single animating purpose seems to have been an orgiastic delight in violence and destruction. This was linked with wickedness on a wider, more historical scale. It seems, for instance, that they deliberately chose the anniversary of Hitler's birth as the day of slaughter, the same day that Harris posted an Internet message which read 'Today is my last day on earth. Be prepared.'

It is hard to think that there is not *some* connection between this obsessive interest in the regular contemplation of images of violence, and the real violence which followed. It is a point to which I will return shortly. For the moment, however, let it be observed that there is no reason to think that there is any straightforward (or even indirect) *causal* link here. Speaking at the time, the American President Clinton remarked on the availability of violent images on television, video and the Internet. He noted, in the course of his address, the role of the Internet as a conduit for dangerous information – how to make bombs for instance – and wondered whether the greatly increased exposure to such material among recent generations makes them more prone to violence. To very many people such a contention seems hardly more than common sense. Yet those who would defend the claim that, at some level or other, the depiction of violence causes violence, have to explain why it is that vast numbers of other young people, similarly exposed, never come near to committing acts of this magnitude.

It might be replied that this is not a reasonable requirement. Not everyone who is exposed to the 'flu virus gets 'flu, after all, and just as this does not lead us to doubt the causal connection between the two, why should it do so in the other case either? There is thus no *special* difficulty in the psychological case. Or so it might be thought. In fact, let us leave aside the interesting matter of numerical proportions. (Large numbers of people exposed to viruses do succumb to them; only a tiny number of those 'exposed' to depictions of extreme violence turn extremely violent.) The position is importantly different in another way. Broadly speaking, our understanding of physical disease is well advanced, so that in the second case we have at least the makings of an explanation, one couched in terms of an underlying germ theory. By contrast, in the first case, as I observed in an earlier section, we simply have no such theory. With respect to the phenomenon of the multiple murderer, scientific psychology is as mystified as the rest of us. In other words, we have a theory which gives us reason to think that when 'flu occurs, the virus is its cause; we have no theory to justify us in thinking that when the murderous mind is present, the obsession with images of violence is part of its cause. For all the best psychological science allows us to know, it may instead be simply one more indicator of its presence (violent types are attracted to violent images), and no more its cause than shivering is the cause of 'flu.

At best, the jury is still out on the relation between pornography and violence. Despite the intuitive conviction of many people to the contrary, there does not appear to be convincing empirical evidence of the harmful effects of pornography. No study has revealed any clear statistical connection between those who are exposed to such material and those who engage in violent or perverted acts. Even the seemingly plainest and most telling instances cannot clinch the matter. This is partly because the theories of psychological motivation with which they must ultimately be supported allow interpretation in different directions. The most compelling examples usually cited are those of killings which appear to act out some video nasty (not, we should note, a claim that was made about Columbine). But it is just as plausible to think that the connection is not cause and effect. It may be rather that the psychology of someone who is fascinated by such images is also the psychology of a killer. This, for all we know, could well be true of Klebold and Harris.

Something of the same is to be said about the extension of the argument from fiction to fact, according to which the reporting of violence stimulates crimes by providing ideas and models for criminals, so called 'copycat crimes'. On this theory, ideas are suggested to would be criminals, which they then set about realising in their own locality. This may indeed happen, but where crimes do appear to be copycat, this shows only that their form has been determined by reports from elsewhere; it does not show that the impulse to unspeakable wickedness has been prompted by the reporting. It may be plausible to think that Klebold and Harris formulated their plans to imitate the exploits they saw on television or discovered on the Internet (though there is no evidence of this), but it is much less plausible that until they started surfing no thought of committing murder and mayhem had entered their heads. Once more, it seems to me, we need hard evidence, both about patterns of crime, and about the motivations of actual criminals, evidence which we do not have.

Precisely because of our lack of hard evidence it is naive to imagine (as perhaps President Clinton imagined) that we can estimate the contribution that watching pornographic videos can make to the balance of forces within the mind of the killer. Even if we knew that Klebold and Harris dwelt at great length on the videos they watched (which we do not, as a matter of fact, know) we could not attribute any clear causal weight to this. After all, censors also spend a large amount of time watching these materials and do not turn violent as a result. There is no more reason to think that watching violent videos was the cause of Klebold and Harris's state of mind than that it was simply more evidence of it.

This line of argument may be applied more generally. It is a familiar thought that people whose newspapers and television screens are regularly filled with reports of violence, though they do not themselves turn criminal, will, so to speak, become inoculated against its horror and as a result become more accepting of it. That is certainly one possible outcome. It is equally possible, however, that the reporting of violence increases people's revulsion in the face of its consequences, and strengthens their repudiation of it. Neither one of these reactions is any more or less possible that the other, and that is as far as reasoning in the abstract can take us. To discover most people's actual, as opposed to possible, reaction we need solid, and extensive, social inquiry. This would provide some real evidence, but it is evidence of a sort that we do not have as yet. Studies that have been attempted along these lines have resulted in very uncertain or conflicting conclusions. There is reason to hold that violence begets violence. We ought not to confuse this with a quite different thesis – that the *depiction* of violence (factual or fictional) begets violence. On behalf of this thesis people are also inclined to invoke the principle of *res ipse loquitur*, and deny the need for evidence. But in fact that depicted violence causes real violence is a complex and ambitious thesis that has yet to be established.

It seems then, that neither the exploration of personal psychological histories, nor attention to unusual external causes gets us very far in answering the question 'Why did they do it?' Faced with the evident inadequacy of the most obvious lines of inquiry, some people conclude that at bottom, actions like these are simply inexplicable, and that a major part of our problem is that we desperately want to make sense of something that cannot be made sense of. This was the view of Rochelle Brundson, one of a positive army of 'counsellors' who arrived in the aftermath of Columbine. If so, however, what is to be done? How are we to come to terms with events like these? Brundson, in common with most counsellors, saw the problem in terms of coping with the emotional effects of victims, relatives and a wider public. 'There is always the question of why', she says, '[But] the best we can do is to encourage them [the other pupils] to talk about their feelings and get it out into the open.'[2] My own view is that behind such a claim there is a hopelessly inadequate conception of counselling, closely allied to what has

---

[2] Quoted in *The Daily Telegraph*, 23 April 1999.

been called 'the pressure-cooker theory of emotion'. However, I have written at length on this elsewhere and will not repeat the arguments here.[3] More to the point for present purposes is the observation that while the response of Brundson and others was common, another (not necessarily in competition) was no less common – the call for prayers for the victims and their families, and prayers, indeed, for the whole nation. How could prayers help? It is in attempting to answer this question that the connection between the events at Columbine and the wider philosophical concerns of this chapter will be revealed.

v

How can prayer help? Let us ask a slightly different question; how is prayer *supposed* to help? The answer, it seems plausible to say, is that by praying, those who are suffering the effects of evil are assisted in some way, and assisted by an external power which comes to their aid. This may be the outcome of their own prayers, or the prayers of others, but the central idea is that, in the difficulties they face (however we characterise these), a source of strength becomes available to them which is other than they have within themselves. And that it becomes available as a result of *asking*. In short, in orthodox terms, Christians who pray do not merely aim to focus on, or pour out their hearts to God, but to seek His aid, in the Person of the Holy Spirit, the Comforter (which is to say, 'strengthener').

Now the first point I want to make about this conception of prayer is that it invokes the idea of a spiritual *agency*. In this it is to be distinguished from meditation. Whatever merits and advantages the latter has, its function is to assist us in composing ourselves and inducing within us a tranquillity that we need. Any form of meditation (yoga, say) is thus a method of securing a given mental outcome – calmness instead of perturbation, for example. This is why it is so easily construed (rightly or wrongly) as a special form of relaxation. Furthermore, meditation is *essentially* subjective. That is to say, while there is nothing

[3] See Graham (1990b), ch. 3.

contradictory in the idea of meditating upon an object, even a distinctively Christian one – the sufferings of Christ, for example – the act of meditation is wholly internal, the bringing about in ourselves of a certain outcome and effect, one which is valuable to us in the face of the stress and distress we will otherwise undergo. TM, or transcendental meditation, can be rightly so described. It is meditation on that which transcends ordinary experience. But this does not imply that whatever it is that is transcendent is an independent agency responsible for the effect brought about by meditating upon it. Rather, the efficacy lies in the practice of meditation itself.

In the case of prayer, by contrast, it is precisely because I apprehend the inadequacy of my own natural resources, however assisted they may be by accumulated techniques of meditation, that I ask for supernatural *help*. The question, of course, is whether such help is actually available. The natural-istic assumptions of 'our modern sensibility' suppose that it is not, and this is why such a sensibility can make space for meditation but not for prayer. The widespread credence given to this assumption also explains why outwardly religious people are easily persuaded nowadays that the prayers they utter should be thought of as a form of meditative exercise.

It is important to note that this last possibility – interpreting prayer as a form of meditation – makes it difficult to formulate the criteria, still less assess the facts, with respect to the efficacy of prayer. Imagine that someone prays and, as such people have often reported, experiences a 'peace that passes all understand-ing'. This outcome, even if we are fully convinced of its occurrence, is equally compatible with its being, *really*, medita-tion. It follows that the questions we are here concerned with cannot (contrary to some televised experiments) be rationally settled by the gathering of empirical evidence. Rather, if we are to make any significant progress in their investigation, it must be in terms of their explanatory adequacy in a wider frame-work. And this framework includes the explanation of evil.

The point to be emphasised at the present juncture is this. Of the pupils and teachers who underwent the appalling events of Littleton, their families and friends, the people who sought to

help them, and the rest of us who merely learned about what
had happened, a great many sought refuge in prayer. In so
doing, however, they departed to this extent from 'our modern
sensibility' by looking to a spiritual supra-naturalistic agency
that could be called upon for help. They did so, I think, not just,
or not entirely because they had no other course open to them.
Rather, they were moved by a sense, common to those who
experience heart-breaking tragedies and acts of almost unbelievable horror, that the veil of ordinary experience had been
drawn aside to reveal a far different, deeper, and on this
occasion darker, dimension. This is what religious experience
often is, a sudden and dramatic 'sense of something far more
deeply interfused', to quote Wordsworth. It can be prompted by
good people and events no less than by evil people and terrible
events, the former resulting in a sense of the Divine, the latter in
a sense of the Satanic. In both cases it generates the thought (or
perhaps it would be better to say 'the sense') that the flow of
everyday experience takes place within a far larger context than
that with which we are ordinarily aware. To put the point
succinctly, the nature of the human condition is something that
probably passes our *comprehension*. But it does not always pass
our *apprehension*, and it is events like the episode at Littleton that
regularly bring people to the belief that they have apprehended
it.

It is true of course that very many of those who turned to the
consolation of traditional religion did so against an equally
strong assumption that the events with which they were trying
to cope had some underlying naturalistic explanation which
psychology or sociology might uncover, or that they were
'senseless'. There is an evident conflict between these views,
however. It would be a more coherent way of thinking about
such things if the appeal to supernatural agencies for help were
invoked precisely because it was by supernatural agencies that
they believed themselves to have been assailed. This is the
connection with evil. We need the help of God, it seems more
consistent to say, because the other world we have suddenly
encountered has brought us face to face with Satan. In the
words with which I have entitled this chapter, events such as

Columbine impress it upon us that we are in a world where forces of darkness operate, and because of this we need forces of light. As St Paul says 'Our struggle is not against human foes, but against the cosmic powers, the authorities and potentates of this dark age, against the superhuman forces of evil in the heavenly realms' (Ephesians 6:12 REB).

So far, however, for all that has been said this is merely a requirement of coherence, and as has been pointed out many times, coherence can be achieved no less easily by denying the premise as by affirming the implication. It is open, at least so far as consistency goes, for the naturalist to claim that since there is no Holy Spirit for prayer to invoke, the best position is to continue to assert the senselessness, and abandon the prayer. This is true. At the same time, as before, the equal consistency of these two positions does not mean that there is no way of breaking the deadlock. We can have reasons for preferring one coherent position to another. What deadlock-breaking moves might be available to us here?

VI

The first is this. As we have seen, our modern, humanistic, scientific sensibility lacks an adequate explanation of evil. Combining conclusions arrived at in both this chapter and the previous one, we can now say that this amounts to a double failure. Humanism cannot explain (so to speak) the evil of evil, and naturalistic science, even of a well-informed psychological kind, cannot explain its occurrence. So, if there are alternative explanations that do accomplish these tasks, there is reason to prefer them. Second, in the sort of circumstances I have described, people do, as a matter of fact, have a strong inclination to pray, which is to say that a standard reaction to events of great evil is to seek supernatural aid. It is true of course that this fact does not in itself make sense of their doing so; people engage in all sorts of unintelligible practices – astrology, superstition and magic being among the most obvious. Still, the fact is that the practice of prayer is almost universal across time and space; it is the modern Western world that is out of step in this respect. This gives us an added reason for pursuing alternative explanations of evil, if these explanations would at the same time make the instinctive prayers of ordinary people intelligible.

The problem with naturalistic explanations of the occurrence of gross acts of evil is that those who commit them, as we have seen, exhibit all the usual elements of rationality. They acquire relevant information, plan their actions, interpret them purposefully, and pursue them with devastating effectiveness. It is for these reasons that they are not to be classed with the Miss Shepherds of this world, who fail in precisely these respects. Even so, there is one further possibility, a possibility consistent with naturalistic humanism – that they can be understood as having a hugely, and hideously, distorted set of values. By this account, Harris and Klebold thought their acts of slaughter 'a good thing to do', a wonderful way in which to depart from this world, a glorious climactic act of revenge on those whom they loathed. They were not sick in any clinically identifiable sense, let us all agree. Rather, in an ancient phrase, what they did was to say 'Evil be thou my good.'

Many people find this sort of claim plausible, partly, I think, just because it seems to rescue 'our modern sensibility' in the face of scientific failure. But is it plausible? To begin with, on the face of it 'evil be thou my good' is flatly contradictory; it requires that one and the same thing be recognised as evil *and* affirmed to be good. To avoid this contradiction, we might say that what we actually mean is that the perpetrators of great evils mistakenly believe the evil to be good. Unfortunately, to make this move is to return to problems encountered in the last chapter. Humanism holds that the final court of appeal in matters of goodness is what human beings value. In which case, these human beings cannot have made a mistake; they simply valued something very different from the majority of their fellows. But in this case we are then left with the difficulty – why were *they* so different? – a question which returns us to the seemingly intractable problem of explaining their occurrence.

What I think this well known phrase – 'evil be thou my good' – aims to capture is a feature of wrongful (or sinful) action that Augustine famously points to in his *Confessions*. Augustine's example, in comparison to those we have been considering, is rather trivial – the theft by him and some boyhood companions of pears from an orchard. Still, the same feature emerges. Augustine did not want the pears. In fact he threw them away almost immediately. What attracted him was the doing of *wrong*. It is the knowing inclination to do wrong that we need to explain. Its explanation lies, or is at least illuminated by, the claim with which I ended a previous section. An alternative explanation to psychological illness or social malformation is that Harris and Klebold were seduced by evil. The problem, as I there observed, is that of moving from this to the further, metaphysically more ambitious implication, that in this case no less than that of the ordinary everyday instance, there is not merely seduction, but a seducer.

I shall say, as a tentative account of what went on in Columbine, that the images of violence on which the two boys (and their companions perhaps) dwelt, developed and explored had the effect of bestowing upon acts normally found deeply repellent a certain allure. The proper description of their resulting view is probably this: 'What a way to go out!' I say this is the proper description because it expresses not an affirmation of the kind 'evil be thou my good' but a more inarticulate feeling of exhilaration. They were, we might say, *charmed* by the image. The charm lies in its audacity, its dramatically exceptional character, the light, colour and noise of destruction, an *image* to which *real* blood and terror are essential elements. Perhaps we should not regard 'charmed' here as a metaphor, but as a necessary return to an older conception. In fact, unaccompanied by any of the same atavistic overtones, the phenomenon of Harris and Klebold fits exactly Mariama Ba's description of witchcraft in Cameroon – an 'intermingling of two worlds, the living world and the world of the imagination'.

It might be replied, by the modernist, that as metaphor this may be all very well, but as *explanation* it fails to make any real headway with the issue. Does it really amount to saying any more than that they came to see bad things in a good light, which is just what the supposedly inadequate explanation said?

And does it not assume precisely what was said earlier to be unknown – the harmful effects of pornography? In which case, it leaves unanswered the very question in which we are chiefly interested: why *these* boys?

Let me admit at once that I am not here claiming to offer an obvious or an especially easy alternative. Whatever way we look at these things, events like the massacre in Columbine are deeply perplexing. Nevertheless, in so far as we are to be rational, we must prefer better explanations to less good ones. At the same time, anyone who employs the argumentative strategy of 'inference to the best explanation', as I am doing here, must acknowledge that the best explanation, which, because it is the best, is the one rationality requires us to believe, may nevertheless, unbeknownst to us, be false. In cases like these we see in a mirror darkly; if and when all becomes clear, it may well turn out that we saw very imperfectly.

The hypothesis that evil is the outcome of supernatural spiritual agencies may thus be erroneous. I shall seek to address some further difficulties in the next chapter, but for the moment the chief point to observe is that it is not obviously subject to the objections just canvassed, and that it has something to offer us as an alternative to the non-existent explanations of naturalism. Principally it locates the explanation in a defect of the will rather than a defect of perception or belief, and it can give some account of what has made that will defective. It does not say that Harris and Klebold came to think of bad things as good. On the contrary, it holds that they came to find the very badness of bad things attractive, just as St Augustine did in a much more minor way. In short, they rationally *willed* the wicked. It is a topic to which we will have occasion to return in the next chapter.

But why them? Here again my non-naturalistic alternative has something to say: these boys were *chosen*, just as a seducer chooses his victim, and they were worked upon, not by straight-forward deception, bribery or psychological manipulation, but through their own agency. In their taste for violent pornography they displayed a susceptibility that made them suitable candi-dates for Satanic purposes, individuals who could be successfully seduced by evil. There was a spirit, in short, that saw them as *willing victims*. The moral psychology of naturalism, which dominates 'our modern sensibility' makes the phrase 'willing victim' largely unintelligible since the first part implies activity, and the second passivity. Yet a less theoretically influenced understanding of human psychology regularly recognises such a category (as do some legal systems). In the light of the demonstrated deficiencies of naturalism, should we not adhere to the uses of ordinary language?

'Perhaps', it might be replied, 'but despite the plausibility of all that has been said none of it amounts to an argument that shows, or even makes probable, the existence of a tempter.' Nor does it. All I have shown is that we have reasons to *postulate* one. What reasons? The first is that naturalistic humanism can offer no account adequate to the phenomenon. The postulation of forces of darkness can. The second is that it accords better with the natural apprehension people have that they have encountered something 'beyond the veil'. But a third lies in a further feature of this particular example. One of the pupils who died at Columbine High School was Cassie Bernall, a recently converted evangelical Christian. There is some uncertainty about the facts here, but initially at any rate eyewitnesses reported that as Bernall cowered in the school library she started to pray, only to be confronted by one of the gunmen who pointed a weapon at her head. 'Do you believe in God?' 'Yes', she said, and with the remark 'There is no God', he shot her in the temple. One witness to this specific event is recorded as saying that his voice sounded 'like Satan was trying to talk through him'.

Now there is relatively little hard evidence to support this account of the matter; though none to refute it either. Following her death Cassie Bernall's mother published a book entitled *She said Yes: the Unlikely Martyrdom of Cassie Bernall.* The title is somewhat misleading. The author does not in fact make great play of the purported exchange, and expresses her own uncertainty about its accuracy. More interesting, to my mind, is the fact that Cassie Bernall had herself shown interest in satanism, and underwent a faltering Christian conversion in the context of difficult teenage years. What her mother portrays is a context leading up to the massacre in which it was true that many of the young people concerned were moving in an atmosphere charged with a sense of the satanic and the fight against it. If this is so, it goes some considerable way to confirming my earlier contention that the whole encounter struck those involved – including Klebold and Harris, perhaps – not merely as an instance of extremely and unusually bad behaviour, but participation in a far deeper aspect of experience, for whose narration the language of possession and prayer proved apposite.

In short there is a (relatively) simple explanation of what went on at Columbine. This was yet another instance of something most peoples at most times have believed in – the battle between elemental forces of good and evil – a battle in which the Prince of Darkness was on this occasion assisted by the wealth of technology readily available to those who were, as a result of their engagement with it, more readily seduced into becoming his agents. By this account, the regular watching of violent videos did not *cause* their subsequent action, a contention, let it be repeated, for which there is no satisfactory evidence. Rather, it made them ready targets for someone else's 'crafts and assaults'.

None of this proves or even makes more probable than not the hypothesis that there are spiritual forces operating on a cosmic level, though it is worth observing again that the modern Western world is unique in finding this difficult to swallow. I do not believe in fact that there can be either a logical demonstration of the necessity of supernatural spiritual entities, or (for different reasons) any straightforwardly empirical evidence of their existence. What there is, however, is an interrelated set of considerations showing, contrary to the firm conviction of modernism, that we have reason to take seriously the postulation of a cosmic drama within which our moral lives are set. This is unquestionably an idea regularly invoked by people who find themselves facing the sorts of evil this chapter has been concerned with. Moreover, should it turn out that there are further and other contexts in which such a postulation has explanatory value, this will strengthen its plausibility. The next step in my argument, accordingly, consists in showing that this same story enables us to make progress with another of the topics of this book – the traditional problem of evil examined in chapter three. Before returning to that topic however, the next chapter can usefully begin by saying something more about the drama itself.

CHAPTER 5

The transformation of evil

There was war in heaven: Michael and his angels fought against the dragon; and the dragon fought and his angels, and prevailed not, neither was their place found any more in heaven. And the great dragon was cast out. That old serpent, called the devil and Satan, which deceiveth the whole world; he was cast out into the earth, and his angels were cast out with him. And I heard a loud voice saying in heaven, Now is come salvation, and strength, and the kingdom of our God, and the power of his Christ: for the accuser of our brethren is cast down, which accused them before our God day and night. And they overcame him by the blood of the Lamb, and by the word of their testimony; and they loved not their lives unto death. Therefore rejoice, ye heavens, and ye that dwell in them. Woe for the earth and for the sea: for the devil is come down unto you, having great wrath, because he knoweth that he hath but a short time. (Revelation 12.7, AV)

Does this wonderful passage, quoted here in the translation which (to my mind) lends it its greatest power, record something that has actually happened (in any sense)? *Was* there war in heaven? *Is* Satan cast out, and come down to us with great wrath because he knows his time is short? The reason to believe that this is so is that it provides us with the best available explanation of evil, and since evil is something which cries out to be explained, we ought to believe the best explanation. In the previous chapter I argued that when we examine episodes of great evil carefully, and reflect on people's responses to them, we can discover substantial grounds upon which to give serious consideration to cosmic narratives of this sort. In this chapter and the next, I shall further argue that the narrative structure of Revelation's cosmic story has explanatory advantages with respect to another aspect of evil, and that in its light the Christian understanding of morality is both made more intelligible and shown to be more adequately in keeping with what we might call 'our moral experience' than are secular alternatives. In short, it explains (as they cannot), the twofold sense that the moral dimension of human life is both inescapable and of great importance. Before proceeding to the next stage of the argument, however, it will be useful to provide a résumé of conclusions arrived at up to this point. This will serve as a reminder of the context within which these further arguments gain both strength and relevance.

I

What chapter one showed is that there is no such thing as Christian ethics, at least as this is normally understood. This is to say, there is no set of ethical principles that we can identify as being distinctively and essentially Christian. We should not take this to mean that Christian theology bears no relation to morality. It does. But what it has to say about it relates not to the content but to the significance or *meaning* of morality as a dimension of human thought and practice. The content of morality is to be determined by the processes of reason that every moral agent, Christian or non-Christian, must employ – logical consistency, conceptual clarification, impartial inquiry, adequacy to the facts, and so on. Whether or not this procedure could in principle be short-circuited by divine revelation (as Muslims, for instance, believe the Koran to short-circuit it) is not a matter of any consequence to the Christian understanding of morality because the New Testament contains very few, if any, express revelations. This contention accords, in fact, with a critically historical approach to the Gospels. Despite the widespread scepticism induced by Enlightenment thinking, a scepticism as marked among Christian as among non- and anti-Christian scholars, rigorous, critical and clear-sighted historical investigation *can* produce substantial conclusions about the historical Jesus. These conclusions however, relate primarily not to what he *taught*, but to what he *did*, as well as to what he was perceived by the early Christians to have done. The best account of the historical Jesus, then, is not that of Christ as a religious teacher, one who propounds a system of ethical doctrines. There simply is no such set of 'teachings' to be recovered, try as we might. What there is is a highly plausible historical reconstruction, from Gospel and other evidence, of Christ as a self-conscious actor, one whose words, stories and symbolic actions combine to make an impressive claim to a special place in the divine plan, and which, for that very reason, explain why he was killed.

This conclusion – that Jesus was a doer rather than a sayer of the word – turns out to be of some significance when we turn our attention to evil. Evil, as a recurrent feature of human experience, needs to be explained in at least two respects. First, there is the necessity of providing a philosophical explanation of its intrinsic character, its reality as evil. Second, there is a need to explain its occurrence. These two questions are interconnected. Any satisfactory explanation of why evil things happen must include reference to their intrinsic nature and not merely appeal to their causal antecedents. In previous chapters I have argued that the humanism and the naturalism characteristic of 'our modern sensibility' cannot in fact give a proper account of the nature of evil or its occurrence. A humanistic understanding of value construes the negative character of evil as a function of human attitudes to it. It thus opens up the undesirable possibility of eliminating evil not by changing the world, but simply by amending our attitudes. This implies that if only we did not care about the bad things that happen, they would not exist, in the sense that they would no longer be evil. This, I contend, is a *reductio ad absurdum* of any underlying conception which can have this as one of its implications. In short, evil is disturbing whether or not anyone is disturbed by it. In so far as they are not, far from demonstrating its non-existence, this reveals, rather, the benighted condition into which human beings can fall. As Augustine says of the wars, plagues, earthquakes, famines and bloodshed that are such a marked feature of human experience:

Let every one who thinks with pain on all these great evils, so horrible, so ruthless, acknowledge that this is misery. And if anyone either endures or thinks of them without mental pain, this is a more miserable plight yet, for he thinks himself happy because he has lost human feeling. (Augustine 1998: XIX §7)

But in any case, who, seriously, can hold that the Holocaust would cease to matter if only we could induce in ourselves the state of not being concerned about it?

Second, we need to explain why evil things happen. The resources available to 'our modern sensibility' are those of a naturalised science. Within such a framework the only possible explanation seems to lie with some form of malfunction, social or psychological. However, close examination of dramatic instances of unspeakable wickedness shows that they do not prove amenable to explanations of this sort. On the contrary, the most plausible account of these occurrences interprets them as working through the rational agency of their perpetrators, and not as aberrations which arise from the subversion of that agency. There is, as a result, good reason to question the fundamental categories of naturalistic conceptions of mind, and to make conceptual space for a rather different idea – that human agents can be seduced into subservience to (rather than subverted by) an external power, and/or willingly submit to it. It is in this way that the conceptions of both Satan and the Holy Spirit are made more plausible, and are to be connected to human action and events in the world, conceptions which, as a matter of fact, can be found implicit in the natural response of many people to evil events.

Both ideas are antithetical to the naturalistic and humanistic ways of thinking within which these important issues are commonly explored, of course. But perhaps we should regard this as a measure not of modernity's enlightenment, so much as its confinement. Viewed in this way, there is thus reason to return to some supposedly 'pre-scientific' ideas, ideas which, if we formulate them carefully enough, can be separated from the primitive and atavistic overtones normally associated with them. In other words, the postulation of spiritual powers need not be conceived in terms of voodoo, witchcraft, fairies or hobgoblins.

The stage is thus set for a fresh approach. There is additional interest in such an approach because it makes the ancient radically new. Its novelty lies in its incompatibility with our modern sensibility, and yet it achieves this novelty not by some act of futuristic imagination but by redeploying ideas current as long back as the world of Second-Temple Judaism, the world in which the Jesus of the Gospels operates. The philosophical task, of course, is to make this approach plausible as well as interesting. In order to do so it is necessary to say something more (in this and the next chapter) about the nature of spiritual agency other than that of human beings, or to put it in more traditional language, the workings of spiritual corruption, and of divine grace. It is also necessary to consider further the explanation of episodes of evil. It is with evil I shall begin, but from another point of view – the traditional 'problem of evil' – thereby returning to the topic of an earlier chapter.

II

In chapter three I discussed the problem of evil. My interest there was in the further implications of there being some successful version of an argument that derives the non-existence of a good God from the fact of evil. In the face of evil, however, Christian thinkers have frequently formulated alternative responses, 'theodicies' that aim to 'justify the ways of God to man'. The general form of these theodicies is of as much interest as the detailed arguments they employ. In the main they seek to offer some compensatory advantage such that, while on the surface the evil we see is unconditionally bad, in fact it is outweighed by other goods that it implies. Sometimes this move invites us to assess the balance of good over evil in a larger context, one that includes paradise as well as earthly existence. The idea is that, though as things generally go we are restricted by ordinary experience, this may be a limited part of the picture. There is scope to hold, and some reason for Christians to believe, that the evils the innocent suffer in this world are more than compensated for by the bliss which is their reward in heaven. If so, then we cannot properly take account of evil within the frame of this world alone.

An alternative, but similar strategy is deployed by the argument from 'secondary goods'. This holds that if it were not for primary evils – pain, disease and death – such admirable traits as compassion, courage and heroic self-sacrifice would not exist. It is these things which 'shine like a jewel' (Kant) in 'the darkness of these times' (Wittgenstein). Evil, in other words, is a necessary condition of the existence of the even better. This is true not only (or even) because of another world, but in this one.

Such lines of thought have consistently attracted support. Yet upon closer examination they are not very satisfactory. Consider the first. In the normal everyday legal case, compensation is in order when, and because, a great evil has been done. Such compensation does not outweigh the evil, however. Still less does it cancel it out. On the contrary, it is called for precisely in acknowledgement of the fact that what has been done is an *irremediable* evil. In this respect compensation is to be contrasted with reparation, which *undoes* evil (or is intended to). Suppose, for instance, you damage some piece of my property, during my absence and unknown to me, and then repair the damage before my return, leaving me in my ignorance. In this case, though something bad has happened to my property, you cannot be said to have harmed me. If however, despite the restoration of my property, I am inconvenienced in some way, then compensation is in order, precisely because I have been (mildly) harmed, but in a way that cannot be undone. My *property* can be made as good as new; the *inconvenience* cannot be repaired. As a result, it can only be compensated for.

The same point holds when we apply the idea of compensation to our understanding of God's relation to His creatures. If He has constructed a world in which, for whatever reason, innocent children suffer and die, the compensatory bliss they receive in heaven (assuming they do) does nothing to repair or undo this loss. Rather, if they are given compensatory bliss because they deserve it, this precisely serves to underlines the fact that they were victims and recipients of a great wrong, something which ought not to have happened. The plain implication of this is that heavenly bliss can only *mitigate* earthly torment; it cannot *justify* it. If we are in search of a theodicy, what we want to know is not what God is going to do about these things now that they have happened, but why they were ever permitted in the first place. Accordingly, as a theodicy, the appeal to compensatory bliss fails – and manifestly I should say.

The argument about secondary goods fails too, though not in quite the same way. Let us suppose it to be true that were it not for pain, disease and death there could be no expressions and exercises of compassion, courage and so on. (This is not obvious; I can sympathise with failure that has caused no pain, for example.) Even so, and precisely in so far as this *is* true, there is a further dimension to be considered. These very same things are no less the necessary conditions of secondary *evils*; were it not for pain, disease and death, there would be greater limits to cruelty, callousness and murderousness. If God had not created the possibility of excruciating physical pain, there would be much less scope for the good offices of surgeons and physicians. But equally, the activities of torturers would be severely constrained. On the face of it, the existence of secondary goods seems to be matched, if not overshadowed, by the existence of secondary evils. Though it is not easy to know how such estimations are to be made, at best the two would appear to cancel each other out, and from this it follows that the secondary goods argument simply fails to accomplish what it sets out to. It does not show that the world is better for containing the primary evils it does.

What these considerations demonstrate, I think, is that these two familiar theodicies cannot withstand much critical scrutiny. But they share a deeper fault, and one whose exploration is more to the point in the present context. Both aim at a calculation, the purpose of which is to estimate whether the amount of evil we encounter in experience is greater or less than the good that accompanies it, arises from it or depends upon it. This strategy, whether couched in terms of secondary goods or compensatory bliss, ignores a possibility which ought to be considered – that engagement in calculation, estimation and comparative weighing is a wrongheaded approach to the problem of evil.

To appreciate what is wrong about it, it is useful to look again briefly at the Free Will Defence. It is important to note that it is possible to appeal to free will in the context of the problem of evil in two different ways. The first, which is the appeal Plantinga makes and which was explored in chapter three, seeks only to show that the traditional version of the problem of evil does not present us with a deductively valid argument. If the defence works it does not 'justify the ways of God to man' but shows only that from the simple fact of evil we cannot *deduce* that God is not good (and hence not God). Any purported deduction founders on the fact that, in a world with other free beings, God's responsibility for what happens is, so to speak, cut across by the responsibility of these other agents (both human and non-human). Certainly, He has created them, but having done so His greater power makes Him no more responsible for what they do than a government's greater power makes it responsible for the deaths that follow its refusal to concede to a terrorist's moral blackmail.

This invocation of free will does not morally *exonerate* God, however. Rather it converts the problem of evil into an inductive argument, in the face of which He still has a case to answer. The plausibility of this version rests upon the claim that *at some point* morality requires us to constrain the activities of even free beings, that God (if there were one) could be faulted for allowing these other beings too much freedom, and thus being willing to permit a level of evil incompatible with a good God. In the earlier discussion of the inductive version of the problem of evil I was not concerned to deny this. My aim, rather, was to turn the tables on the sceptic, and ask whether what was impermissible for God was not also impermissible for us. A Free Will *theodicy*, by contrast, would seek to address the sceptic's basic contention and deny that there is too much evil in the world to be incompatible with the existence of a good God.

Now making such a position plausible depends upon the claim that the value of freedom outweighs the woe it brings in its train. To many this seems wholly implausible in the light of history. Is it conceivable that the freedom of Hitler and his henchmen, for instance, could be so much more valuable than the horrors they inflicted on so many million Jews? Or that the importance of Stalin's personal autonomy could outweigh the 'Harvest of Sorrow' he inflicted on the Ukraine in the 1930s (not to mention the sustained agonies of the Gulag)? Actually, however compelling the rhetorical force of these questions, it remains difficult to know how such calculations could plausibly be made, and for this reason it is usually possible for the ingenious theist to find some way of getting God off charges of this sort. But to my mind there is a far more telling objection. A Free Will theodicy (as opposed to a Free Will Defence), no less than the arguments about compensatory bliss and secondary goods, at some level or other involves the comparative weighing of good and evil in the conviction (or at least the hope) that the former will outweigh the latter. It is here that the principal error lies.

What is this error, exactly? Consider a plain case of a necessary evil – major surgery. To say that this is a necessary evil is to say, first, that it involves pain, anxiety and risk, and second that these are unavoidable if a greater good – restoration to health – is to be achieved. Of course, (odd though this might sound) the *necessity* of the pain, anxiety and risk, is a *contingent* matter; were we to find a medical technique that could accomplish the same ends painlessly and with much less risk, major surgery would not be necessary at all, and there could be no justification for inflicting the suffering it involves, and no reason to accept it. (The history of dentistry vividly demonstrates how contingently discovered new techniques can render the pain of old ones unnecessary.) It is only if it is not technically possible to do otherwise, that the term 'necessary' evil applies. Now with God, all things are possible, and for this reason it seems that the same move cannot be made with respect to the evils that beset us in the world He has created. Or at least some of them, for it is here that the special interest of a theodicy built upon free will lies (as opposed to those appealing to compensatory bliss or secondary good). A Free Will theodicy seems to show that some evils are logically necessary, logically necessary, that is to say, to the realisation of freedom, and hence beyond the will even of God.

If this is true, however, any such theodicy still faces a serious difficulty; it succeeds not so much in justifying evil, as eliminating it. Let us return to major surgery. It is not difficult to imagine a small child, who understands only in part what is going on, experiencing the pain and suffering she undergoes in hospital as an unqualified evil. From her point of view, we might say, it is pain and suffering pure and simple. Yet the child's devoted parents have wished this upon her, despite all her pleadings. How can this be? In this case, of course, the reason is plain, and easy for others to appreciate; the parents understand the larger picture, one in which the anticipated benefits make all the child's distress worthwhile, and worthwhile *for the child*, whether she understands this or not. It is true, certainly, that were there any less painful alternative, they would choose it. Not to do so would indeed be the infliction of evil. But as it is, the child's pain and suffering are not, strictly speaking, evil at all. They are more properly thought of as *costs* (albeit strikingly high ones), costs outweighed by anticipated benefits. In this respect, however, they are no different *in kind* to the much more modest demands life can make on us. There is nothing about them that moves us from the spectrum of good *versus* bad to that of good *versus* evil. To think otherwise is like making the mistake of supposing that purchases automatically cease to be good value if only they cost a large enough amount of money. This is evidently false. We cannot make judgements about the value of a purchase irrespective of what it is the purchase of, and consequently mere price tells us nothing. The truth, rather, is that *any* level of cost can be counterbalanced and outweighed by a sufficiently great benefit; billions of dollars could be good value for a greatly improved health service in a large country, while a few pence could be poor value for an ineffectual remedy for a headache. Mere price cannot determine good and bad value.

If this is correct, it follows that none of the three strategies for dealing with the problem of evil that we have considered is adequate to its task. Upon analysis, whatever other merits they may have, all of them fail to make conceptual space for a qualitative shift from the merely bad to the truly evil, and the effect of this is that evil is accounted for by being cancelled out. Such strategies purport to show that, in the end, those things we take for evil are no more than costs worth paying for the benefits that follow. What is actually required is an account of evil that acknowledges its ineliminably evil character, and at the same time shows how it can be overcome. In other words, what we need is something like the Hegelian concept of *aufheben*, namely that which preserves and at the same time *transforms*. The elements of this idea lie in the structure of narrative, and it is the power of narrative form, a topic touched on briefly in an earlier chapter, that illuminates the deficiencies of the alternative we have been considering.

III

In a narrative, the *order* of events matters. In other words, their significance lies not merely in the events themselves but in their place in the narrative. To illustrate this point, let us return one last time to the medical example. Suppose that what we have to deal with is a cancerous growth, and that there are two ways in which it might be treated. The first of these consists in radical surgery. This form of treatment removes the growth straight away, but involves a long and painful recuperative period afterwards. In this case, the cost follows the benefit. An alternative cure, let us imagine, employs chemical treatment which is horrible to undergo, but at the end of which the growth will have withered away. In this case, the cost precedes the benefit. For the purpose of judging their respective merits, however, this difference in order is of no consequence. All that matters is whether the total experience involved is one that results in a higher net benefit than that estimated for the other. What we are comparing are sequences of events, certainly – benefit followed by cost, cost followed by benefit – but sequences with a merely chronological not a narrative order. Both possibilities, we could say, are to be viewed as temporal singularities.

Now this is in fact the way in which the history of the world is conceived by the theodicies we have been considering. Each of them, in its own way, views the world from creation to the *eschaton* (or in the case of the first, a little longer), as a single, enormously long episode, whose total costs and benefits can be estimated and compared. In semi-technical language they are *synchronic* conceptions. If this were the right way to view matters, however, salvation history would not really be history at all, merely a single event which, taken as a whole, proves better rather than worse (on whatever scale of 'better and worse' might be appropriate to the concept of 'salvation').

To put it at its most modest, this conception is plainly at odds with a more familiar, more orthodox, and essentially *diachronic* conception, which sees salvation as a matter of God's mighty works *in history*. This contrast between the synchronic and the diachronic is very important for my purposes, because the fact that the synchronic conception construes the meaning and value of human life as ordained by God in terms of a sort of profit-and-loss account, means that it fails to do the one thing that animates this entire book – take evil seriously. By contrast it is precisely this, or so I shall argue, that a properly diachronic or narrative conception of God's relation with the world can do.

How does it do this? Recall that in a narrative structure it is not merely the intrinsic character of events that matters, but the order in which they occur. A useful illustrative example will be found in that episode of intellectual history which has shaped so much of the course of Christian theology in the last one hundred and fifty years, namely the advent of evolutionary biology.

In human history, as a general rule nothing of consequence appears *ex nihilo*. This does not quite mean, however, that history is a 'seamless web' within which there are no specially notable events, because we can in fact meaningfully speak of, and identify, turning points and decisive moments. This is true of the history of science, and *a fortiori* the history of biology. The growth of science exhibits a steady accumulation and development of knowledge and understanding (what, following Thomas Kuhn, we might call 'normal' science), but this does not conflict with the contention that there have been relatively infrequent great discoveries, and some specially fertile periods ('revolutionary' science, in Kuhn's terms in *The Structure of Scientific Revolutions*). So, for example, evolutionary ideas were gathering pace some time before Darwin, but it is with the publication of *The Origin of Species* that they were brought together, developed and expanded to a degree that allows us to describe Darwin as the father of evolutionary biology, and thus one of the greatest scientists of all time. Not infrequently, historians of ideas regard a claim like this as a challenge, a popular assumption waiting to be disproved by the facts of the past. Is it really true that Darwin should be accorded this towering status? One simple way in which his claim to fame could be undermined would be by the discovery of an earlier exposition of the same ideas. In this particular case, there is of course a contender – Alfred Russel Wallace – who is sometimes said to have anticipated Darwin's discovery by several years. Historians of ideas have rarely concluded that claims on Wallace's behalf to be the originator of evolutionary biology (he himself made no such claim) do overshadow Darwin's, because, it seems, his investigations merely prompted Darwin to publish the *Origin* earlier than he might otherwise have done. But I am not here concerned with this factual basis of this particular episode in the history of science (fascinating though it is), only with its usefulness as an illustration of the character of narrative. *If* it were true that Wallace had formulated the fundamental concepts of modern biology before Darwin, then whatever popular opinion might think, Darwin would not be the father of the theory of evolution. The important point to note, for my purposes, is that this conclusion follows, not from the truth or scientific importance of the ideas expounded in *The Origin of Species*, which are what they are, but merely from the timing of their formulation in an historical sequence.

What this shows is that the significance of *The Origin of Species* for intellectual history derives not solely from the intrinsic merits of the ideas it contains – their truth or comprehensiveness – but crucially from the relation of their formulation there to other events in the history of science. To discover that

Wallace anti-dated Darwin would not alter the cogency of Darwin's theory. But it would transform its significance in intellectual history. It is this notion of transformation that I want to explore.

IV

An action, event or state of affairs is transformed, I shall say, when its nature and consequences remain the same, but its meaning or significance is altered by its place within a narrative context. To take a familiar example. The assassination of the Archduke Ferdinand in Sarajevo on 28 June 1914 is commonly said to have started the First World War. For a long time, however, historians have regarded this as a mere 'trigger' of such dramatic consequence only because of larger political currents. As with the example of Darwin, I am not concerned with the truth about the particular case but only with making a conceptual point about narrative understanding. The meaning or significance of the Archduke's assassination can change as more information is gathered and a larger historical picture constructed. Changes of this sort, it is important to see, are not changes in the event itself, which happened as and when it happened. Of course there are historical questions of this kind too. The precise date of Henry VIII's marriage to Anne Boleyn, for instance, is a matter of some difficulty and dispute.[1] But such questions are essentially 'first order' and it is only once we have established the historicity of the event – that it happened and (usually) when it happened – that the question of its significance can be tackled. Any change in the significance we come to lend it must arise, therefore, not as a result of our shifting its date (which is literally impossible of course), but considering afresh its place in a wider narrative – in the case of the Archduke's assassination, 'the origins of the First World War'.

In making this point I do not mean to backtrack on the remarks about historical method which I made in chapter two.

[1] See MaCulloch (1996), Appendix I.

To say that basic historical data must be woven into a narrative if their meaning and significance is to be determined does not re-introduce a radical distinction between 'fact' and 'interpretation' in history. To repeat what I said there, a good historical explanation is nothing more, and nothing less, than a convincing claim about a more complex and inclusive realm of fact. All that has been added here is the further contention that such explanations will take the form of narratives. Nor is narrative understanding restricted to historical inquiry narrowly conceived. It is central to many areas of thought and reflection, notably the legal and the moral. In fact another point of great importance about it is that narrative can determine *moral* meaning. A very straightforward example is the infliction of suffering. Two acts of inflicting suffering could, from the point of view of the pain and distress caused to the victim, be identical and yet morally quite different. This is true in the case of assault and punishment. A violent attack upon an innocent party and the punishment meted out on the attacker can be equally bad experiences to those who undergo them. Indeed, according to the conception of punishment known as the *lex talionis* they *ought* to be identical in this respect. Consequently, their moral difference cannot lie in the intrinsic character of the experiences, and must rather be found in their respective contexts. Punishment is punishment only if it follows an offence, retaliation is retaliation only if it follows attack, which is why the expression 'getting your retaliation in first' has a dark kind of humour about it. Similarly, capital punishment and murder are identical in that they take the life of a person against his or her own will. This is a shared feature that the confusing idea of 'judicial murder' exploits, and the confusion arises from a failure to grasp that the moral difference between the two is not to be found in their consequence – killing – but in the place of such killing in a narrative. Capital punishment can only be inflicted on someone who has previously committed a capital crime. This does not imply that capital punishment is thus automatically morally justified; it implies only that the task of justifying capital punishment will be quite different to that of justifying murder, and that if both are morally objectionable (as many believe), they are so on different grounds and not because they both 'come to the same thing'. The common feature they share will lead us to think them morally identical only if we remove them from the narrative context which gives each its moral meaning.

v

Once we have grasped the importance of narrative in the determination of meaning and significance, especially in the moral sphere, we can see how widespread its deployment is. As a first step in returning us to the central topic of this chapter, let us consider one more historical example – the Peninsular War of 1808–14. This was a war against the Napoleonic French in which the Duke of Wellington commanded a British army with allied Spanish and Portuguese soldiers. Forced to retreat into Portugal, it became evident that if Wellington was to make any progress in the war it was essential that he break out from the French imposed confinement, re-enter Spain and drive the French army back over the Pyrenees, which eventually, against considerable odds, he did. In fact, though his name remains forever associated chiefly with the defeat of Napoleon himself at Waterloo, it was the Peninsular War which established his reputation as a military campaigner of genius.

Three battles that took place in the course of this war are worth comparing. A marked feature of the Siege of Badajoz (April 1812) was the death of thousands of civilians at the hands of British soldiers uncontrollably engaged in an orgy of slaughter. This atrocity was repeated at the Siege of San Sebastian (August 1813). On this occasion the unspeakable acts committed by ordinary British soldiers and their non-commissioned officers were only a little less terrible than those at Badajoz. It may seem odd, therefore, that the British were feted as heroes by the Spanish after San Sebastian. Yet from the Spanish point of view, whatever the headcount of civilian suffering, the two sieges were importantly different. The difference lies in the fact that between the two sieges the Battle of Vitorio (21 June 1813) took place, a victory for the allies (thanks in part to Napoleon's ill-fated attack on Moscow) which effectively turned the course of the war. In short, however horrible its actions, at the Siege of San Sebastian the army under Wellington was an army of liberation, while at Badajoz it was an army in retreat. That is to say, the significant difference did not lie in the amounts of death and violence. As a matter of fact, allied losses at San Sebastian were heavy, and the indiscriminate slaughter which followed very similar. The important point was that the Siege of San Sebastian took place *after* Vitorio, Badajoz *before* it. In short, it is their respective places in the whole narrative of the Peninsular War that makes the difference.

It is important to underline one significant feature of this whole episode. While generally the Owl of Minerva, as Hegel says, takes its flight at dusk – which is to say that understanding is usually a product of hindsight – sufficient of the narrative was discernible by August 1813 to inform contemporary Spanish attitudes. They witnessed much the same degree of terrible civilian suffering, but they saw it occur in a context of success rather than failure, of advance rather than retreat. The point might be generalised. Let us agree that wholesale death and injury in war is always horrible, whenever it occurs. But it makes a difference whether it occurs before or after the decisive battle of the war. This difference, let it be stressed, is not one between the two events considered intrinsically. As I was at pains to point out with earlier examples, intrinsically the event remains what it was; the appalling degree of violence, suffering and death is not *reduced* by diachronic difference. But it is transformed from the point of view of meaning. Given that its intrinsic horror is not any the less, how *could* the Spaniards view San Sebastian differently? The answer lies in its meaning; San Sebastian *meant* liberation. This is not a compensatory difference, but a narrative one.

Before and after Vitorio is only one aspect of the larger context. It also matters where the origins of the war lie. The British army under Wellington, however appalling its conduct on these occasions, was an army of liberation and not, like the French, an army of imperial conquest. Wherever armies meet, there will inevitably be killing and suffering. To take the moral measure of it, however, we cannot simply count the dead and injured. Death and injury inflicted by an army of liberation in the course of mopping up operations is not on a par, morally or militarily, with death and injury inflicted by an army engaged in aggressive conquest.

These observations are not intended to minimise the horrors of war, still less offer some comfort to militarists. Elsewhere[2] I have set out at greater length the important distinction between militarism and a belief in the possibility of just wars. Here the point is not to assess the morality of warfare but to indicate the importance for moral assessment of a narrative structure such as this example displays. The example has not been chosen at random, however, for the case of war allows us to return to the opening sentence of the quotation with which this chapter began – 'There was war in heaven'. Can the points that have been made about historical narrative and moral meaning be carried over to the theological understanding of evil?

It may be useful to recall how we came to start out upon the discussion of narrative. In section II of this chapter I argued that the traditional theodicies by which Christian philosophers have most often attempted to reconcile the experience of evil with the existence of a good and omnipotent God are essentially *synchronic* conceptions and that in this way they leave no room for a more familiar, more orthodox, and essentially *diachronic* conception, which sees salvation as a matter of God's mighty works *in history*. By contrast, the passage from Revelation precisely offers us a cosmic narrative. It ends with these words: 'Therefore rejoice, ye heavens, and ye that dwell in them. Woe for the earth and for the sea: for the devil is come down unto you, having great wrath, because he knoweth that he hath but a short time.' Now if we were to accept this brief narrative as part of the cosmic history of the world, it would throw a certain light on evil. There has been war in heaven, which is where the fundamental struggle between good and evil takes place, and Satan has been forced to retreat to the earth. So, while the denizens of heaven can rejoice, the occupants of the earth and

<hr>

[2] In Graham (1997a).

the sea should be warned that woeful things have come upon them. Not for the first time, of course, because we may assume that hitherto satanic powers fought on earth as well as heaven. But now that Satan has been defeated in heaven, the earth can expect to suffer even more at his hands. This is not because Satan is staging a comeback. On the contrary, his great wrath, in the face of which the earth and sea will suffer, arises precisely from his enraged recognition of defeat, his sure and certain knowledge that 'he hath but a short time'.

This narrative conception does not, with respect to evil occurrences, deny their reality or place them within a cost–benefit framework which shows their badness to be outweighed by the good which they generate. These, alone, are points in its favour. But more positively it provides us with a new understanding of the present evils of this world, one which alters what I have called their moral meaning. They become explicable as horrible acts in the final raging struggle of an evil intelligence that knows itself to be defeated. To understand them in this way does not eliminate them, ameliorate them, or counterbalance them. It *transforms* them. However terrible they may be, they can now be seen in a different light, just as the civilian slaughter which followed the Siege of San Sebastian was to be viewed differently from that at Badajoz, and most importantly, it casts them in a light compatible with hopeful moral agency. The cosmic narrative thus secures for us just the sort of understanding we need if we are to take evil seriously and still engage meaningfully in moral endeavour. This thought is not new. On the contrary, it signals a return to ideas that predate 'our modern sensibility'. As Peter Brown observes, in late antiquity

the devil was given a vast but strictly mapped-out power. He was an all-embracing agent of evil in the human race; but had been defeated by Christ and could be held in check by Christ's human agents. The Christians were convinced that they were merely mopping up on earth a battle that had already been won for them in heaven. (Brown quoted in Clark 1984: 56)

'Perhaps so', it may be replied, but what reason have *we* to regard this narrative as in the remotest degree plausible? It is only if we have grounds to think it true that such a transformation really takes place. There are, as it seems to me, two lines of thought which need to be considered in the course of exploring this question. First, there is, so to speak, an 'internal' one, the issue of whether there is good reason to regard this cosmic narrative as Christian. Second, even if there is, there remains the (to some minds all-important) question whether whatever its Christian authenticity, there is any positive reason in its favour that should incline us to accept it. On the first point I shall argue, both that the central ideas of battle and victory are recurrent Christian themes and that they accord with our best understanding of the historical Jesus. On the second point I shall consider and attempt to overcome two obvious objections: that it presupposes a metaphysical agency – Satan – whose existence we have no reason to postulate, and that even if the idea of a satanic power were to be conceded, this offers us nothing in way of a better explanation of evil since it rests upon a certain circularity.

These issues are the topics of the next few sections. Their examination will set the stage for a sixth and final chapter where I advance a more positive and hence more compelling consideration in favour of this cosmic narrative – that it provides a rational ground for hopeful moral endeavour.

VI

As the passage with which this chapter began amply demonstrates, The Revelation of St John the Divine is written in very colourful language. Moreover, it represents itself as a vision and not as history, not even a heavily theological history such as we find in St John's Gospel. For all that, it is evident that the driving concern of Revelation is the significance of the historical Jesus, the 'Lamb' to whom it makes reference again and again. Indeed, as Richard Bauckham has demonstrated, Revelation is remarkable for its relatively early endorsement and exposition of a very high Christology. A central theme of this Christology is the victory of the Lamb over powers of darkness, a real victory despite the tribulations of the early Christians for whose chastisement and encouragement Revelation was written. This theme of victory over suffering and death (John is especially concerned with them in the form of persecution and martyrdom) both informs and accords with a central tenet of Christianity over two millennia – that in the death and resurrection of Jesus we witness a decisive victory in the war of good against evil, God *versus* the Adversary. The motif of *Christus Victor* is repeated century after century in the most familiar Easter hymns.

> For Christ, arising from the dead,
> From conquered hell victorious sped
> He thrusts the tyrant down to chains
> And Paradise for man regains.   (Seventh century)

> How Judah's Lion burst his chains
> And crushed the serpent's head;
> And brought with him, from death's domains,
> The long imprisoned dead.   (Eleventh century)

So much is confirming evidence of Brown's contention about late antiquity, but the same theme continues in Christian hymns of subsequent periods.

> The strife is o'er, the battle done;
> Now is the Victor's Triumph won
> O let the song of praise be sung.
> *Alleluia.*   (Seventeenth century)

> Love's redeeming work is done;
> Fought the fight the battle won.   (Eighteenth century)

> Thine be the glory, risen, conquering Son,
> Endless is the victory thou o'er death hast won.
>   (Nineteenth century)

This repeated imagery of battle, victory and liberation from the assaults of the enemy allows us to infer that, even if this theme is somewhat muted nowadays, the Christian religion has over a very long time put forward an explanation of evil pretty much along the lines of the cosmic narrative I have described. Christian belief from earliest times has held that our experience of evil is the outcome of a fundamental struggle between forces of light and forces of darkness, a struggle in which the death of

Jesus of Nazareth proved to be a decisive victory. And the proof lies in his 'glorious resurrection'. There are many Christians in the modern period, of course, who will claim that all this sort of talk must be understood figuratively or metaphorically. (Marcus Borg in *The Meaning of Jesus* is a specially plain example.) It is quite unclear, I think, what such interpretation amounts to in the end, and whether it can truly accommodate the fact that Holy Week and Easter remain the central focus of the Church's year. But a more telling argument in favour of construing the talk of battle and victory in a more substantial way (I avoid the term 'literal' because I am quite unsure how the contrast between literal and metaphorical is supposed to work in this context) is that it secures a much clearer connection with what we can know about the historical Jesus.

It is in this way that the convergence of historical and theological questions which was discussed in chapter two comes to be of special significance. Much that needs to be said has already been said, in fact. In examining our knowledge of the real Jesus I was at pains to stress that the best historical account we can arrive at is one which focusses upon what he *did* rather than what he *taught*, but that what he did is importantly related to his self-understanding and the understanding his disciples and other early Christians had of his mission. According to E. P. Sanders:

The hard evidence is this: he talked about a kingdom; his disciples expected to have a role in it; they considered him their leader; he was crucified for claiming to be king. (Sanders 1994: 322)

At an earlier stage in the book, Sanders has given us an account of how Jesus understood the kingdom about which he talked.

[T]he kingdom expected by Jesus is not quite that expected by Paul – in the air, and not of flesh and blood – but not that of an actual insurrectionist either. It is like the present world – it has a king, leaders, a temple, and twelve tribes – but it is not just a rearrangement of the present world. God must step in and provide a new temple, the restored people of Israel, and presumably a renewed social order, one in which 'sinners' will have a place. (Sanders 1994: 232)

There is a question, I think, whether the contrast with the

Pauline conception is quite as Sanders suggests,[3] but however this may be, as we saw in chapter two, the most important historical question is why his proclamation of a kingdom should have led to his death. On this point N. T. Wright writes as follows:

[D]iscussion . . . over the last generation of scholarship has come up with two main focal points: the *titulus* and the Temple. The 'title' on the cross, indicating the reason for Jesus' execution, is widely agreed to be genuinely historical. Jesus dies with 'the King of the Jews' written above his head. This is not, after all, so surprising; crucifixion was the regular way of dealing with would-be Messiahs. What is at issue is why anyone thought to lay that charge against Jesus, and why, despite so much apparent evidence to the contrary, it stuck. And the main answer to that question has to do with Jesus' action in the Temple, which most now agree was the proximate cause of his death . . . Jesus' action in the Temple constitutes the most obvious act of messianic praxis within the gospel narratives . . . it spoke not just of religion but of royalty. . . not just of cleansing but of judgement. Jesus was claiming some sort of authority over the Temple and its life . . . This was not so much a matter of *teaching* as of *symbolic action*. (Wright 1996a: 490, emphasis original)

Wright draws the first two volumes of his monumental study of the historical Jesus towards a close with this summation.

I propose, as a matter of history, that Jesus of Nazareth was conscious of a vocation; a vocation given him by the one he knew as 'father', to enact in himself what, in Israel's scriptures, God had promised to accomplish all by himself. (Wright 1996a: 653)

And what God had promised to accomplish was 'the real return from exile, the final defeat of evil, and the return of YHWH to Zion' (652). I, for my part, conclude that the cosmic narrative of war in heaven with which we began, as well as being repeatedly affirmed by Christians across the centuries, is wholly consonant with what we can really know of the historical Jesus.

VII

Important though this conclusion is against the background of over a hundred years of scepticism about the historical Jesus, it

---

[3] See Wright (1997).

is likely to be regarded by many readers as of largely scholarly interest. It is the second line of inquiry I promised to explore that is of greater contemporary interest. Whatever Jesus and first century Jews and Christians thought about this cosmic narrative, what should *we* think? Have *we* any reason to subscribe to it?

The reality of evil, traditional Christianity asserts, is best explained by the reality of Satan. But *is* Satan a reality? Does the Devil exist?

Nothing commends Satan to the modern mind. It is bad enough that Satan is spirit, when our worldview has banned spirit from discourse and belief. But worse, he is evil, and our culture resolutely refuses to believe in the real existence of evil, preferring to regard it as a kind of systems breakdown that can be fixed with enough tinkering. Worse yet, Satan is not a very good intellectual idea. Once theology lost its character as reflection on the experience of *knowing* God, and became a second-level exercise in *knowing about*, the experiential ground of theology began to erode away. 'Although mythologically true', Morton Kelsey writes, 'the devil is intellectually indefensible, and once it was realized that the conception of the powers of "evil" was "only" a representation of peoples' experience, no matter how accurate, the devil began to fade . . . With only sense experience and reason to go on, and with no rational place for an evil first cause, enlightened people simply dropped the devil from consideration. With psychic experience no longer admissible as evidence of his reality, the devil was as good as dead.' (Wink 1986: 9, emphasis original. The quote is from Kelsey 1974.)

Wink (and Kelsey) neatly summarise here many of the points about 'our modern sensibility' that I have been making. Actually, despite the remark about the inadmissibility of psychic evidence, there is a not inconsiderable psychological modern literature on the subject, of a strictly empirical kind. By contrast, however, there is very little modern philosophical discussion of this question. There are exceptions. Winks's impressive three volumes on *The Powers*, though not strictly philosophy, have much in them of philosophical interest. And in an interesting and innovative book – *From Athens to Jerusalem* – Stephen Clark makes a substantial case for taking the idea of daemons seriously, though the context in which he does so is that of truth and consciousness rather than morality and action which is my concern here. (The two contexts are clearly related, of course.) Another instance, more directly focussed on Satan is an essay entitled 'The Devil' by R. G. Collingwood, whose views on the nature of history were discussed at an earlier stage.

'From the crafts and assaults of the Devil, good Lord deliver us.' So we pray; and the prayer certainly answers our need . . . But most people who have responded to the prayer must have asked themselves how much more than this they meant; whether they believed in a devil at all, and if so what they imagined him to be like. (Collingwood 1967: 171)

Collingwood thinks that

There is no doubt that common belief has been tending more and more to discard the idea of a Devil [but that] a world rudely awakened once more to the conviction that evil is real may come again to believe in a Devil. But if it returns to the same belief it has gradually been relinquishing, the step will be retrograde. (Collingwood 1967: 172)

In other words, what is required is a revised conception of Satan. To repeat a contention of Winks's, we need to distinguish between the mythic and the mystificatory. This revision need not make it less orthodox. On the contrary, in Collingwood's view, critical revision may well lead us to an idea more in accord with orthodoxy in so far as it enables us to avoid the popular misconceptions induced by the heresy of Manichaeism (the contention that God and Satan are two opposed, but equally independent, beings). '[T]he vital question', Collingwood claims, 'is not, Does the Devil exist? but rather, What conception have we of the Devil?' (Collingwood 1967: 171). His subsequent argument dismisses a good deal of the 'evidence' that is to be found in contemporary psychological literature, as well as the sorts of consideration I have myself adduced. It comes close, if I understand him correctly, to replacing the first question with the second. Yet, though it seems to me true that there is no point in asking about the Devil's existence unless we are clear about the kind of thing whose existence is in question, in the end we cannot quite rest content with conceptual clarification but must engage in a measure of metaphysics also.

Collingwood is right, nonetheless, to give the conceptual

question priority, and I shall follow him in this. However, to make these questions in any way plausible, some concession must be made towards 'our modern sensibility', some attempt at domesticating of the concept of spiritual powers. One way to do this is to begin with an expression that uses this sort of language and yet is not, or does not appear to be, metaphysically suspect. One such expression is 'the spirit of enterprise'.

'The spirit of enterprise' is not merely a fancy way of talking; it really does seem to figure in an explanatory structure of some consequence. In particular, it has an important role to play in accounting for the economic history of the United States of America. So great has been the triumph of human ingenuity in the US, that it is difficult to remember just how much it has overcome. To those settlers who first arrived there, Phoenix, Arizona, or St Paul, Minnesota were places just about as inhospitable, and unpromising, as it is possible to imagine. Both locations share the savage climatic conditions common to the other great land masses of Asia and Africa. It is easy, when one experiences these conditions, to understand why, over innumerable centuries, the indigenous people of Central Asia and Central Africa failed to make much economic headway. The climatic and geographical difficulties seem so daunting that mere survival is a remarkable achievement. How could we reasonably expect the progressive growth and development typical of more temperate climes? And indeed it is something we have not seen. Yet the very same conditions in North America, combined with immigrant rather than indigenous people, produced, eventually, the wealthiest places on earth.

What explains the difference? The answer is complex, no doubt, but it is a familiar suggestion that in the US there arose a spirit of enterprise which did not materialise in the other two continents. The historical accuracy and explanatory adequacy of such a claim may be disputed. That is not our primary concern here, however. While it is necessary to make out something of a case for this as the *actual* explanation, the chief interest lies in showing it to be a *possible* explanatory factor, one which we have reason to take seriously.

On the most substantial interpretation, talk of the 'spirit of enterprise' in this context provides a reasonably clear and certainly familiar appeal to a spiritual agency as part of the explanation of human affairs. Why call it a spiritual *agency*? The answer lies in the fact that the spirit of enterprise typical of the 'boosters' and 'go-getters' described by Daniel Boorstin in the third volume of his study of *The Americans*, was something which *appealed* to individuals, by which they were *drawn*, and in which they got *caught up*. These are active ways of speaking. On the face of it they imply an agency external to that of the people on which it acts.

Now one obvious response which the proponent of modernism is likely to make is that I have laid absurdly undue stress on a few verbs. The phrase 'spirit of enterprise', such a critic will allege, is a mere figure of speech and is not to be taken literally in the way that I suggest. To treat it literally is a case of a *façon de parler* being not merely allowed, but positively encouraged to mislead us.

I have no doubt that the obviousness of this objection will strike many readers. Yet the appeal to the figurative is not as unproblematic as it may appear. To begin with, if 'spirit of enterprise' is a mere figure of speech, how is it to be cashed out? What is the non-figurative version? It seems that those who interpret it figuratively are committed to finding some reductionist account of the phenomenon, some real *explanans* which the figurative language merely summarises. What could this underlying reality be?

A first suggestion might be that the 'spirit of enterprise' is nothing more than shorthand for the existence of large numbers of enterprising people. There is this to be said for such a suggestion; what we are trying to explain are the different economic histories of North America and (say) Central Africa, and it has already been admitted that part of the difference lies in a contrast between immigrant and indigenous peoples. Might this not be where the whole of the explanation lies? After all, it has been observed many times that emigrants are self-selected; they are people who have the initiative to choose to emigrate, and for this reason we may expect that they will not simply replicate their behaviour in the circumstances which they have elected to leave. Consequently, the great waves of emigration to the US undoubtedly had a higher element of the enterprising among them than among any randomly selected cross section of population. The immigrants, in short, were (plausibly) more industrious and innovative than the compatriots they left behind. If so, this is all we need to explain the different outcomes; we can attribute the effects to different kinds of people, and need not call on any occult agencies. The phrase 'the spirit of enterprise' is just a short hand expression for this widely shared characteristic.

Possibly. But what this leaves out are the very great differences *between* immigrant groups, differences which make it difficult to generalise about their mentality. Some were indeed seeking new opportunities – the Scots, by and large, for instance. Others were merely escaping destitution, the post-famine Irish being one of the most notable examples. Still others were seeking to escape persecution. What forged in them some measure of single mindset was not so much the mentality they brought, as the mentality they *joined* – the pursuit of the American Dream as it is commonly known. In other words, an important part of the success of these immigrant groups lay in what they came to, and not merely, nor even as much, in the individual motivations they brought with them.

Even if this is accepted, an alternative reductivist interpretation of the spirit of enterprise is available. In explaining a macro-effect we must appeal not merely to individuals, but to individuals in concert. When we say that they were embued by the same spirit we mean that they subscribed to a common ideal and accordingly acted in a collaborative collective endeavour – making a New World *together*. Not surprisingly, the net effect of this was more than the sum of its individual parts. Once more, however, this seemingly obvious account of what we mean by the spirit of enterprise encounters equally obvious objections. Contrary to the picture it paints, in the economic sphere the US was built upon individualism. Those who moved West were frequently isolated individuals, reliant entirely upon their own efforts with little or nothing in the way of communal institutions and support. What *animated* them? Even the institutions we are inclined to think of as comprising the fabric of communal life and showing evidence of common purpose – schools, colleges, churches, museums, and so on – in most cases arose from the particular enthusiasms (and often commercial success) of individuals. In short, the emergence of community across the US is to be explained in terms of the advances made by individuals; it is not the collective power of existing communities that explains those advances. Their animating spirit gave rise to the fabric of community rather than the other way about.

A third plausible suggestion is culture. The spirit of enterprise, it might be said, is nothing more mysterious or arcane than a cultural milieu in which some individual drives are preferred and promoted over others. Now it is worth observing that this is not how the expression 'a culture of enterprise' functions in economics and related studies. There, what is referred to as a culture of enterprise consists in the deliberate construction of economic conditions and incentives (often by government agencies) whose purpose is to give a marked advantage to small businesses started by individuals. Sometimes they work and sometimes they don't, but they presuppose and do not constitute, though they may to a degree engender, an enterprising spirit. In any case, a culture in this sense did not exist in nineteenth-century America and cannot therefore be a plausible explanatory factor. Of course, those who speak in this way usually have in mind something other than an institutional framework. The difficulty is to lend this more amorphous sense of 'culture' a character more determinate than *je ne sais quoi*.

It is important to see that this is not a dispute about terminology. I am happy to replace the expression 'spirit of enterprise' with 'enterprising culture', though I think that the second is the less clear of the two. The point is that, whichever expression we use, once we have eliminated explanations in terms of numbers of enterprising people, deliberate collective endeavour and the creation of a culture of enterprise in the narrow sense, we seem to be left with the necessity of positing something else, another agency – the spirit/culture of enterprise – as an irreducible *explanans*.

Culture in this wide sense is an *explanans* because it *forms* those who belong to it and cannot be construed as a summation or accumulation of their interests, beliefs and motives. In short, it is what Hegel calls 'Geist', and what in accordance with his conception I am calling 'spirit'. The facts, I am inclined to say, give us most reason to rest content with this as the basic explanation.

There remains, of course, the question of its metaphysical status. A humanistically minded critic might think that there is nothing much here with which to disagree. Even if we can neither locate nor characterise this sort of 'spirit' precisely, we still have no reason to invoke any element of the supernatural, other than the fact alluded to in the last chapter, that some experiences have a tendency to induce a sense that our ordinary lives are 'really' set within some larger cosmic context. This sense, as it seems to me, is an important datum which itself requires explanation, and should not be dismissed as a residual superstition, an aberation in the modern mind (as humanistic naturalism tends to, and in the end must, dismiss it). But be this as it may, the principal point of this excursion into the idea of a spirit of enterprise is to give some philosophical substance to the concept of a spiritual agency without the overtones of mumbo-jumbo. And it *has* been given sufficient substance if the following is agreed: that the spirit of enterprise has a real explanatory role, that it cannot be reduced to human agents, individually or collectively, and that it makes sense to describe its operation in the same sort of language that we describe human agency.

The critical reader, I imagine, will want more than this, a detailed exploration of the metaphysics of such agencies. But just how much more is required? In his attempt to interpret the 'powers and principalities' language of the New Testament for the 'modern' mind while remaining faithful to the original, Walter Wink makes an illuminating suggestion:

What might we learn if we listened to the ancient myth on its own terms and tried to decipher, by an act of interpretative divination, what is moving within it? The ancients regarded the spiritual Powers as non-material, heavenly entities with specific characteristics or qualities . . . What I propose is viewing the spiritual Powers not as separate heavenly or ethereal entities but as *the inner aspect of material or tangible manifestations of power* . . . that the 'principalities and powers' are the inner or spiritual essence of an institution or state or system; that the 'demons' are the psychic or spiritual power emanated by organisations or individuals or subaspects of individuals whose energies are bent on overpowering others . . .

Let me illustrate. A 'mob spirit' does not hover in the sky waiting to leap down on unruly crowds at a soccer match. It is the actual spirit constellated when the crowd reaches a certain critical flashpoint of excitement and frustration. It comes into existence at that moment, causes people to act in ways of which they would never have dreamed themselves capable, and then ceases to exist the moment the crowd disperses . . . As the inner aspect of material reality, the spiritual powers are everywhere around us. Their presence is real and inescapable. The issue is not whether we 'believe' in them but whether we can learn to identify our actual everyday encounters with them – what St Paul called 'discerning the spirits'. (Wink 1984: 104–6, emphasis original)

I should admit immediately that I have omitted from this quotation elements that seem to me questionable in the sense that they detract from the substance of the conception of spiritual powers that Wink wishes to advance. I regard these omissions as defensible because my purpose is not simply to deploy or to defend what he has to say. As it seems to me, there is here the kernel of an idea which will serve well in the present context, suitably amended.

We need to give some account of the reality of spiritual powers that does not construe them as eternal entities who 'hover in the sky waiting to leap'. In other words their principal characteristic cannot be that they are not explicable in terms that make sense. The first question, then, is that of their reality. Returning for a moment to the spirit of enterprise and its role in the history of the United States, we can deploy something of Winks's account by noting that this spirit is indeed plausibly thought of as the inner aspect of a tangible manifestation. The spirit of enterprise is invisible; it cannot be seen heard or counted. Yet it has a role to play in the explanation of what happened. So too with Satan at Columbine. He too was invisible and depended for his activity on the presence of visible, tangible agents – Klebold and Harris. Understanding their intelligence, their wilfulness, and the social and psychological background that they possessed, however, does not account for all that they did. Rather, it seems plain that 'they were caused to act in ways of which [others] would never have dreamed themselves capable' and that it was 'the inner aspect of material or tangible manifestations of power' which enabled them to do so. In short, as a traditional hymn says, 'There's a spirit in the air.' It is a phrase which modernity has no difficulty in employing. To attribute a reality greater than that which modernity attaches to it, it is sufficient to give it an *irreducible* explanatory role, of the sort that the spirit of enterprise has, and to be able to attribute to it specific characteristics in specific circumstances. What more, metaphysically, is required? To demand more, as it seems to me, is to make it a condition that the spiritual be construed as material, an impossible undertaking of course.

VIII

The preceding section was intended to make some headway with the conceptual question that Collingwood sets for us, and with the metaphysical implications of that conception. What sort of conception of the devil should we employ? The answer is, if we take the spirit of enterprise as our model, that we should think in terms of an agency independent of human beings whose activity is to be described in the same sort of language, in terms, that is to say, of intentions, aims and purposes. When we apply this idea to the explanation of evil we have reason to postulate a spirit to which traditional language gives the name of Satan. We have reason to deploy such a postulation *if* it can be made to do explanatory work that alternative conceptions cannot do.

   Is there, then, a spirit of evil at work in the world? Here, as it seems to me, it is sufficient to recall the arguments of chapter four. I argued there that when we consider carefully the phenomena of the multiple murderer, or the evils of Stalinism, Nazism and the Hutu onslaught in Rwanda, explanations in terms of individual psychologies or sociological conditions can be seen to fail dramatically. By contrast, the substantial interpretation of ideas such as the seductive power of evil that are customarily thought to be mere figures of speech, does offer us a good deal (though not everything) in the way of understanding these distressing phenomena. It is further worth observing, as I noted previously, that this sort of explanation is not altogether absent from the modern world. Though daemonology is highly unfashionable, people still turn to prayer and the invocation of divine assistance, a response endorsed by Clark: 'In such trouble we can only pray to be assisted, hope that we are following the right way, confirm or correct our vision by careful hearing of our fellows visions' (Clark 1984: 85). One such (ancient) visionary is Mother Julian of Norwich. In *Revelations of Divine Love* she writes:

Then, before he spoke to me, God allowed me to look at himself for a considerable time, and, as far as my simple mind could take it, to dwell on all that I had seen, and its significance. And, without voice or speech, he framed in my soul these words: 'By this is the Fiend overcome.' These words were said by our Lord, and referred to his passion which he had shown me earlier.

By this our Lord revealed that it is his passion that overcomes the Fiend, and that the Fiend is as evilly disposed now as he was before the incarnation. However hard he works, just as often he sees all souls escape him, saved by the worth and virtue of Christ's precious passion. This is a grief and a shame to him, for whatever God allows him to do turns to our joy and to his shame and woe. It is just as much a cause of grief when God gives him leave to do his work as when he is not working, because he can never do all the evil that he wants. His power is in God's control. (Julian 1966: 83)

Actually, archaic though this might sound, as I observed earlier the language of possession continues to be used – 'something came over me', 'something got into him', and so on. It is true that these are normally taken to be mere markers for something else, we know not what, even by those who speak like this. Yet if it is the very same naturalism that inclines us to think in this way, the arguments of this chapter give us reason to conclude that there are more substantial grounds to accept them as they stand than to postulate a purportedly 'scientific' explanation of which we have not even the most basic elements.

But what of this anti-modernistic, or more accurately pre-modern alternative? If, as I have argued, the reality of Satan turns on the ability of the concept to explain where other conceptions fail, we must address this question: Does the appeal to an evil spirit really explain anything? At this point we arrive at the second objection I undertook to consider – that the explanation of evil in terms of a satanic power is circular. It is an accusation made expressly by Colin McGinn in *Ethics, Evil and Fiction*. In considering the explanation of evil character he writes:

One answer, historically prominent, is that there is a dark satanic force that underwrites [the psychology of evil]. The devil intrudes upon our psychology to make us prefer the pain of others to their pleasure. In extreme cases Satan actually takes possession of us, substituting his psychology for ours. This is a religious answer. I shall not discuss this answer in any depth, mainly because I do not accept the background religious assumptions. Let me just note that the answer does not really explain what needs to be explained anyway. It does not tell us what the evil person finds appealing about the pain of others; it simply offers to tell us what causes him to have the evil impulses to begin with. Moreover, the invocation of the devil simply raises the same question about his psychology: why does he find the pain of others worth pursuing? The devil's psychology raises our puzzle in its most intense form without resolving it. What *does* make Satan tick? It is no answer to say that he is Satan. So this kind of explanation cannot satisfy us. (McGinn 1997: 72)

This passage neatly formulates two fundamental objections to the satanic hypothesis. First, to appeal to such a force at best identifies the external cause of evil character, and does nothing, therefore to illuminate its nature. Second, it explains the evil psychology of the wrongdoer in terms of the evil psychology of the cause (Satan) and is thus no explanation at all. Now with respect to the first of these objections, it may be replied that McGinn is operating with a duality which I gave reason to reject at an earlier stage. There, I cited the example of seduc-tion as a way of operating upon others that is not merely causal, but works upon and through the will of the seduced. Seduction as opposed to rape, works on people who may literally be described as 'willing victims'. McGinn, in the chapter from which this passage is taken, does discuss the nature of (sexual) seduction, but he construes it as a form of pure manipulation. 'In seduction, especially of the innocent or reluctant, the object is made to abandon his normal values and desires by being swept up in bodily ecstasy' (McGinn 1997: 77). This is incorrect in my view, though it is true that my concern is with seduction more broadly conceived than the purely sexual. On my account, the seducer does not cause me to abandon my values, but rather brings me to apply my values differently. The importance of this difference lies in its bearing on the force of the first objection McGinn has to the satanic hypothesis. If it is true, as I suggested, that Satan seduces (some of) his victims, and the nature of seduction is as I construe it, then explaining the actions of (some) evil doers by reference to Satan is not a matter of merely pointing to an external cause. It illuminates precisely in the same way that the story of a seduction well told reveals the relevant state of mind of the seduced as well as the seducer.

In the preceding few sentences I included the qualification 'some'. This is because I see no reason to suppose that Satan is to be invoked as the explanation of every act of every evil doer. There may indeed be evil characters who are wholly responsible for their own actions. (I shall return shortly to McGinn's definition of the evil character). What we want to explain, very often, is the evil *actions* of those who are not obviously evil *characters*. What is far more puzzling than the sustained attitude of (for instance) sadistic people, is the behaviour of the seemingly normal and ordinary. This, indeed, was the puzzle with many of the mass murderers described in the last chapter. Jeffrey Dahmer was not without moral sensibility; Dennis Nilsen was a representative of his union, acting effectively in the better, even best, interests of his colleagues. He did not take pleasure in their pain and frustration, but to the contrary, sought conscientiously to diminish the difficulties they encountered in their working lives. The same point can be made about other evils on a larger social scale. What is puzzling is how people who continued to care for their families and friends could play their part in the concentration camps, how there was enormously widespread participation in the slaughter of Tutsis by large numbers of ordinary Hutus who, afterwards, far from boasting, recognised only too well the evil of what they had done, and shrank from admitting it. McGinn sets out on his explanation of evil by describing two psychological types – G-beings and E-beings as he calls them. The problem exhibited by the horrors we seek to explain lies precisely in the fact that the perpetrators cannot be confined to this second class. Nilsen and Dahmer did evil things; they were not obviously evil beings on McGinn's definition.

If there are E-beings, then Satan has no need to seduce them; they are already on his side. But has McGinn in any case offered us a satisfactory definition of their character? At the start of the chapter he asserts his 'basic idea . . . that an evil character is one that derives pleasure from pain and pain from pleasure [in other people]' (McGinn 1997: 62). In illustration he cites the standard literary example – John Claggart, the master-at-arms in Herman Melville's *Billy Budd*. Now as it seems to me, this example does not in fact bear out his definition. It is not so much that Claggart takes pleasure in the pain of others; if this were the case, there is no special reason for him to have made Billy his victim. Rather, Claggart hates the natural innocence and virtue that are so evident in Budd. The root explanatory notion is not Claggart's evil character, but Budd's virtuous one. Evil, it is of the greatest importance to see, has no character of its own. Hatred of good is *essentially* negative, a point that Collingwood (in accordance with St Augustine) is at pains to emphasise, as is Clark: '[I]t is the central thesis of theistic and semi-theistic doctrines that the principles and powers of the world are not merely "out there" but "here within"' (Clark 1984: 194).

This way of construing matters – the deeply negative nature of evil – has a decided advantage over McGinn's, whose account of these matters in effect comes close to the 'evil be thou my good' conception discussed in chapter four. It is an implication of his requiring any explanation of evil to tell us what the evil person finds positive about the pain of others. As a result the basic motivation of the evil character is just what it is in the good character, namely the pursuit of pleasure. The difference can only lie therefore in its object. The G-being takes pleasure in other people's pleasure; the E-being takes pleasure in their pain (and pain in their pleasure). But why is this not simply a different, perhaps statistically abnormal psychology, like the psychology of those who are fascinated by mud, say? What makes it an *evil* one? McGinn *asserts* that it is evil, of course, and further asserts that, though pleasure is good thing, we cannot attribute any value to the pleasures of the sadist. But why not? If pleasure is a good, it is a good irrespective of its object. Any assertion to the contrary, such as McGinn's, seems to me an arbitrary stipulation. A more consistent (if unpalatable) view would hold that the pleasure the sadist takes to some degree *offsets* the pain to his victims. There is at least this much to be said in favour of the rapist; he enjoys his activities. I take it that such an implication is not merely unpalatable but intolerable, and it is precisely for this reason that McGinn stipulates to the contrary. But the stipulation is required, I think, precisely because in the end McGinn, being a good naturalist, has no real explanation to offer. In fact though

statistically evil is probably rarer . . . [n]either hedonic law [the pleasure of the E-person or the G-person] is more intrinsically intelligible than the other, not when you get right down to it; both are basic and brute from the point of view of folk psychology. So there is nothing more mysterious about acting on the evil disposition than acting on the virtuous one. (Of course, the latter is more *justifiable*, but that is another question.) (McGinn 1997: 83)

Thus, we can say no more about the evil disposition than that it is basic to human psychology, and we must conclude that the question of its wrongness is not connected with moral psychology at all, but 'another' question. By contrast, I think, my characterisation brings the psychological and the moral questions together. On my alternative account the evil person hates the good. This both explains why evil characters do what they do, and what is wrong with it; the explanation lies in the fact that they are motivated by hatred and its wrongness lies in the fact that the good is the object of their hatred.

According to the cosmic narrative I am defending, the supreme hater of the good is Satan. With respect to those (rare) human beings who share his hatred, we can say that they are already on his side; he has no need to recruit them. With respect to the far more numerous and much more troubling cases of those human beings (to be described as weak and foolish, perhaps) who become the instruments of evil, we can now deploy traditional language to explanatory purpose and say that they are seduced by the 'crafts and assaults of the devil'.

No part of this story is subject to the criticisms McGinn brings against it. Satan's evil character – hatred of the good – is not being called upon to explain other evil characters, who quite independently hate the good, but to explain the evil actions of those who are not directly motivated by hatred of the good, and Satan's crafts consist precisely in being able to work upon their wills. He is not, therefore, merely an external cause (a topic upon which there is more to be said shortly).

To summarise: the traditional Christian cosmic story of war in heaven which has led to war on earth provides us with a narrative framework which better explains both the existence and the nature of evil than the humanistic and naturalistic alternatives which underlie 'our modern sensibility'. A further defect of that sensibility, I have argued, is that it cannot ground hopeful moral endeavour. It sets the idea of absolute moral requirements at odds with practical reason, and makes moral endeavour at best a fruitless, if heroic, gesture, one that would be better served by seeking the destruction of the world.

IX

Is there not, though, another circularity in this explanation, one which McGinn has failed to identify? Let us return to the problem of evil. Surely, if God is all powerful, He has it in His power to prevent the existence of Satan (and evil human beings like him) from the outset. Evil people, and evil spirits, Satan chief amongst them perhaps, exist only because He permits them to. If God is Creator and Satan really does exist, then God is responsible for Satan's creation also. By tradition, of course, Satan is not created as an evil spirit; on the contrary, he is a fallen angel. But even this does not appear to let God off the hook. If He is omniscient then He could foretell Satan's future conduct, and must accordingly have permitted it. Precisely the same point applies to lesser evil beings. In either case, then, is not God ultimately responsible for the evils that beset the world, even if (as my explanation both in this and the previous chapter suggests) they are evils of Satan's doing? It seems to follow that any explanation of the evils of this world in terms of evil agencies, whether human or superhuman, leads back to God and thus raises the traditional problem of evil once more, albeit at another level. There may have been war in heaven, as a result of which Satan is driven to wreak his destructive anger on earth in the form of plagues, famines, earthquakes, wars and so on. But it is still God who has created this whole scenario. How then can He be the *summum bonum* upon which the meaningfulness of moral endeavour is supposed to rely?

At this point we need to consider again, and a little more closely, a presupposition which I earlier disputed – that what God has created He is responsible for. If, as the Free Will Defence claims, God cannot be held to be responsible for the evil actions of human beings who do wrong, there is no reason to think that the same logical point does not apply to the actions of other agencies. If we allow that God is justified in not destroying us the moment we put a foot wrong, then so too may He treat his other creatures, Satan included. Of course, as we saw, there is a further question about how far God can justifiably allow other agencies, whether human or not, to go. This is the inductive problem of evil to which (I argued) a Free Will theodicy cannot provide a wholly satisfactory answer, because the finger of blame *can* rightly be pointed at God, and not just at these other beings, if He allows them to go too far. The crucial question is, of course, how far is too far?

Now with respect to Satan we are, in a sense, on more solid ground than we are in other cases because, if the cosmic narrative we find in *Revelation* is to be believed, far from being allowed to go on and on, Satan has been defeated, and his time, by cosmic if not by our standards, is short. So, if it is true that God's justice depends upon His not allowing Satan a free hand then, in principal at least, His justice is secure; Satan is not merely constrained; he is beaten.

However, the criticism we are here considering refuses to accept that the Free Will defence, which supplies the first crucial move in this strategy, can be taken to have the final word. If we are to avoid the heresy of Manichaeism we must assert that God alone is the creator and that Satan is not an independent power of evil but owes his existence to God. As such Satan may be the Prince of Darkness, and thus responsible for (most of) the evil things that happen, but God, being creation's King, is responsible for there being evil at all.

This is a very long-standing problem in philosophical theology, as is evidenced by the fact that it receives extensive treatment in the writing of the first major Christian philosopher, Augustine of Hippo. However it is Augustine, in my view, who formulates a solution that is broadly correct. He says this:

> It is not permissible for us to doubt that the contrasting appetites of the good and the bad angels have arisen not from a difference in their nature and origin – for God, the good Author and Creator of all substances, created them both – but from a difference in their wills and desires. For some remained constant in cleaving to that which was the common good of them all: that is, to God Himself, and His eternity, truth and love. Others, however, delighting in their own power, and supposing that they could be their own good, fell from that higher and blessed good which was common to them all and embraced a private good of their own. (Augustine 1998: XII §1, 498)

How does any of this help us with our difficulty? The answer lies in the subtle distinction Augustine here draws between nature and will. The nature of the fallen angels (Satan in short) is God's doing, but evil flows not from their nature – what they were made to be – but from their will, whose origin lies with them alone.

> God's enemies are so called in the Scripture not by nature, but because they oppose His authority with their vice. They have no power to injure Him, but only themselves; for they are His enemies

not because of their power to harm Him, but because of their will to resist Him. (Augustine 1998: xii 3 501)

It is a mistake, he thinks, to suppose that their nature, for which God is responsible, is the cause of their evil will, because that will has *no* cause.

[A]n evil will is the efficient cause of evil action, but nothing is the efficient cause of an evil will. For if anything is the cause, this thing itself either has a will or it has not. If it has, the will is either good or evil. If it is good, who is so foolish as to say that a good will makes a will evil? For in this case, a good will would be the cause of sin, and we cannot believe anything more absurd than this. On the other hand, if this thing which is supposed to make the will evil has itself an evil will. I now inquire what made it so. (Augustine 1998: xii §6 505)

In short, to take this line leads either to absurdity or to infinite regress. Some other analysis is required, and Augustine supplies it.

Let no one, then, seek an efficient cause of an evil will. For its cause is not efficient, but deficient, because the evil will is not itself an effect of something, but a defect. For to defect from that which supremely is, to that which has a less perfect degree of being; this is what it is to begin to have an evil will . . . to seek the causes of these defections . . . is like wishing to see darkness or hear silence. (Augustine 1998: xii §7 507–8)

God is the (ultimate) cause of everything, but it does not follow that he is the explanation of everything. This would follow only if we were to suppose that all explanation is causal, and this is something which it has been my aim to deny at various points in the argument so far. When we turn our attention to the will of free agents, whether human or angelic (i.e. superhuman), explanations must be couched in terms of rationality/irrationality, and not in terms of causality. Augustine's account of evil as deficiency (or in more traditional language 'privation') may imply, as it has often been taken to imply, an absence of explanation, because of the general metaphysical principal that from nothing nothing comes. But *if* there is reason to interpret Augustine in this way, there is consequently reason to modify his account a little. Furthermore, the Augustinian account of evil is often taken to mean that evil is not anything, but the lack of something. Now once again, this *may* be the correct interpretation of Augustine (it is not a question upon which I propose to dwell), but if it is, it is not one that we are ineluctably obliged to follow. We can accept the idea that the evil will has no efficient cause, and at the same time consistently hold that evil will is the efficient cause of evil deeds. (I myself have found nothing in Augustine that denies this.) It follows that evil actions and occurrences have a causal explanation – the will of those who caused them – but that we are not thus committed to an infinite regress, because these wills have themselves no causal explanation. The explanation, rather, lies within them; these are wills that hate the good.

But *why?* What *is* the explanation? Here we need the sort of explanation that Augustine supplies – 'delighting in their own power, and supposing that they could be their own good, [they] fell from that higher and blessed good which was common to them all'. Clark, too, emphasises the negative character of evil motivations. 'The art of thought, very often, is to know what *not* to think, what path *not* to follow, what theories to forbid ourselves to use. Demon-possession is what follows when we have abandoned the right way' (Clark 1984: 192, emphasis added). This, as it seems to me, is a *rational* explanation, which is to say one which renders the outcome *intelligible*, but does not supply necessary and sufficient conditions as a causal explanation is often thought to do (though perhaps incorrectly). The difference can be illustrated by considering once more the example of love, love of another human being. Someone who is in love may explain the state of their affections by referring to features of the beloved. In so doing, assuming they refer to certain features, they make that love intelligible; but they do not make it rationally obligatory. I can find the love you have for someone intelligible (as opposed to unintelligible) without thereby being rationally obliged to love them myself. In short, there are explanations that are not causal in the sense that apprehending the antecedent does not of necessity produce (in me) the consequent. So too with Augustine's explanation of the evil will. People can come to 'delight in their own power, and suppose that they could be their own good' and thus 'fall from that higher and blessed good which is common to all and embrace a private good of their own'. Precisely this (or something very like it) is to be seen at work in the episode at Columbine, I am inclined to say. We can understand it, without imputing necessary and sufficient causal conditions, which is why the talk of conditioning by violent pornography on the internet is both inept and inadequate.

I conclude that the cosmic narrative of Revelation does indeed have explanatory power, and in the absence of better, this gives us good reason to subscribe to it. It remains to show, of course, that the same story has other advantages, namely the ability to make morality meaningful. In attempting this important additional task, it is necessary to explore further the deficiencies of humanism and to say something about the relation of human action to divine grace. These are the topics of the next, and final, chapter. But before that there is this question to be addressed – 'In the absence of better?' Why should we suppose that the Christian narrative is the only alternative to 'our modern sensibility'? Before proceeding to the topics of the next chapter it would seem necessary to say something in defence of an apparently indefensible exclusivity.

x

One alternative to modernity is a return to pre-modernism. This is the course I have advocated. But an alternative, currently far more fashionable, is postmodernism, the view that the exclusive character of the naturalistic scientism of modernity is to be replaced by the acceptance of a plurality of possible alternative narratives. Why not accept, welcome even, this open-ended option? The answer lies to a considerable degree with topics discussed in chapter one. Postmodernism rests, in part, on the supposition that the contemporary world is a pluralistic one, both comprising and rejoicing in a wide variety of 'perspectives'. I have already expressed my doubts about this. There is in fact a striking uniformity in contemporary moral opinion, and we are led to think otherwise only by a distorting emphasis on changing attitudes to sexual morality. What really feeds the idea of radical pluralism, I argued, is not an impassive empirical observation of 'the way we live now' but a sceptical philosophical presupposition – the assumption that reason cannot in principle determine the respective merits of the various claimants to cogency. I deny that this is so, and question also the 'facts' of pluralism. But however this may be, what is the alternative on offer? The answer is – radical humanism, the belief that, in the words Plato attributes to Protagoras, 'man is the measure of all things'. It is a view, as I have had occasion to note, that some espousedly Christian thinkers have endorsed. Thus to repeat a quote from Don Cupitt: 'All meaning and truth and value are man-made and could not be otherwise.' But even if they are man-made, they are nonetheless susceptible to criticism, including the criticism of the ultimate attribution of 'man-madeness'. The case for a return to the pre-modern, as opposed to an advance to the postmodern, thus rests upon the adequacy of humanism, one of the two strands I have identified in 'our modern sensibility'. This, set in a theological context, is the topic of the next and final chapter.

CHAPTER 6

The theology of hope

The title of this chapter is also the title of a book by Jürgen Moltmann – *Theology of Hope* – one of the best-known works of theology this century and at one time highly influential. The aim of this concluding chapter, however, is not to assess or even examine Moltmann's theology of hope. This is because it was formulated largely in the light of a perceived challenge to Christianity from an alternative Marxist analysis of history and society, a 'challenge' that must now seem somewhat passé. In the wake of the collapse of the Soviet Union in the 1980s and the changes that China underwent in the 1990s, in short the demise of communism, it would appear that, while God is not yet dead, Marxism certainly is. Accordingly, my purpose here is not to explore the details of Moltmann's theology of hope, but the wider conceptual context within which we might try to assess the merits of *any* such theology. Since many of his concerns are now outdated (in my view), I shall refer to only two themes in his book that seem to me of continuing interest and relevance – the place of hope in the pursuit of understanding and the logic of promise with respect to the future. Both these ideas are important for the topic with which this chapter is concerned– the *rationality* of hope and its relation to the value and meaning of human life. In the course of exploring the issues that surround this theme, my further purpose is to draw together both the subjects and the conclusions of preceding chapters.

I

What makes it rational to hope for this rather than that? What makes it rational to hope at all? The connection between these general questions, and the more focussed question of the theology of hope is not so very far to seek. Indeed Moltmann himself provides an illuminating principle for thinking about the two, and this is the first of his lines of thought upon which I propose to draw.

In the Middle Ages, Anselm of Canterbury set up what has since been the standard basic principle of theology: *fides quaerens intellectum* [faith seeking understanding] – *credo, ut intelligam* [I believe so that I may understand]. This principle also holds for eschatology, and it could well be that it is of decisive importance for Christian theology today to follow the basic principle: *spes quaerens intellectum* [Hope seeking understanding] – *spero, ut intelligam* [I hope so that I may understand]. If it is hope that maintains and upholds faith and keeps it moving on, if it is hope that draws the believer into the life of love, then it will also be hope that is the mobilizing and driving force of faith's thinking, of its knowledge of, and reflections on, human nature, history and society. Faith hopes in order to know what it believes. (Moltmann 1967: 33)

Actually, although Moltmann treats them interchangeably, the two versions of the new principle here proposed do not have quite the same implications, and it is the first rather than the second that I want to employ. While the second makes hope a necessary condition of understanding (in the way that Anselm almost certainly meant faith to be), the first more modestly makes hope merely a ground upon which to seek further and deeper understanding. That is to say, the idea of hope seeking understanding takes the hope that I find in myself and others, or more generally the hope without which action seems to be pointless, as the starting point of an investigation into its rationale. The root idea is that it is rational to subscribe to whatever beliefs are required to make hopefulness intelligible.

It must be acknowledged that there is a question whether Moltmann's substitution of hope for faith carries with it the full implications of the original principle, whether, that is to say, hope is a mode of knowledge in the way that Aquinas (for instance) construes faith as being. But even if we suppose, with Aquinas, that faith is to be given epistemological precedence over hope, we can still interpret hope as *a* ground of belief, and importantly a ground which may decide matters upon which the more usual ground of evidence leaves us uncertain. It is a separate question, of course, whether there need be anything in this sort of rationale that we could properly call theological, whether, that is to say, the rationality of hope ultimately lies in a divine *logos*.

It is this further question that is of greatest interest for present purposes, certainly. It is only if the rationality of hope implies a theology, in at least some contexts, that it can serve to further amplify the cosmic narrative which the previous chapter sought to elaborate and (to a degree) defend. One way of proceeding, then, is to consider what the alternative might be. As we shall see, to do so combines, in fact, an exploration of both the wider issue of rationality and the narrower one of theology. The alternative to theology, of course, is one important aspect of that 'modern sensibility' which it has been the purpose of this book to probe and question – hope based on humanism.

In an essay entitled 'Humanism and Reform' the philosopher A. J. Ayer, at the time of writing President of the British Humanist Association, wrote:

In one sense, humanism is a harsh doctrine. To insist that life has only the meaning that one succeeds in giving it, that we have only this short amount of time to experience any happiness or accomplish anything of value, is all very well for people who are living in easy circumstances and have been given the opportunity to develop intellectual and cultural interests. For those who are ignorant, helpless and in material want, it is small consolation to be told that their miseries will end with death; and throughout history the majority of human beings have been in this condition. It would, therefore, be insensitive if not hypocritical for humanists to preach their doctrine unless they believed that the values which they set upon human experiences and achievement were capable of being realized not merely by a privileged minority but by mankind in general. Even if they cannot be assured that this will ever be so, they at least have the moral obligation to do what they can to make it possible. (Quoted in Rogers 1999: 281)

It is not often that humanists admit the darker side to their doctrine. In reality, humanism is an even harsher creed than Ayer allows, something the ambiguities in his argument (if such it can be called) disguise. If humanism is true, the vast majority of human beings at all times, including the present, have had worthless lives. This is because their lives have contained little or nothing of those things which alone make them valuable from a humanistic point of view. This is the harsh side of humanism which Ayer here acknowledges. Yet despite what he seems to imply, the further truth is that the honest humanist has indeed nothing more to offer than 'the small consolation . . . that their miseries will end with death'. This is because the fact, if it were one, that the values which humanists set upon human experiences and achievement are *capable* of being realised by humankind in general, is no consolation to those who, as a matter of fact, will never realise them. How can it make my life valuable to know that, though it isn't, it could be? Only the actuality, not the possibility, can render lives worthwhile from a humanistic point of view. (Ayer, in the passage quoted, equates value and meaning; I shall subsequently draw a distinction between them.)

But there is yet another and not much less unpalatable implication of humanism. Contrary to what Ayer says, the wealthy and privileged humanist has good grounds upon which to discount any talk of a moral obligation to seek reform of the world with a view to improving the lot of the poor and the ignorant. These grounds flow from a logical principle generally agreed, that 'ought implies can'; if the end result of our actions *cannot* be accomplished, we are under no obligation to attempt them. Insensitivity and hypocrisy, to which Ayer refers, are not to the point; the fortunate humanist's moral indifference is legitimated by practical impossibility. This is a result of the plain fact that there are very few circumstances, if any, in which he or she will have a realistic chance of increasing the humanistic value of the general run of people's lives. The comparatively wealthy can do little to secure a lasting improvement in the lives of the poor, an unhappy fact confirmed by the repeated need for, and repeated failure of, charitable aid programmes which aim to redistribute resources from people in wealthy countries to people in poor ones. Even if this were not so, even if the prospects for such improvement were brighter, it would still be the case, since the past cannot be altered, that nothing will allow the humanist to escape the conclusion that the vast majority of all human lives ever lived have been worthless and meaningless.

Now it is likely be said that I am here being too pessimistic about the chances of ameliorating the human condition, and too consequentialist in my interpretation of moral obligation. Consider the second objection first. Within a Kantian framework, a framework that makes much of the principle 'ought implies can', moral endeavour does indeed require an assurance of success, but it secures this by divorcing action and consequence. It is actions not consequences that matter morally, and this means that there is one thing of which we *can* be assured; if we *try* to do right we will be successful – *in trying*. No step-motherly nature (to quote Kant again) can rob us of good intention; it can only rob us of efficacy. *Pace* the consequentialists, efficacy is not of moral relevance; we have met our moral obligations if we have tried to meet them.

Or so the Kantian alleges. There are many doubts to be entered against this conception of morality, some of which have been touched on at earlier stages in the argument. This is not the place to explore them further however.[1] It is sufficient to assert only that moral intent must have *some* issue if it is to bring moral merit; I cannot go down in history as, say, a liberator of slaves, unless I have successfully liberated at least some slaves. To have tried to do so unsuccessfully may be very praiseworthy, but it still means my moral hopes were dashed. What is true, however, and on this the Kantians can agree with Ayer, is that the *assurance* of success is not a pre-condition of moral obligation. If it were, our scope for moral endeavour would be drastically reduced. Since requiring assurance of success would imply that we can only meaningfully undertake programmes of moral reform whose outcome is not in doubt, and since these

---

[1] I have discussed these issues at length in Graham (1990a), ch. 4.

will always be very few in number, moral endeavour could be of little significance in our lives.

Nevertheless, in so far as we think that, morally speaking, efficacy matters as well as intention we will have to give some account of what makes the chance of success realistic. One obvious way of attempting to do this lies in an appeal to probability. Between assured outcome and total failure lies likelihood, and it is the realm of likelihood that is relevant to almost all courses of action. Probability, it is commonly said, is the guide to life, and viewed in this way, it seems natural to hold that if a morally desirable outcome is probable enough, we are under an obligation to attempt it, while if it is sufficiently *im*probable, our obligation to attempt it lapses. The crucial question, of course, is how probable is probable *enough*? We could state this question differently; how much reason do we need to make rational the hope that our moral endeavours will succeed to a degree compatible with lending at least some importance to efficacy? This returns us to the issue with which this chapter began: what is the basis of reasonable hope?

An intuitively appealing answer is that a hope is reasonable if there attaches to it an outcome which inductive reasoning shows to have a probability greater than 0.5 (where 1 represents a certainty and 0 an impossibility). Let us accept for the moment that this is the case (allowing that such estimates can be further complicated by the probability of partial as opposed to complete success) and return to Ayer's contention, that a humanistic value system both implies and sustains a programme of reform. In the light of the foregoing analysis, what this means is that relatively wealthy and privileged humanists have an obligation to seek economic and political reform if it is inductively more probable than not that the general run of humankind can be brought thereby to have humanly worthwhile lives. Is this inductively probable? The relevant evidence is hard to accumulate, but I should have said not. We know there to be enough truth in Burns's claim that 'the best laid schemes o' mice an' men/Gang aft a-gley' to doubt whether there is much prospect of intentionally ameliorating the condition of most human beings. This is not to say that life for the poor and disadvantaged has not got better over time. Arguably, at least on some measures, it has, especially in the West over the last two hundred years. (I say 'arguably' because if the general run of people are wealthier, more have died in wars, persecutions and other conflicts than ever before.) What is far more contentious is the suggestion that the human condition has been bettered as a result of the self-conscious intention and design to better it. If, despite the general improvement in the lot of human beings, this second claim about deliberate programmes of action is false, then we do not have any inductive basis for thinking that reform can be hopefully pursued now.

To many minds the contention that humanity has not much improved the lot of the poor will seem absurd. It is as evident as anything can be, they will say, that the spread of greater prosperity, better health, longer life expectancy and higher levels of educational attainment to ever larger numbers of people was the mark of the nineteenth and twentieth centuries, and that these outcomes followed from programmes of social and political improvement, technological innovation and economic reform. For my own part, I do not think that this is at all obvious, but let us suspend the question. There is this further question. If the human condition has been bettered, what has been the agency of its amelioration? Plainly, though individuals have played a part from time to time, and sometimes a very striking one (Wilberforce and the abolition of slavery is a questionable, but a not implausible example), no serious historian subscribes any longer to the 'great men' conception which attributes large scale transformations to actions of individuals. No doubt political leaders have played some part (for evil as well as good, let it be observed), but it is a combination of general trends – expanding populations, cultural accumulation, technological innovation, increasing commerce, political liberalisation and the growth of education (alongside other factors no doubt) – that have transformed the West – to the extent that it has indeed been transformed.

Could these changes be the outcome of the collective power of the state? It is difficult to sustain the belief that it is. To think otherwise is to attribute a degree of power to the state that is quite implausible. To begin with, it is only relatively recently that the state has taken to itself powers and responsibilities with such a large-scale remit. It was only in the second half of the twentieth century that the civil and economic power of the state grew to the proportions we now take for granted. But more importantly, having done so, the state has been the instrument of disaster more often than it has been the instrument of improvement. The state's potential in this regard is a feature of the much more limited states of earlier times, in my view, but we have only to consider the twentieth century's most conspic-uous attempts to use the extended power of the state in the spirit of humanism to effect major transformations and im-provements in the lot of ordinary people, to see how spectacu-larly they go wrong – the Bolshevik's socialist programme in Russia, the Nazi's attempts to create a Third Reich out of greater Germany, Mao's cultural revolution in China, Castro's policies in Cuba, the Khmer Rouge's brutal attempt to wipe the slate clean in Cambodia; the list is not endless, but it is long, and it points to human misery on a gigantic scale, a scale so large that it is difficult to imagine still less comprehend. Schemes of humanistic political improvement, if the twentieth century is anything to go by, have an exceptionally bad record.

It might be replied, of course, that I have slanted the evidence in my favour by choosing only the worst examples and sup-posing, illicitly, that these movements began as sincere attempts to improve economic and social conditions. A fuller picture, such a critic will allege, must include the liberal democratic governments of the West and the major increases in prosperity, education, health and life expectancy that the same century has witnessed as a result of their activities. I am myself persuaded that the calamitous projects of socialism, communism, fascism and so on are of the greatest importance in assessing the hope-fulness of political programmes inspired by humanistic ideals, but however this may be, the additional supposedly positive evidence does not alter things much. Take just the case of the United States. First, there is good reason to hold that the astonishing internal prosperity of the US owes relatively little to state action. We are led to think otherwise by the doctrine, not to say dogma, of economic planning. Yet the facts are that management of the modern economy under the guidance of economic theory is at best a very imperfect science (and if Paul Ormerod, in *The Death of Economics*, is to be believed, a profoundly misconceived one[2]). Despite the claims of politicians, it seems to be the case that in general 'successful' governments have *presided over* economic growth rather than engineered it. This may be true, even, of Roosevelt's New Deal. The cause of growth in Western economies, including that of North America, is far more deep-seated than political programmes. Secondly, if the US is very far from being the 'Great Satan' that some Islamic countries have regularly declared it to be, many, perhaps most, of the US's excursions abroad in the interests of democracy and human rights have at best failed and at worst compounded the problems they ostensibly sought to address. This may have more to do with ignorance than malfeasance, but the fact remains.

The same could be said of France, Belgium, Portugal and (perhaps to a lesser extent) the United Kingdom, all of whose internal and external policies of improvement have had only a very uncertain connection with their effects. Arguably indeed, the self-conscious divesting of colonies, supposedly in the interests of their greater freedom and prosperity, has for the most part resulted in precisely the opposite. Nor is the picture improved if we consider the combined action of states in concert, the so called 'international community'. Consider for instance, international action in post-colonial Africa. In his justly celebrated account of the Rwandan genocide of 1994, compellingly entitled *We Wish to Inform You That Tomorrow We Will be Killed with our Families*, Phillip Gourevitch has detailed how the unbelievable horror of the events that took place there was intensified rather than ameliorated by the response of the United Nations (in particular the Security Council), its High Commission for Refugees, and almost all the other international aid agencies involved, both governmental and charitable. There may never have been an episode of more intense

---

[2] It should be noted, however, that Ormerod's work has met with a very mixed reception, and has failed to cause the waves it was intended and initially expected to.

suffering and death, yet it took place in an era of international co-operation, the end of empire, and a drive to development. I shall assume, not altogether plausibly, that the intentions of all these agencies were good; this does not alter the fact that their actions were ignorantly inept beyond the point of culpability and that even greater harms resulted than if they had failed to engage in the situation at all.

It is a mistake to generalise from a single instance, of course, but there are many more episodes that bear the same interpretation – the Ethiopian famine of 1984, for instance, the UN-sponsored action against Iraq in 1991 or the action of NATO against Serbia in Kosovo in 1999. All three led to a demonstrable increase in human suffering. The upshot seems to be this. If we take historical experience seriously, dispassionate assessment suggests that a very low probability of success attaches to 'schemes of political improvement', whether pursued by individuals, by states, or by the 'international community'. All this is consistent with the empirical fact of improvement, of course. In many places the lot of ordinary people has improved by a large factor. It would be foolish to deny that the people of Europe, for instance, were vastly better off in the twentieth than in the fourteenth century, in terms of humanistic values. The question at issue is not the fact itself, but its explanation. At the same time, it is worth recording that this is not a universal fact; it seems incontestable that the condition of sub-Saharan Africa, never very good, worsened in the second half of the twentieth century, and this despite the deliberate efforts of international aid organisations, both government and non-government.

These are unpalatable conclusions for the reforming humanist because they call seriously into question the credibility of humanism as a moral creed by which to live. The intentional action of human beings individually or in concert at best accomplishes little and at worst is detrimental. Adam Smith's famous conception of an 'invisible hand', that somewhat mysteriously turns the striving for individual good into a collective benefit, has frequently been misunderstood and misrepresented (often by its admirers), but there is little doubt, to my mind, that more faith is to be placed in it than in the visible hand of the state.

Humanism's implication is plain. The vast majority of human lives have lacked the values that make life worth living, a very great many lives will go on lacking them, and where this is the case there is nothing a convinced humanist can expect, or be expected, to do about it. The future may hold more promise (who can say). Serfdom came to an end in Europe, we know not why exactly. It was not by anyone's design, and was neither expected nor predicted by those who might have been in position to anticipate. Perhaps the lives of the common people in sub-Saharan Africa will undergo a similar change in the next fifty years. But if they do, there is every reason to believe that this will be serendipitous (from the point of view of individual and collective action) and hence of no relevance to moral endeavour. In short, the creed of the humanist is not, as is often falsely supposed, one of enlightened optimism, but either blind confidence or enlightened despair.

II

This is true, however, only if we tie the assessment of humanism to the standard of effective action. There is another version of the humanist ideal that might be defended – a creed that *affirms* the human spirit rather than attributes to it a peculiar efficacy. Indeed, in general the phrase 'the triumph of the human spirit' refers to the assertion of value and meaning in human endeavour precisely in the face of impossible odds. The human spirit, on this conception, triumphs not when it masters the human predicament and succeeds in placing it under control, but when it endures in the face of defeat. To be truly human is to persist in the face of (literally) insurmountable odds. It is this version of humanism, as it seems to me, which presents the most powerful alternative to the theology of hope, and which supplies the most plausible support for Kekes's claim, which I quoted in the Preface, that 'Christianity is another way of succumbing to false hope'.

James Fitzjames Stephen is a nineteenth century writer of

whom few now know, brother, in fact, of the much better known Leslie Stephen, and thus the uncle of Virginia Woolf. In his own day he gained some celebrity by being the author of a work entitled *Liberty, Fraternity and Equality* in which he offers trenchant criticisms of John Stuart Mill. The larger part of this book is concerned with detailed (and often effective) dissection of Mill's arguments in *On Liberty* and *The Subjection of Women*, but in his Conclusion Stephen turns to some of the themes with which I have been concerned. In contrast to Mill, Stephen held to the truth of the Christian religion, but he acknowledged, as who at that time and subsequently could not, a deep uncertainty which previous ages had not felt, an inability to assert with complete assurance the truth of that in which he strove to believe. As a result he relinquishes the medium of vigorous argument to enter upon a more reflective strain, and contents himself in the end with the articulation of an attitude to life. In his expression of this, I think, he captures very effectively (if unintentionally), a heroic humanism that can be contrasted with the optimistic reformist humanism against which I have been bringing objections. Stephen describes the human condition thus:

We stand on a mountain pass in the midst of snow and blinding mist, through which we get glimpses now and then of paths that may be deceptive. If we stand still we shall be frozen to death. If we take the wrong road we shall be dashed to pieces. We certainly do not know if there is any right one. What must we do? 'Be strong and of a good courage' [Deuteronomy 31:6–7]. Act for the best, hope for the best, and take what comes. Above all let us dream no dreams, and tell no lies, but go our way, wherever it may lead, with our eyes open and our head erect. If death ends all we cannot meet it better. If not, let us enter whatever may be the next scene like honest men, with no sophistry in our mouths and no masks on our faces. (Stephen 1967: 271)

Whatever Stephen may have intended, he here expresses an ideal that can be interpreted as an approach to life shorn of (false) theological comforts, one which eschews as sophistry the cosmic narrative I have been attempting to rehabilitate, and reviles the pious mask it would encourage us to assume. Of course, there are elements in the passage just quoted which a thoroughgoing heroic humanism of the sort we are now considering would abandon. It is not merely that we do not know if there is any right path. There *is* no one right path. Among the multifarious attitudes possible for us, we must choose. Here, heroic humanism and the anxieties of the existentialist come together. For existentialists contend that the aspects of life with which I have been concerned – the importance of moral integrity, the existence of terrible occurrences, the futility of human endeavour – have no rational ground or explanation. Their slogan, indeed, is that human life is *absurd* – which is to say, lacking in any sense or meaning. The challenge of human existence is to acknowledge this fact without recourse to sophistry or masks. The question is though: then what? The existentialist/humanist answer is to affirm the human spirit, the ability to endure, in the honest acceptance that this really is the condition in which we find ourselves, and by this endurance and acceptance our lives are graced with as much significance as we can hope.[3] 'Only endure' might be said to be the existentialist's slogan, to which the humanist adds a rather more attractive element of enjoyment, in so far, it should be added, as the way the world treats us makes enjoyment of life possible.

There is no denying – or at least I have no desire to deny – that there is something admirable about such an attitude. At the same time there seems something paradoxical in the idea that nothing means anything except the honest recognition that nothing means anything. *Could* this be true? Moreover it is not unreasonable to suppose that there is something foolishly (if heroically) self-denying in the refusal to accept, or even consider perhaps, the idea that it may not be so. We long for good news, and after a while its continuing absence may seem to sanction the idea that the best attitude is one which no longer expects it. As a matter of human psychology, some such often seems to be the case, yet for all that, unbeknownst to us, there may yet *be* good news. Is it really a mistake, sophistry or a mask, to keep this possibility open? More than that, might it not be rational to

---

[3] I discuss the cogency of one literary expression of this idea, namely Lewis Grassic Gibbon's, in 'The Moral Vision of *Cloud Howe*'.

conduct our lives in the light of its possibility? Existential humanists have been described (by Alasdair MacIntyre) as 'disappointed rationalists', people who having sought an explanation have found none but nevertheless go on believing that there ought to be one. Only this way can we explain their *angst*, and its supposed overcoming.

But the very idea that there *ought* to be an explanation, to which as it seems the humanist clings, can in my view provide an avenue. It is at this point that the principle of *spes quaerens intellectum* comes to be of some consequence.

What is needed is hope. Hope indeed, is a necessary virtue even in scientific epistemology: 'the only assumption on which (the scientist) can act rationally is the hope of success'. In this area, hope is a necessity if we are to remain sane. To set out upon the road to saintliness we need to be able to hope that the evils of this world can be, and will be, remedied. Nor can this trust be in our own powers, which cannot touch the mass of suffering. We also need to believe that it is not ourselves alone who share imaginatively in the distress of things, and set ourselves to heal them. We need to believe that, in some hidden way, something is on our side. (Clark 1984: 46. The quote is from Peirce)

. . . If the universe is not founded on anything remotely like the values we 'project' then nothing that we do or value is more than a pastime. (Clark 1984: 199)

As everyone versed in the strengths of formal reasoning knows, logic has its limitations. In particular, logic alone cannot determine the order of argument. To repeat a common adage, one man's *modus ponens* is another man's *modus tollens*. Its application to the present context is plain. Faced with the argument that what I have called reformist humanism renders moral endeavour hopeless, and that heroic humanism insists on resting content with (not to say emphasising) the absurdity of human existence, so far as logic goes, we are free to persist with our hopes and reject either version of the humanist creed. In other words, to the extent that hope continues to seek understanding, it will not find it in a humanistic conception of value. Even the version that is more admirable (in my view) denies that there is any understanding to be had.

In the minds of many readers, I have no doubt, this alternative inference will have been arrived at too speedily. The deep-seated presumptions of the present age can hardly be so easily dispelled. I believe that both the conclusion and the arguments for it can be spelt out at greater length and in yet more convincing detail, but since I would claim that at many points in preceding chapters the elements of this spelling out have been put in place, I do not propose to rehearse them yet again. Certainly additional evidence and argument may need to be brought, but the more pressing task for present purposes is to ask whether, were the rejection of humanism to be adequately made out this would in turn create any opening for theology. And on the surface, at any rate, it will surely seem that it does not. If in the face of historical experience, humanism fares badly, how much worse must religion do? Put to the same test, it seems that the Christian religion (with which I am here exclusively concerned) gives us, if anything, even less ground for hope. Is it not true (as a familiar philosophy of history holds) that it took humanistic Enlightenment to rescue Europe from the ravages of the religious wars of the sixteenth and seventeenth centuries, and that it was only when theological seriousness was abandoned (in the way my first chapter noted) that a good measure of pluralistic peacefulness could take hold, with increased freedom and prosperity following in its wake? Even if we consider the twentieth century, the evidence appears to point in the same direction. Certainly there have been catastrophic and monumental secular experiments, but if we take only one of the examples already cited, Christianity seems also to have failed. This is the case of genocide in Rwanda. As I have implied, I regard the events in Rwanda as the most dramatically appalling violent slaughter of one set of human beings by another ever recorded (notwithstanding the Holocaust, ghastly though that was), and possibly (allowing for our historical ignorance) the worst that has ever occurred anywhere. Yet this happened in a largely Christianised society. If the aim and the hope of Christian missionaries in the nineteenth century was to replace darkness with light, Rwanda stands as empirical refutation of their efforts, and thus their hopes. Murky though the picture of responsibility is, and will remain in all probability, there seems little doubt that Christian affiliation, even Christian priesthood, cannot be correlated with a witness to good over evil in the murderous spirit that seems to have seized the Hutus, and led in a few short weeks to 800,000 Tutsi deaths. All the preaching and converting that had gone on over the preceding one hundred years counted for nothing, apparently.

The trouble with this counter attack is that to appeal to the 'evidence' in this way presupposes a metaphysic that is precisely the one at issue. Christian cosmology, at least in its orthodox and traditional forms, supposes that the world in which we live is not one ultimately governed by causes and effects which may be subsumed in ever more comprehensive laws, but by spiritual agencies which operate in accordance with will, intention and desire. We can be more or less economical in our ontology of these spirits. At the most minimal, in addition to human agency, there is only God. On a more prolific interpretation, there are angels and daemons, perhaps the active agency of the communion of saints, and the hidden but constant presence of Satan. For present purposes, it does not matter how economical or extravagant we are in our ontology. The point is rather that the spirits, whether one or many, are not to be manipulated by means of a knowledge of their workings as the world of physical causality is. We plead with God to aid us, we ask the angels for their assistance, we combat the forces of darkness in the language of prayer not with magical formulae. And their responses are those of intentional agents. God, it has frequently been said, can answer our prayers with a 'No' as much as with a 'Yes'; the mere fact of praying cannot be guaranteed to secure any particular outcome. Consequently, the evidence that prayer does or does not 'work' cannot amount to the assemblage of observations into a law-like regularity. So too with citing facts about conversion. Conversion does not bring into existence a causal precondition of better times. We may reasonably hope that it will make a difference, but conversion also brings into existence yet another battlefield.

I am aware, of course, that this talk of spiritual agencies is profoundly unfashionable to the point of seeming atavistic and obscurantist. Though it is an issue which previous chapters sought to address, it is one to which I will return briefly. For the moment, however, my purpose is simply to observe that the evidence of history cannot be called upon to refute the Christian's contention that God is on our side in the way that it refutes the naturalistic assumption that either individually or collectively we have the means of securing the moral outcomes we desire. To take the case of Rwanda again. Anyone who gives serious credence to the traditional cosmic story outlined in the previous chapter will believe, as St Paul accurately perceived, that the victory of Christ over sin, though an ultimate one, did not immediately dispel sin from the world. The war against Satan has been won, but there are still residual battles to be fought. And in the course of those residual battles the prowling lion not only seeks whom he may devour, but does so with temporary success. Long-standing theological controversy surrounds the issue, but I shall assert that conversion to Christianity is a necessary and not a sufficient condition of being found at the last day on the side of the angels. Otherwise how are we to explain the evident fact that seemingly sincere Christians can end up conniving in works of wickedness? Human weakness, it is plausible to suppose, continues to be subject to the 'assaults and crafts of the devil' and we may thus expect that among the number of those who are sworn in and paid up, even prominent, Christians there will be agents of evil. As Augustine emphasised powerfully, the present dispensation is one in which two cities are intermingled, and the City of God cannot be empirically identified with the church on earth.

III

But if this is true, how are we to tell the difference, and if we cannot, how are Christians to secure the hopefulness of moral endeavour any more than the humanist can? At this point there is reason to return to Moltmann, and the second of his themes that I think of continuing relevance. Moltmann finds the key concept for anticipation to lie not in inductively based prediction but in 'promise'.

A promise is a declaration which announces the coming of a reality that does not yet exist. Thus promise sets man's heart on a future history in which the fulfilling of the promise to be expected. If it is a case of a divine promise, then that indicates that the expected future does not have to develop within the framework of the possibilities inherent in the present, but arises from that which is possible to the God of that promise. This can also be something which by the standard of present experience appears impossible. (Moltmann 1967: 103)

All that empirical evidence gathered from historical experience can show is 'something which by the standard of present experience appears impossible'. Humanism has to rely upon the supposition that the expected future *will* develop within the framework of the possibilities inherent in the present, but by this standard we can only conclude that the things we might hope for in the redemption and transformation of the world are impossible. In the light of humanism, hopeful moral endeavour is thus groundless. Of course we can still 'hope against hope' as we say, and blindly predict that things will get better to the point where the lives of most human beings have value and worth from a humanistic point of view. Perhaps indeed they will. But what such blind faith cannot secure, even if its prediction should turn out to be accurate, is either a ground or an obligation for *action* that has this happy outcome as its aim.

By contrast, this is just what the promise of God can do. We see in a mirror darkly, according to St Paul, then, at the *eschaton*, we shall see face to face, and what we shall see (to quote Tennyson) is

> That nothing walks with aimless feet;
> That not one life shall be destroyed,
> Or cast as rubbish to the void
> When God hath made the pile complete.

Maybe. This is a pleasing picture, certainly, but what *reason* have we to believe in it? The answer lies not in any induction from historical experience – the successes of the Church's prayer for instance – but in the fact that an almighty benevolent God has promised that it shall be so. To quote Moltmann again:

In the covenant, God in his freedom binds himself to be faithful to the promise he has given; and if this covenant extends to a future in which fulfilments are to ensue, then it cannot be regarded as an historical fact, but is to be understood as an historic event which points beyond itself to the future that is announced. (Moltmann 1967: 121)

Now it does not require an excessively critical mind to think that we are not much further forward here. We can say, certainly, that within this framework of thinking there is reason to believe in the hopefulness of moral endeavour; *if* an almighty benevolent God has made such a promise, then we have reason to think that, whatever historical appearance may suggest, human efforts to work for good and against evil are not fruitless, and indeed that it is participation in such work itself, and not the outcomes our efforts secure, that makes life meaningful. But what reason do we have to adopt this framework? The answer lies in the principle of *spes quaerens intellectum*. Our reason to adopt the framework of ideas is that it makes sense of hoping. In short, the theology of hope I have just sketched is a doctrine we can live by; the humanism with which I have contrasted it is not.

IV

There still seems to be something lacking. At best the argument shows that rational hope needs a theology. What it does not show is that we need rational hope. In the last paragraph I asserted that the theology of hope is a doctrine we can live by. Could we not, acknowledging all that has been said, live by something less? After all, the theological baggage that this account of the rationality of hope brings is very considerable. Although considerations have been adduced to think that the pre-modernistic conceptions which the contemporary world has for the most part abandoned are not perhaps as misguided and intellectually worthless as is generally supposed, and that they can be given an interpretation that eliminates a good deal of their atavistic overtones, even so, the theology of hope, as it has been expounded, asks us to accept ideas so at odds with 'our modern sensibility' that the burden of proof unquestionably lies with anyone who seeks to dislodge it. More importantly, that burden will only have been discharged if it can be shown that there is no alternative.

Yet, it seems that there is an alternative. Let us agree that humanists, who reject the realms of the supernatural, can only live in hope, and cannot make that hope rational within the terms of their creed. Even so, there is a good deal to be said on their behalf. First, despite an earlier remark, they need not in fact 'hope against hope'. Even if there are no solid empirical grounds for thinking that human action individually or collectively can secure a greater and permanent improvement of the human condition, this is no reason against what we might call unmediated hope. I hope it will happen, a humanist might say. I have no special reason for this hope, but I can still hope. And so long as my life is worth living, and those of many others, I have reason to persist in doing what I can, both for myself and for others. No doubt there will be failures, but some successes too. And as long as my life and those of some others can possess and for the most part retain a good measure of the value humanism espouses, there is no reason to discount or denigrate their worth. Still less is there any reason to seek their end. Surely this much is true. A great many people find life worth living, and do so because their lives contain those very things that humanists believe to be valuable. Why should they cease to do so because they have no solid ground for the aspiration that the world will eventually be transformed?

Both the observation and the question require a response if the argument I have been developing in this book is to have any claim on 'our modern sensibility'. What is to motivate dissatisfaction with the limited view and the limited aspirations they both express and endorse? This is the issue with which I shall conclude. It is here that the distinction between value and meaning, to which I promised to return, is of some significance.

What is the meaning of life? This is a question people not infrequently suppose to be that with which philosophers contend. Accordingly, the expression 'my philosophy' is usually thought, in some way or other, to signal an answer to this question. Yet professional philosophers generally deny that they have anything special to say on this subject. Indeed, not infrequently they deny that the question can itself be made meaningful. This is partly because asking it seems to launch us on an infinite regress; if I say the meaning of life is x, this simply raises the further question 'what is the meaning of x?', and so on *ad infinitum*.

There is, I think, something correct about this suspicion. This much is true certainly. If we were to suppose that the question had a single determinate answer which might be expressed in one (or a few) short sentences, then we would be deeply mistaken. There is no formula (even a long one) that could be the answer to this question in the way that there may be an answer (albeit technical and complex) to the question 'What is the cause of cancer?' Even so, this should not be taken to imply that the question 'What is the meaning of life?' is nonsensical. Though it does not admit of any straightforward answer, it does signal an area of reflection in which more and less intelligent things can be said. This is evidenced by the fact that one answer seems plain enough – there *is* no 'meaning of life'; life is what you make it – an answer that marks the humanism I have been questioning in this and previous chapters.

Accordingly, it seems, what questions about the meaning of life open up is not so much the possibility of rival 'theories' but alternative lines of reflection, and it is one of these I want to explore by drawing a distinction between value and meaning. That human beings value things is incontestable, and that the things they value give them the motivating reason to go on living seems equally certain. We might wonder, as philosophers persistently have done, whether the things we typically value have some other 'objective' value, independently of our valuing them, a topic upon which I have touched from time to time. But however we answer it, there is a further issue; what do the things we value *amount* to? This is a question that is reflected in a familiar way of thinking, and in my terminology it is a question that signals a distinction between value and meaning. It is a fact that we commonly mark a difference between the experiences with which life has presented us (good or bad) and those things we have accomplished. The question 'What have you done with your life?' looks, generally, for an answer couched in terms of accomplishments rather than experiences. In other words, 'I had a good time' will not do.

It might be thought that this is something of prejudice. Why should having enjoyed life not be enough? The trouble is that enjoyment seems too neutral with respect to its different objects. People can (and regularly do) enjoy the trivial and the bad. But if enjoyment is not enough, what will make the difference? One answer, with which I find it hard not to have a deep sympathy, is that in one way or another I have left the world better than I found it. In adopting this perspective we do not need, for present purposes, to be specific about what counts as 'better' here. It is sufficient that we have the idea of transcending our own good, but necessarily ephemeral, experiences (which are not to be decried of course) and pointing to something which, in some sense or other, we leave behind, whether moral, aesthetic or intellectual.

This way of thinking might be described as a belief in the greater value of those things that endure. According to William James this is precisely the idea that lies at the heart of what he calls 'the religious hypothesis'.

Science says things are; morality says that some things are better than other things; and religion says essentially two things.

First, she says that the best things are the more eternal things, the overlapping things, the things in the universe that throw the last stone, so to speak, and say the final word. 'Perfection is eternal' – this phrase of Charles Secrétan seems a good way of putting this first affirmation of religion, an affirmation which obviously cannot be verified scientifically at all.

The second affirmation of religion is that we are better off even now if we believe her first affirmation to be true. (James 1912: 25)

Now the idea that the best things are the most enduring things is one to which there is substantial reason to subscribe. Imagine that, in response to the question 'What have you done with your life?' I specify some accomplishment which, as it happens, is wiped away without trace shortly after my death. Would it not be right to regret this? Or better, perhaps, is it not evident that we have reason to prefer the circumstances in which this is not so? Accordingly, do we not have reason to take such steps as we can to ensure it? It is the belief that we do that explains (amongst other things) the interesting and important human practice of last wills and testaments, by means of which (somewhat curiously) we both try to, and do, continue to exercise an influence on the world of the living when we ourselves are beyond the grave.

So we might amend the question 'What have you done with your life?' to the question 'What is your legacy to the world?' and thereby reveal this important dimension to human existence – that it seeks to reach beyond its three score years and ten. Can it do so, and for long? The natural impulse seems to be: if it is good, let it continue to endure for as long as possible. If this is our attitude then we find here an indisputable difference with other values – happiness and enjoyment most notably. It makes no sense to think that we can make these persist beyond the grave. Perhaps, if a good God wills it, they will be restored to us. Such is many people's hope of heaven, but it is plain that this is something that must be done for them, not something they can themselves secure or even contribute to. By contrast, the ways in which we try to lend meaning to our lives do imply that we can continue to influence the way the future goes, and it would be difficult to deny that this in turn implies a hope that we may do so.

It is in this way that we are obliged to revisit the question of hope. 'Blessed are the dead who die in the Lord, for they rest from their labours, and their works shall follow them' (Revelation 14:13). So the Bible tells us, and it makes a certain sense. If our works are to follow us, this is made much more likely if and in so far as they are taken up and sustained by an agent 'with whom is no variableness, neither shadow of turning' (Epistle of James 1:17). In short, a common conception of what it is for a human life to mean something other than the personal satisfaction of its possessor finds its most adequate justification in the supposition that there is a God who is on our side, and that we have reason to believe this chiefly because He has promised that it is so.

Of course, if this is true, God is not on our side because of what we will, but because of what He wills. That is why the right way to think about human accomplishments is a matter of assessing their compatibility with the God who made all and controls all. There is one of Cranmer's inimitable prayers which expresses just this thought.

Almighty God, who alone canst order the unruly wills and affections of sinful men: Grant unto thy people, that they may love the thing which thou commandest, and desire that which thou dost promise; that so, among the great and many changes of the world, our hearts may surely there be fixed, where true joys are to be found.

It would be foolish to claim that the philosophical arguments which I have been exploring, and the conclusions I have drawn from them, provide a proven basis for the intellectual cogency of this prayer. Yet, as it seems to me, enough has been said to show that there is more here than beautiful and moving language (as undoubtedly there is). There is also an underlying idea which, in the light of its own concerns, the modern world has been foolish, and mistaken, to abandon. But the very fact of the language being moving has an important evidential role too. To quote William James once more, from a lecture expressly devoted to the question 'Is life worth living?':

This life *is* worth living, we can say, *since it is what we make it, from the moral point of view;* and we are determined to make it from that point of view, so long as we have anything to do with it, a success.

Now in this . . . I have assumed that our faith in an invisible order is what inspires those efforts and that patience which makes this visible order good for men. Our faith in the seen world's goodness (goodness now meaning fitness for successful moral and religious life) has verified itself by leaning on our faith in the unseen world. But will our faith in the unseen world similarly verify itself? Who knows?

Once more it is a case of *maybe*; and once more *maybes* are the essence of the situation. I confess that I do not see why the very existence of an invisible world may not in part depend on the personal response which any one of us may make to the religious appeal. God himself, in short, may draw vital strength and increase of very being from our fidelity. For my own part I do not know what the sweat and blood and tragedy of this life mean, if they mean anything short of this. If this life be not a real fight, in which something is eternally gained for the universe by success, it is no better than a game of private theatricals from which one may withdraw at will. But it *feels* like a real fight – as if there were something really wild in the universe which we, with all our idealities and faithfulnesses, are needed to redeem; . . . For such a half-wild, half-saved universe our nature is adapted . . . [T]he dumb region of the heart in which we dwell alone with our willingnesses and unwillingnesses, our fears and faiths . . . [h]ere is our deepest organ of communication with the nature of things; and compared with these concrete movements of our soul all abstract statements and scientific arguments – the veto, for example, which the strict positivist pronounces upon our faith – sound to us like mere chatterings of the teeth. (James 1912: 61–2)

In short, there is evil, and any moral crusade against it rests for its rationality on the supposition that there is hope in the crusade, otherwise our lives amount to no more than 'a game of private theatricals from which one may withdraw at will'. In 'the dumb region of the heart' we know this, but it is a knowledge that 'our modern sensibility' cannot explain or accommodate. My purpose in this book has been to show that the region of the heart need not remain dumb. Faced with this choice, it makes more sense of human existence to abandon our modern sensibility and willingly engage in moral endeavour, looking to the God who is our hope.

Bibliography

Augustine (1951), *Confessions*, trans. F. J. Sheed, Sheed & Ward, London.

(1998), *The City of God against the Pagans*, ed. and trans. R. W. Dyson, Cambridge University Press.

Ba, Mariama (1986), *Scarlet Song*, trans. D. S. Blair, Addison Wesley Longman, Harlow.

Bailey, D. M. (1948), *God Was in Christ: an Essay in Incarnation and Atonement*, Faber and Faber, London.

Bainton, Roland H. (1960), *Christian Attitudes Toward War and Peace*, Abingdon Press, Nashville, TN.

Bauckham, Richard (1996), *New Testament Theology: the Theology of the Book of Revelation*, Cambridge University Press.

Bauckham, Richard, ed. (1998), *The Gospels for All Christians*, T. & T. Clark, Edinburgh.

Bennett, Alan (1994), *Writing Home*, Faber, London.

Bernall, Misty (1999), *She said Yes: the unlikely Martyrdom of Cassie Bernall*, Plough Publishing House, USA.

Boorstin, D. J. (1974), *The Americans: the Democratic Experience*, Vintage Books, New York.

Borg, Marcus J. and N. T. Wright (1999), *The Meaning of Jesus: Two Visions*, Society for the Promotion of Christian Knowledge, London.

Bornkamm, Günther (1973), *Jesus of Nazareth*, trans. I. and F. McLusky, Hodder and Stoughton, London.

Brink, David O. (1989), *Moral Realism and the Foundations of Ethics*, Cambridge University Press.

Brown, P. (1971), *The World of Late Antiquity*, Thames and Hudson, London.

Bruce, F. F. (1985), *The Real Jesus*, Hodder and Stoughton, London.

Burridge, Richard A. (1992), *What are the Gospels? A Comparison with Graeco-Roman Biography*, Cambridge University Press.

Chilton, Bruce and J. I. H. McDonald (1987), *Jesus and the Ethics of the Kingdom*, Society for the Promotion of Christian Knowledge, London.

Clark, Stephen (1984), *From Athens to Jerusalem*, Clarendon Press, Oxford.

Collingwood, R. G. (1967), 'The Devil' in *Religion and Understanding*, ed. D. Z. Phillips, Basil Blackwell, Oxford.

Croce, Benedetto (1965), *Guide to Aesthetics*, trans. Patrick Romanell, Bobbs-Merrill, Indianapolis, IN.

Cupitt, Don (1980), *Taking Leave of God*, SCM Press, London.
  (1984), *The Sea of Faith: Christianity in Change*, British Broadcasting Corporation, London.

Devine, T. M. (1999), *The Scottish Nation: 1700–2000*, Penguin, London.

Dodd, C. H. (1980), *The Parables of the Kingdom*, Fount Paperbacks, Collins, Glasgow.

Evans, C. Stephen (1996), *The Historical Christ and the Jesus of Faith*, Clarendon Press, Oxford.

Fergusson, David (1998), *Community, Liberalism and Christian Ethics*, Cambridge University Press.

Glover, Jonathan (1999), *Humanity: a Moral History of the Twentieth Century*, Jonathan Cape, London.

Glover, T. R. (1921), *Jesus in the Experience of Men*, SCM Press, London.

Gourevitch, Philip (1999), *We Wish to Inform You that Tomorrow We Will be Killed with our Families: Stories from Rwanda*, Picador, London.

Graham, Gordon (1990a), *Living the Good Life*, Paragon House, New York.
  (1990b), *The Idea of Christian Charity*, Collins, London.
  (1997a), *Ethics and International Relations*, Blackwell, Oxford.
  (1997b), *The Shape of the Past*, Oxford University Press.
  (2000), 'The Moral Vision of *Cloud Howe*', *Aberdeen University Review*.

Grant, Michael (1977), *Jesus: an Historian's Review of the Gospels*, Charles Scribner's Sons, New York.

Hare, John E. (1997), *The Moral Gap*, Clarendon Press, Oxford.

Hibbert, Christopher (1997), *Wellington: a Personal History*, HarperCollins, London.

Hume, David (1902), *Enquiries*, ed. L. A. Selby-Bigge, 2nd edition, Clarendon Press, Oxford.
  (1947), *Dialogues Concerning Natural Religion*, ed. Kemp Smith, Norman, Thomas Nelson, London.
  (1976), *The Natural History of Religion*, ed. Wayne Colver, Clarendon Press, Oxford.

(1978), *A Treatise of Human Nature*, ed. P. H. Nidditch, Clarendon Press, Oxford.

James, William (1912), *The Will to Believe and other Essays in Popular Philosophy*, Longmans, Green and Co., London and Bombay.

Jeremias, Joachim (1978), *The Parables of Jesus*, SCM Press, London.

Julian of Norwich (1966), *Revelations of Divine Love*, Penguin, Harmondsworth.

Kant, Immanuel (1956), *Critique of Practical Reason*, Bobbs-Merrill, Indianapolis, IN.

(1976), *Groundwork to the Metaphysics of Morals*, Hutcheson, London.

Kekes, John (1990), *Facing Evil*, Princeton University Press.

Kelsey, Morton (1974), 'The Mythology of Evil', *Journal of Religion and Health*.

Kieran, Matthew (ed.) (1998), *Media Ethics*, Routledge, London.

Kierkegaard, Søren (1938), *Journals*, ed. A. Dru, Princeton University Press.

(1992), *Either/Or*, Penguin, Harmondsworth.

Kolakowski, Leszek (1982), *Religion*, Fontana Paperbacks, Collins, Glasgow.

(1998), *God Owes Us Nothing*, University of Chicago Press.

(1999), *Freedom, Fame, Lying and Betrayal*, Penguin, Harmondsworth.

Kuhn, Thomas S. (1970), *The Structure of Scientific Revolutions*, University of Chicago Press.

Leyton, Elliot (1984), *Compulsive Killers*, New York University Press.

Mackie, J. L. (1977), *Ethics: Inventing Right and Wrong*, Penguin Books, New York.

MaCulloch, Diarmaid (1996), *Thomas Cranmer*, Yale University Press, New Haven, CT.

McGinn, Colin (1997), *Ethics, Evil and Fiction*, Oxford University Press.

Markham, Ian S. (1994), *Plurality and Christian Ethics*, Cambridge University Press.

Marshall, I. Howard (1977), *I believe in the Historical Jesus*, Hodder and Stoughton, London and Sydney.

Masters, Brian (1993), *The Shrine of Jeffrey Dahmer*, Hodder and Stoughton, London.

(1995), *Killing for Company*, Arrow, London.

Melville, Herman (1986), *Billy Budd, Sailor and Other Stories*, Penguin, Harmondsworth.

Mill, John Stuart (1975), *Three Essays*, Oxford University Press, London.

Moltmann, Jürgen (1967), *Theology of Hope*, trans. A. Leitch, SCM Press, London.

Nagel, T. (1970), *The Possibility of Altruism*, Oxford University Press.

Nietzsche, Friedriech (1973), *Beyond Good and Evil*, trans. R. J. Hollingdale, Penguin, Harmondsworth.

Ormerod, Paul (1994), *The Death of Economics*, Faber and Faber, London.

Plato (1973), *The Last Days of Socrates*, trans. Hugh Tredennick, Penguin, Harmondsworth.

Renan, Ernest (1870), *Vie de Jesus*, Paris.

Rogers, Ben (1999), *A. J. Ayer: a Life*, Chatto and Windus, London.

Sanders, E. P. (1993), *The Historical Figure of Jesus*, Penguin, Harmondsworth.

(1994), *Jesus and Judaism*, SCM Press, London.

Scott, Ernest Findlay (1938), *The Validity of the Gospel Record*, Nicholson and Watson, London.

Schleiermacher, Friedrich (1968), *On Religion: Speeches to its Cultured Despisers*, trans. John Oman, with an introduction by Rudolf Otto, Harper and Row, New York.

Schweitzer, Albert (1910), *The Quest of the Historical Jesus: A Critical Study of its Progress from Reimarus to Wrede*, London.

Stanton, Graham (1997), *Gospel Truth? Today's Quest for Jesus of Nazareth*, Fount, HarperCollins, London.

Stephen, James Fitzjames (1967), *Liberty, Fraternity and Equality*, Cambridge University Press.

Strauss, David Friedrich (1846), *The Life of Jesus Critically Examined*, trans. George Eliot, London.

(1971), *Der Christus des Glaubens und der Jesu der Geschichte*, ed. H.-J. Genscher, Gutersloh, Mohn.

Swinburne, Richard (1979), *The Existence of God*, Clarendon Press, Oxford.

Thomas, Keith (1985), *Religion and the Decline of Magic*, Penguin, Harmondsworth.

Turnbull, Colin (1974), *The Mountain People*, Picador, London.

Watson, Francis (1997), *Text and Truth*, T. & T. Clark, Edinburgh.

Webster, John (1995), *Barth's Ethics of Reconciliation*, Cambridge University Press.

Wink, Walter (1984), *Naming the Powers*, Fortress Press, Philadelphia, PA.

(1986), *Unmasking the Powers*, Fortress Press, Philadelphia, PA.

Wolf, Susan (1984), 'Moral Saints', *Journal of Philosophy*.

Wood, P. B. (1990), 'Science and Virtue in Aberdeen' in *Studies in the Philosophy of the Scottish Enlightenment*, ed. M. A. Stewart, Clarendon Press, Oxford.

Wright, N. T. (1996a), *Jesus and the Victory of God*, Society for the Promotion of Christian Knowledge, London.

(1996b), *The New Testament and the People of God*, Society for the Promotion of Christian Knowledge, London.

(1997), *What Saint Paul Really Said: Was Paul of Tarsus the Real Founder of Christianity?*, Lion Publishing, Oxford.

Index